To make it in the music business y
fidence, luck – and good advice. Thi

Tony Hatch has written a guide to
world, steering clear of hidden reefs

He reveals the secrets of success f
'Let's form a group' to the time when
do with the money.

On the way he deals with repertoire, presentation, how to get heard, writing songs, studio technique, arranging, copyright, contracts and finance. He also tells how you become a backroom boy of the pop industry.

The book is not only a must for the budding superstar: it is a valuable handbook for everyone connected with the music business.

THE AUTHOR

Tony Hatch's life is a showbusiness story with a happy ending.

Born in Pinner, Middlesex, in 1939, he went to the London Choir School. He became head chorister of All Souls, Langham Place, London, then went to work as a tea boy in a music publisher's office.

He got a job as an assistant to a record producer, and later spent three years with the band of the Coldstream Guards.

In 1960 he wrote 'Look For A Star', his first major song hit. He began to produce records for Pye with artists like Lonnie Donegan and Emile Ford.

It was in 1964 that he wrote and produced Petula Clark's 'Downtown' – which became an international No. 1 hit and sold 3 million copies.

The following year he wrote 'Where Are You Now', with Jackie Trent. Jackie's recording went to No. 1. They worked together on more songs; and in 1967 they got married and recorded the song which became their signature tune – 'The Two Of Us'.

They continued to collaborate successfully in songwriting, performed in cabaret, worked together in the recording studio, and set up their own music publishing company.

Tony Hatch now appears regularly on ATV's talent show New Faces; writes many television theme tunes; and is involved with the highly successful Sweet Sensation.

ANSWERS TO QUIZ

John Lennon – Art student
Elton John – Office boy
Cilla Black – Cloakroom attendant
Matt Monro – Bus driver
Lynsey De Paul – Commercial artist
Joe Cocker – Gas fitter
Gilbert O'Sullivan – Postal clerk

In the same series:

EMPEROR ROSKO'S DJ BOOK

So you want to be in the music business

TONY HATCH

EVEREST BOOKS LTD
4 Valentine Place London SE1

Published in Great Britain by Everest Books Ltd, 1976

ISBN 0 903925 443 (Paperback)
ISBN 0 903925 958 (Hardback)

Cartoons and diagrams by ALISON SWAN
Music copyist P. BALDWIN

Printed in Great Britain by
Richard Clay (The Chaucer Press), Ltd.,
Bungay, Suffolk

To Jackie

ACKNOWLEDGEMENTS

MICHAEL FREEGARD, F.C.I.S., General Manager, Performing Right Society Ltd.

MADELINE HAWKYARD, Contracts Manager, Pye Records Ltd.

RAY PRICKETT, Chief Technical Manager, Pye Studios

GEORGE ELRICK, F.R.S.A., President, Entertainments Agents Association of Great Britain

OHNNY DEAN, Percussionist

AND MY SPECIAL THANKS TO

BOBBY MELLIN and PAT WILLIAMS – my first employers (£3 15*s.* together with all the pro-copies I wanted)

DICK ROWE – who brought me into the recording world and encouraged my songwriting

LOUIS BENJAMIN and ALAN FREEMAN – Pye Records 1960–70. Ten good years (Say no more)

CYRIL SIMONS and SAL CHIANTIA – Two guiding lights along the way

PETULA CLARK and CLAUDE WOLFF – They had the faith

LES COCKS – Star maker!!

CHERRY LILL – for helping me put this book together

CONTENTS

INTRODUCTION

ANYONE CAN DO IT

Dear Tony Hatch,

Forgive me for writing to you but I would appreciate your advice. My son has written some songs and although I don't claim to be a good judge of popular music they do seem to be very commercial (I think that's the word) and all the family keep asking him to perform them. We bought him a cassette recorder for his 13th birthday and he has recorded them with the help of my sister, Agnes, on the piano.

Would it be alright to send you the cassette for your opinion? I'm sure he will be furious with me for writing to you but I'm certain his future is in music.

Yours sincerely,
Eileen Rolents

Dear Mr. Hatch,

I like your music very much. I would like to be a songwriter or singer or both if possible. I write a lot of songs. I've got about seven hundred and fifty. Would you listen to them. I don't want to send them to a record company because they might steal the ideas. I could come and see you next week as I will be in London. I hope you can help.

Yours sincerely,
John Maxwell

Dear Sir,

A friend of my father has offered to pay for a recording session for a group that I'm lead singer and bass guitarist with.

I am wondering if you know a studio in Exeter and how much it would cost to hire. Is it worth adding violins, etc. or a saxophone. I have lots of ideas about this but don't know whether it would be worth the money.

Yours faithfully,
Alan Dene

There's no mystery about the attraction of the music business. It's glamorous, financially rewarding, ego satisfying, a very pleasurable way of life and, more than anything, it seems that anyone from a wages clerk to a property heiress can find success. Strangely, though, it's normally those from more humble backgrounds that achieve stardom and, therefore, really appreciate these rewards.

It isn't any wonder, then, that my daily delivery of mail always contains several letters similar to these. Letters from up and coming songwriters, dreaming of their first hit high in the charts; an appeal from a frustrated singer wondering when he'll become a big star, youngsters forming groups; groups searching for that elusive hit song and recording contracts.

Yes, many believe they can make a career in the music business or at least get a few good years out of it, then retire to the South of France.

You don't have to be born with a silver spoon in your mouth, inherit a fortune or win the pools. You can't buy success in the music business but you *can* find it if you've got talent, ambition, confidence, sound advice and a piece of good luck at the right time.

Don't assume that anyone who has found success started with an advantage that you're denied. Your milkman or you could be next year's discovery. But remember the equation:

Talent + Ambition + Confidence + Advice + Luck = SUCCESS

Talent

So what about talent? Why do I appear to be obsessed by the word? What is talent? To put it simply, it's the facility, the gift that The Good Lord has given us, to express ourselves to and be appreciated by our fellow men. For some it's the ability to be an actor, carve wood, paint a picture, cook, build bridges, design skyscrapers or simply make money.

Within the music business the word talent is often misunderstood. How many times have you heard some misguided critic claim that the singer of this week's chart topper has no talent? The critic is out of order. The talent is there even if it's only the ability to interpret a song attractively enough to persuade the public to *buy that record.*

Des O'Connor may not be considered by all to be another Mario Lanza but you can't refuse to acknowledge his talent as an all-round versatile entertainer who has many devoted admirers.

Elton John and Bernie Taupin may not write cunningly devised rhyming couplets in the George and Ira Gershwin, Cole Porter style but no one can deny their great talent to write rhythmically orientated words that perfectly match today's demand for music with a strong beat, yet have a bit of class about them. The message in song lyrics may have changed between the 20s and today but the desire for poetic imagery is still the same. It used to be 'moon in June'. Hammerstein wrote 'the corn is as high as an elephant's eye'; then Lennon and McCartney gave us 'Eleanor Rigby' who 'puts on a face that she keeps in a jar by the door'.

Just because you don't sing like Sinatra or compose like Coward, don't get an inferiority complex. You may still have something to offer your fellow man. And if you believe in yourself, read on.

(Of course, you may well sing like Sinatra or be walking around with the follow-up to 'Mad Dogs and Englishmen' . . . in which case . . . continue reading. You *still* need advice.)

So talent in the music business is as much the ability to create words and music as it is to sing or simply play bass guitar in a group.

What makes people suddenly 'discover' themselves musically after years of apparently being the same person and doing the same things? I once asked Dick Rowe of Decca Records how I came to write 'Downtown' and produce a world hit with Petula Clark having been associated with her for several years previously. What was the sudden magic? What were the secret ingredients? 'You had something to say,' he said, 'and it was important in its time.' Maybe that's why it often takes someone fifteen years to be an overnight success but this ability to 'communicate' is an important part of talent itself.

Ambition

This ingredient is also very important in the equation for success. It's that burning desire to be there yourself where Gilbert and Elton walk. *Your* picture outside the Royal Albert Hall. Your name on the Star Dressing Room Door at Top Of The Pops. You collecting an Ivor Novello Award, receiving the Grand Prix of the Eurovision Song Contest and walking into your bank (straight into the manager's office), with your first healthy royalty cheque.

And with ambition you must have . . .

Confidence

Confidence that you have the ability to raise your sights high enough to make it, self assurance that the disappointments, frustrations and frequent failures won't put you off your ultimate goal.

Advice

With confidence must be the desire to learn from the mistakes and benefit from the advice that everyone is going to give you. Not all the advice will be wise. You have to decide what can be useful to you, and that's where I believe I can help a little. Through many years in the music business I have seen the same basic mistakes made over and over again. Firstly, whether you're a performer or writer, you never see your own work as others see it. Listen to other people's comments. If there's no bias, then it's fair to say that their views may represent far *more* people. Secondly, whether you're a performer or writer, you're the designer, manufacturer and salesman of your own product. Just like a company producing a new line in household goods you must put time and effort into the initial development. Furthermore you will have to invest money in the promotion and presentation of your product. I'll give you two examples.

If you're a singer, there's no good going on stage looking tatty. Buy a suitable dress or outfit, make your hair presentable. It's worth it. And if you're a writer, don't send a music publisher or record company an unaccompanied voice singing your song on an old piece of tape in an unidentified envelope with illegible lyrics. Nobody's got time to sort that lot out and many good songs must have been rejected simply because they were badly presented. It doesn't need to cost a fortune and throughout this book we'll be looking at various ways to make it inexpensive but effective.

We'll also be looking at songwriting itself, forming a group, contacting record companies and music publishing companies right through to protecting your rights in all your hard work.

I can't write a hit song for you, produce a chartbound sound or make you a star but I can help you to use your talent, ambition and confidence in more useful ways.

There's one more ingredient for success and that is . . .

Luck

Everyone striving for success must have that initial break. Sometimes it's simply being in the right place at the right time, meeting the right people. On other occasions it's the sudden inspiration that gives birth to a great song or the discovery of a gimmick, that can help a solo singer or group to break away from the ordinary run-of-the-mill performance.

So I'll wish you the best of luck. You'll certainly need it.

CHAPTER ONE

FORMING A GROUP

1. GETTING STARTED

There's always been a great attraction in being a member of an instrumental/vocal group. Firstly, there's enormous enjoyment in making music with other people, with a sense of competition to spur your efforts. Secondly, you can learn much from each other and, thirdly, if the group develops musically you are a self-sufficient outfit ready to play anywhere, any time without the necessity of accompaniment provided by other musicians who from one quick rehearsal may not get it together as well as you.

It's possible that you already play an instrument fairly efficiently and have friends who also play other instruments. Maybe you want to set up a group. You'll be influenced greatly by your own musical tastes so make sure you friends have similar tastes or you'll be for ever arguing over whether you're a heavy rock group, folk group, soul group or dixieland band. Even if you and your mates don't have identical ideas at least agree to work on a common group policy. Much time will otherwise be wasted.

The very basic musical requirements for a rhythm group are one drummer, one bass guitar or double bass player, one lead/rhythm guitar or one keyboard player (piano, electric piano or organ). One or all members may sing although it's best to select a lead singer to carry most of the vocal work with the other two providing the backings. Obviously either the bass player or guitarist or keyboard player are better placed to sing lead vocals simply because of the layout of a group but several groups become successful with the drummer singing lead, so it's not a hard and fast rule.

I have sometimes seen (even on New Faces) rhythm groups appearing without a bass player. This is okay for folk groups (who can even do without drums) but certainly not for a normal pop group. You really need that solid sound underneath which really helps to drive the beat along. This goes for the drums also. Unless you're going folky, they are essential.

To the basic rhythm you can always add a keyboard player if you've already got a guitarist. Alternatively you can add a guitarist if your third member (after bass and drums) plays keyboard. My advice, however, in the early stages, is not to go beyond four playing and singing members. If a sensational singer turns up, well you'd be crazy not to make him (or her) lead vocal, leaving everybody else to concentrate on the instruments and backing vocals, but just because you meet someone who plays trumpet don't automatically incorporate them into the group. You won't be ready for it and you probably won't know what to do with it, either. (The trumpet, I mean.)

The reason I advocate a really small group to start with is simple. You are still learning to play your own instrument and probably your friends are in the same position. The larger the group, the greater amount of time will be wasted in getting in tune, looking for chords, discussing arrangements, etc. You'll almost certainly end up wishing you'd never got together. So, for a while, small beginnings. You can grow in time.

Now comes the crunch, and you have to be honest with yourself. Are you and your friends really proficient enough on your respective instruments to at least enjoy yourselves while trying to make music together? If not, it'll be disappointing for you and (if you rehearse at home), a pain in the neck for the rest of the family. So let's ask a few questions.

Guitarists: How long have you been playing? Do you know the basic chord shapes? Can you read a few chords?

If you've been playing a couple of weeks, can only find two chords with difficulty and don't know what they're called then you need a lot more practice before embarking on a group venture. If you can't afford lessons or can't find a teacher then buy a good beginner's guitar tutor book. Most of them are very easily understood and all the basic chord shapes are illustrated. You'll also find advice on how to choose a guitar, how to tune it and how to look after it. Another way to practice on your own is to play along with your favourite records, especially where guitar work may be prominent. This helps your 'feel' for rhythm besides being of inspirational value, stimulating your ambitious nature.

Before you think about working with a group you should be able to play the basic chords fairly efficiently without having to waste time placing each finger down on the strings separately. Nobody expects you to be Segovia overnight but E major, A major, B major, D major, etc. and their equivalent minor chords should not be out of your reach.

At this point I can't stress enough the value of learning to read music in addition to chord symbols. Admittedly, as a guitarist, you can get by on chords alone but learning to read music is not only

. . . a pain in the neck for the rest of the family . . .

knowing what a blob on a piece of paper represents in sound but what it represents in terms of 'time'. When you learn to read music you learn both the note and how long it should be. Chord symbols for guitar will look something like this:

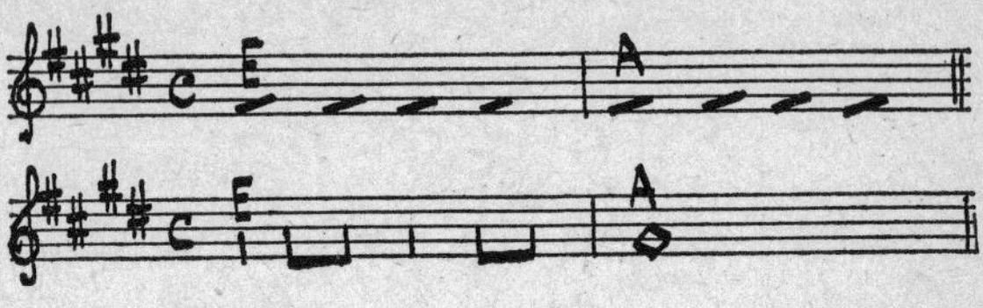

or this

Now these examples appear quite similar although they are totally different, not in respect of which chords are played but how many are played each time the fingers strike the strings.

Basic music tuition in schools normally covers time values but I really do encourage anyone who wants to play music to try and find extra tuition elsewhere, either from books or from a more experienced musician.

The aspiring musician can also obtain names and addresses of music teachers from the classified columns in local newspapers, citizens advice bureaux and local education offices that may have information regarding evening classes.

One day you might want to write or play the following phrase:

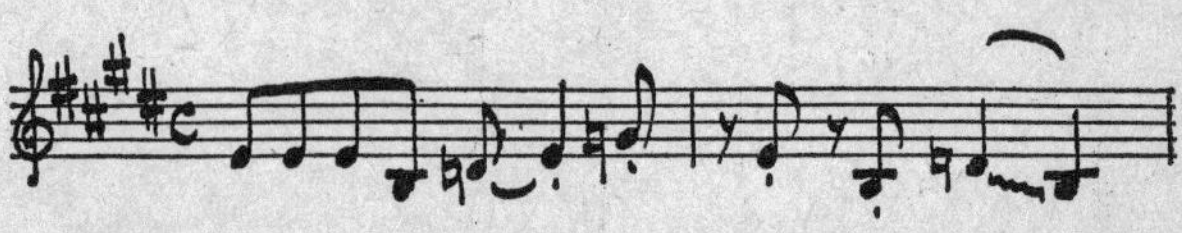

If you have ambitions to leave group work for the financially rewarding world of TV, radio and recording sessions then you will have to be able to read the above sequence of notes as fast as the average reader can read this print.

For the time being, anyway, a fair knowledge of basic chord shapes is sufficient for a guitarist who wants to play in a group. The ability to read these chords should become second nature and likewise when somebody asks you to play E minor 7 instead of E major 7 you should be able to shape that chord quickly, not spending valuable time look-

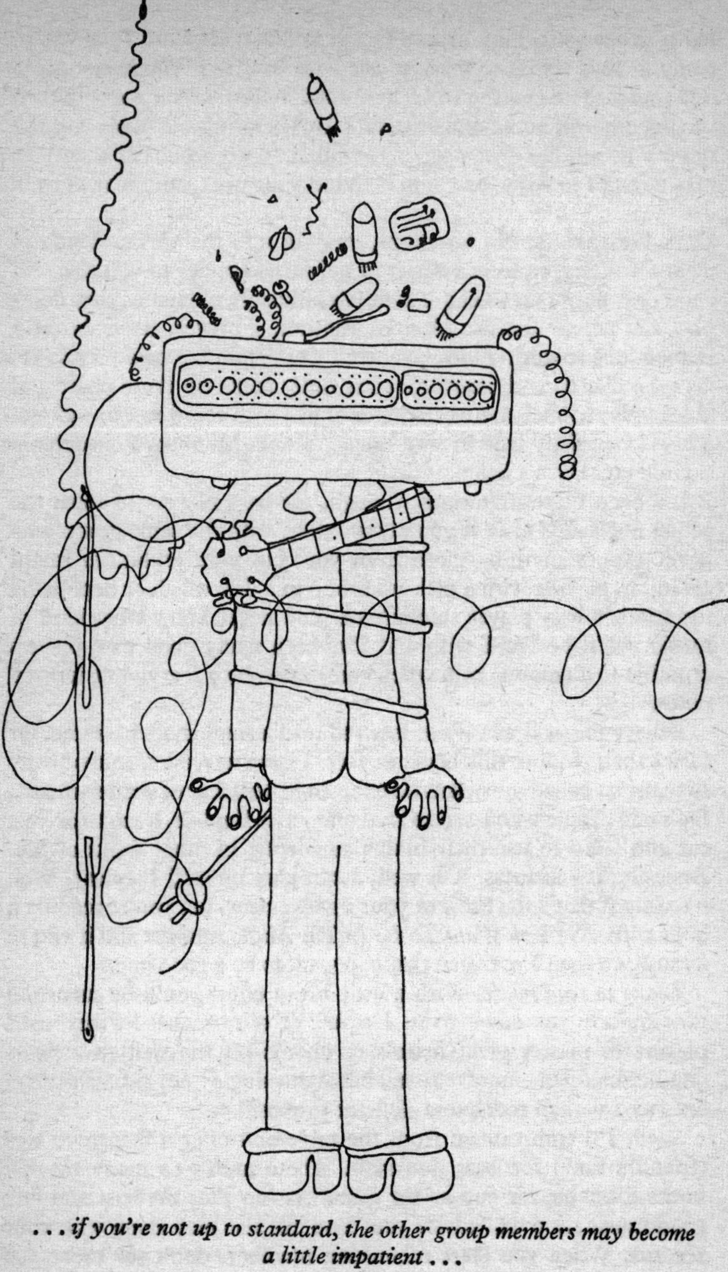

. . . if you're not up to standard, the other group members may become a little impatient . . .

ing it up in your book. If you've reached this standard then you're ready to start trying to make music with others. If you're not up to this standard and you're still determined to form or join a group then be prepared for some embarrassing, exasperating moments and the remote possibility that one of the other more proficient members may attempt to wrap your guitar round your neck, amplifier as well.

Bass Guitarists: No questions, straight into the action. Much of what I've referred to in respect of guitarists applies to you also. All good bass players read chord symbols although, of course, they don't play the actual chords. Modern rhythm, however, depends on a tremendous amount of do-it-yourself work from the bass player. He gets the chords and, knowing what notes make up those chords, is able to play a much more exciting bass line than could ever be written. This is especially true in soul music, Tamla-Motown, Philadelphia Sound, etc. Have a listen to them.

It's even more important, though, for bass players to learn the actual notes. It's okay if you always work with the same group who never expect anything more from you, but your ambitions might extend to playing with a pick-up group in a dance-hall or deputising for another bass player somewhere. You never know what kind of music you'll be faced with and I've seen many good bass players crumble to a nervous ruin when confronted by a few simple written notes.

Believe me, it is so easy to learn to read a single note bass line, far easier than reading this book, in fact. I have never understood why so many so-called musicians develop an instant fear of written music; the same people who learn to read and write English, learn to drive a car and learn to use their brains so adeptly in other walks of life. Basically, it's laziness. 'Oh well, I can play by ear,' they say. Well it's okay if that's the limit of your involvement, but you're reading a book called *So You Want To Be In The Music Business* and if you're a musician then I presume that you want to be a good one.

Learn to read music. With a little bit of effort you'll be surprised how quickly you adapt to it. I agree, of course, that for keyboard players to master great fistfuls of chords off the written copy is another ball-game but we're talking about single lines as bass players are faced with, a much less difficult proposition.

Well, I'll climb down from the table and offer a few more tips (friendly now) for bass guitarists. There aren't so many tutorial books available for you as for guitarists but they *do* exist and any good music shop will advise you. You can also play along with your records. When you start rehearsing together, don't try to be too

. . . many bass players crumble when confronted with a few written notes . . .

clever with your improvisation of the chords and your drummer and guitarist will appreciate this simple solidarity. Work in conjunction with the drummer's bass drum. Nowadays all modern pop sounds blend the two. The bass drum gives good impact to the bass sounds, but not if the two are all over the place with no sense of co-ordination. I often rehearse just the bass and drums on their own, simply to get them together. On your bass and amplifier settings try to achieve a 'clean' clear sound. Many bass players spoil their own work by sounding as if they are playing through a bale of wool.

Drummers: Can you play a simple solid rhythm? Are you developing co-ordination of feet and hands?

You are the foundations, central pillar and main beam of the sound. You have to be rock steady and unshiftable from the basic beat. Many groups (even professionals) have a tendency to race, get faster and thereby substitute a more rapid tempo for the even more important element of 'feel'. You can't really describe this 'feel'. You listen to a group and you say 'it's got a good feel'. It makes you want to move to the rhythm, it makes you feel good and it's achieved by hitting the right tempo and staying solidly together.

The worst thing for an inexperienced drummer to do is to try to be clever when all it really needs is a simple basic rhythm. Forget the flowery frills that will probably disrupt the evenness of your rhythm. They can come later. Just sit down, on your own, and play 'time'. Develop your wrists, develop your touch, work with your bass drum until it feels your foot may fall off. Practise, practise, practise! Try to keep perfect time, and keep it simple to start with.

The other members of the group will appreciate the solidarity of your support more than you realise. You've got to hold it all together and you have the advantage that you only need to concentrate on keeping the rhythm. They have to concentrate on finding the notes and the chords *and* playing rhythmically.

If you can't play for three and a half minutes continuously without collapsing over the kit or contracting temporary paralysis of the right arm then don't offer your services to a group. The drummer's role in the group is hard work but not for the faint-hearted. Make sure you're ready for it.

If you find great difficulty in keeping time I suggest that you buy a metronome, set it to a particular time and play along with it.

Keyboards: Do you know your chords? Can you read and identify them? What instrument will you play?

'Keyboards' has become a general term for all those instruments

. . . if you can't play for 3½ minutes without collapsing . . .

whose method of play is derived from the piano. It includes piano, electric piano, organs of various design, electric harpsichord, clavinette and synthesisers. We'll presume that financial considerations determine your choice.

If you want to be a self-contained outfit then organ and/or electric piano are your best choice. There are some electronic instruments available that are switchable from pseudo-piano sounds to pseudo-organ sounds. The trouble is, unless you purchase a sophisticated and therefore expensive model, you get neither a good piano *nor* organ sound and the whole effect is rather compromised. Another alternative is to rehearse with your ordinary piano at home, hoping that when you start 'gigs' (engagements, paid or otherwise) that the club, bar or dance-hall boasts a suitable instrument. Here again you can run into trouble. You must be certain that your ordinary piano is in tune and in concert pitch or at least very near it. The problem with most pianos in the home is that they are not tuned regularly and are prone to going out of tune rather quickly due to temperature changes, old age or a combination of both. Coupled with that, you can never guarantee what kind of instrument will await you at the gig.

I have heard (even been compelled to perform on) pianos that were old in Queen Victoria's reign and would have been rejected even as firewood. It's all very risky.

Your bass player and guitarist must be able to get well in tune with the keyboard otherwise you never really know if they are to blame for the awful sounds that may be produced. It's hard enough to get your fingers down on a guitar to achieve a chord where every note is in tune without having to fight an out-of-tune piano. So . . . though it may involve some financial outlay I recommend an organ or some kind of electric piano. Don't forget your guitarist, bass player and drummer are committed to expense with their instruments, amplifiers and drum kits so don't think your problem is unique.

On the subject of playing, I concede that good sight reading of keyboard music is very difficult but you must be able to read basic chords using both hands, and since you will almost certainly be called upon frequently to advise your fellow members musically it's well worth studying music from books or a good music teacher.

Besides that, we get back to 'ambition'. You must learn to read music and understand the theory of it if you consider the possibilities of playing for a living as a session musician or even semi-pro part-timer.

Keyboard players are invariably the musical inspiration of groups in which they play. This is possibly because anyone who can play so many notes at one go is automatically considered to be the musical

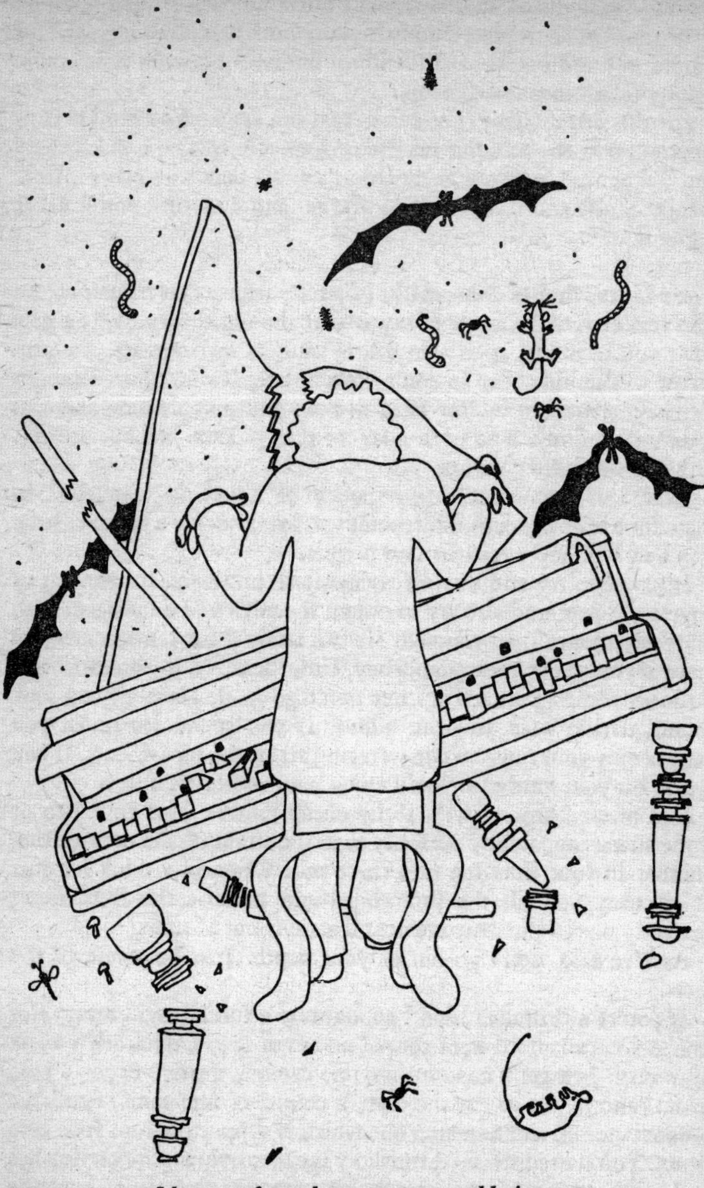

... I have performed on some pretty old pianos ...

genius. I fear this is 'cart before the horse' time. A pianist picks up more musical knowledge simply because both hands are involved (or should be) and a keyboard identifies intervals between notes more readily than other instruments.

Put this advantage to good use. You can see how a chord is constructed, how the bass line fits the pattern, etc. It is far easier to read and write music with the keyboard as a guide than with other instruments. Study musical theory as you go and I'm sure you'll never regret it.

Your Instruments Generally: I do fully realise that finance comes into this area. All I want to say is that the old theory of 'you gets what you pays for' applies in full to musical instruments. A cheap guitar will sound cheap so don't expect more. It won't have strength in its construction, will be hard to keep and play in tune and will sound a bit tinny. The same goes for bass guitars. Drums also improve as the price goes up.

Now I'm not advocating a policy of involving yourselves in incredible H.P. burdens. I just want you to know why a guitar costing £15 new will never really sound perfect.

It's best to try and buy a reasonable second-hand instrument in your early days and also try to obtain the advice of a musician with more experience than yourself. He can study it for ten seconds and know if you've got a reasonable buy. Unfortunately, it *is* an expensive business setting yourself up but don't go mad. Have a good look round, decide what you can afford. If you spend *too* much you won't enjoy your music while worrying about the repayments. If you skimp on your hardware you'll enjoy your music even less.

I've messed around with really cheap guitars. You tune two or three strings apparently perfectly then the strain on the neck getting another in tune puts the first three out. When you think it's just about okay you hit the first chord and because the frets aren't perfectly placed the instrument still sounds out of tune.

As I've said, don't go out of your depth. Just be aware of the facts.

If you're a drummer, don't go and buy a full kit right away. Not unless you can afford it, of course, and even then I think it's a waste of money. Just get a good hi-hat, one cymbal, a snare-drum, a bass drum (and if you've got the cash, a couple of tom-toms) one large (floor standing) and a smaller one which is supported from your bass drum. You'll need sticks (the hickory is expensive) but forget brushes and soft beaters till later. You can buy practice pads which have the same kind of 'bounce' as a snare drum skin for quiet practice when the family are starting to make faint innuendos about the row you're making on the kit. If you don't want to buy a practice pad any firm surface will do to help you develop your technique.

So far I've only dealt with the forming of a basic rhythm outfit as this is undoubtedly the most popular set-up for small-group music. Depending on your ambitions, musical experience and financial considerations there is no harm, however, in considering the addition of wind-instruments to your line-up. Much depends, of course, on what style of music you want to play. Hard-rock bands often benefit from the addition of a tenor saxophone. Folk groups, with their gentler style, sound good when a flute is added.

The only word of advice should be that all wind-instruments are difficult to master and I feel that unless the person playing the wind-instrument is pretty good the overall effect will be rather embarrassing!

Other group line-ups would be like this:

Dixieland, Trad, etc.: trumpet, trombone, clarinet, banjo, double bass, drums, piano.

I would always advise double bass in preference to bass guitar in a trad. or dixieland band. Not only is it more traditionally correct, but somehow the double-bass swings more than its electric brother. You can also use a tuba or sousaphone if you're looking for an authentic turn-of-the-century New Orleans sound. This can be used in addition to or instead of the double bass. If you really want to make foot-tapping music, however, I recommend the double bass as your main bass sound.

There's not a lot of money in this kind of music today (unless you're Kenny Ball) and I think it will be a long time before we see another revival as was experienced in the late 50s and early 60s.

The 'beat' group is really *the* commercial proposition for many years to come, which explains why we shall spend most of our time looking at the various problems of forming, rehearsing, performing in and exploiting this kind of group and its music.

Country Music: The only other form of group music which has outside chances of commercial success is 'country & western'. You've only got to look at the Top 40 Charts, however, to realise that success is normally reserved for solo singers or sometimes duos. So if you're forming a country group your lead singer or singers should be really good and the rest of the group should be used more like an accompanying group to them. For authentic country sounds the addition of 'steel' or hawaian guitar is very useful. Basic rhythm should be provided by a big-sounding acoustic guitar such as a Jumbo, the most popular rhythm guitar by far. Ordinary piano is also often heard in country music but it is dispensable on grounds of mobility. A good self-contained country group is always popular and you don't really want to burden yourselves with piano problems mentioned hitherto.

Another branch of country music is hillbilly. The violin is often heard in this kind of music. Hillbilly is great fun to play but the possibilities of commercial success are limited and it doesn't, therefore, recommend itself as a worthwhile launching pad for the ambitious musician.

Folk Music: There are so many styles even in folk music itself that to categorise them all now would fill the book. If you're thinking of forming a folk group then presumably your taste and appreciation is already channelled and you'll know in which direction you want to go. Guitars, flutes, harmonicas, violins, all make their contribution to folk music in some form.

In recent years the commercial folk music of singer/songwriters such as Melanie, Joni Mitchell, Bob Dylan, Julie Felix and early Donovan has made a great impact on the record buying public. Concert halls are filled to capacity but somehow, because it appears to have a specialised following, television coverage has been restricted mainly to BBC2 programmes.

I still believe there is a great future in folk-rooted music whether it's created by groups or individuals.

As I write these chapters, soul, funky and teeny-beat music dominate the hit parade. Soon I feel there will be a great revival of the free flowing folk style that emanated from San Francisco in the middle 60s. I look forward to it.

2. WHAT TO PLAY

Having decided to form a group, we now look at the 'content' (as we say on 'New Faces').

My advice on what to play is simple. Choose numbers that you can handle.

We'll assume for the time being that you're not writing your own songs so look at the current Top 40, select a song you like, buy the record and a copy of the sheet music if it's available. To start with, select a song that on the record is in the right key for your singers. You don't want the problems at this stage of having to work out a transposition up or down because the song goes too high or low for you. (Mind you, if one of you has the musical ability to do this job of transposition, then good for you and more power to your elbow.)

Most song copies today are set in the same key as the record and have the same 'routine' or arrangement. This helps you tremendously at rehearsal for you can refer to the song copy, play the record and start playing along yourselves with it. If there is no sheet music available then you must write down the chords and words from the record. Here is where your musical knowledge proves to be useful. Anyone can listen to the lyrics of a song and jot them down but how many can identify the chords behind the melody? You will probably find it easier to listen to the record, learn the chords by heart, *then* write them down. (By the way, there's no infringement of copyright in copying down words and chords provided they are used solely by you or your group. If you recopy them, circulate further copies or publish them in any way you could be in trouble.)

Normally, guitarists and keyboard players do this work of finding the chords, so if you're a drummer or bass player without musical knowledge someone else will have to help you.

From the Top 40 select songs that have fairly simple chords and melodies. This will make life a lot easier for you. If you can't play a C minor 9 chord you won't recognise it when you hear it. Play for safety, there are plenty of songs around, simply constructed. If the Top 40 yields nothing for you, pick a standard beat song that you know well.

There is a further reason for choosing popular songs, either current or past hits. When you embark upon your first engagements people will mostly want to hear songs that they know. An inexperienced group can always get away with playing a smash hit, whereas the same group playing some obscure song or a badly written self-composed number will have great trouble in being entertaining.

Although I believe it is always best to copy the recording arrangement, you may wish to make your own arrangements of certain songs. Maybe you feel that the original arrangement is now out of date and a more contemporary setting would be more suitable.

I personally feel that one member of the group should be the main 'thinker' in terms of arranging for the group. If you arrive at rehearsal with no positive plan and everybody throwing in conflicting ideas it can often lead to total chaos.

Here are two conversations overheard at a group rehearsal. The first group achieved nothing. The second made progress.

Conversation of first group:

Bass Guitarist: What are we doing today?
Drummer: Dunno! Let's go to the pictures.

Lead Guitarist:	I thought we might try 'Got To Get You Into My Life' (Beatles classic).
Keyboard Man:	Why? Got any ideas?
Lead:	No, but we can mess around with it and see what happens.
Vocalist:	Have you got the words?
Lead:	No, I thought you'd know them.
Keyboard Man:	Got the chords?
Lead:	No, I thought you knew them.
Keyboard Man:	Well, some of them (tries to play them, gets 8 bars sorta right, then crumbles).
Drummer: (bored)	I just got the new Led Zeppelin album. Great!
Lead:	Come on, man, let's do something.
Bass Guitarist:	What?
Lead:	Can anyone remember what happened after the first part of 'Get You Into My Life?' Play it again, Jerry.
	Etc., etc.

No leadership, not even a useful co-operative working relationship.

Conversation of second group:

Bass Guitarist:	What are we doing today?
Lead:	I wanna have a go at 'Got To Get You Into My Life'. I reckon a lot of Beatles stuff is good for revival and I think we can really update it.
Vocalist:	Got some words?
Lead:	Yea! And I've put the chords down as a basic idea. It should be okay for your voice. There's a copy for each of you. Bill (The Drummer) doesn't need anything cos I want him to 'feel' it. I think we should stick to the original 'feel', anyway, but make it much heavier. I wanna use plenty of harmony on the chorus and leave the verses as solo vocal lines. Let's try and make it really heavy.
Keyboard:	Why don't we start with just a bass riff and build the intro from there.
Lead:	No, I want to hit it really strong from the start. If Bill can give us some heavy triplet stuff across the kit for about four bars it'll help. (To the keyboard) Just smash out two bars of G, then two of F over G Bass, then straight G again, in that sequence.
Bass Guitarist:	What about me?

Lead: Stay basically on the G root, low and solid in a sort of shuffle 'feel'. (Laughter) Sorry I couldn't think of a better word than shuffle, but you know what I mean. Over the top, I've got a few ideas for a riff. Let's try it. Once we've got it together, the intro I mean, we can sing 'Got to Get You Into My Life' in harmony over the top. Just do the intro round and round for a while till it settles. Here we go . . . Er one, two, three, four.
(They try it for a bit.)

Drummer: I don't like all those triplets. Sounds like an explosion in a drum factory. Let me try straight fours on Hi-Hat, opening and closing it, heavy off-beat on snare and thump the Bass Drum.

Lead: Yea, that's good, but you could still throw in a few fills to build the excitement, gets 'em off their backsides and on to the floor, so to speak.

Keyboard: Why don't you put a bit more fuzz on that opening solo, you sound like Bert Weedon at the moment. Etc., etc.

You see that the second group are trying to be constructive. You don't have to write everything down and, in fact, more ideas will germinate if you allow a certain amount of freedom of thought.

Here are a few more tips.

Make sure the key for the vocals is right. Play through the basic song on guitar or keyboard only with the vocals to check the key. Maybe you want a harmony line over the lead vocal line at some point. You may have to lower the key for the lead vocal to accommodate this.

Once the key is set one member of the group can set out the arrangement on paper or work it out in rehearsal.

First consider the intro. It is very important to make this as effective as possible.

The *length* of the intro is your main concern. On numbers designed mainly for the disco your intro can be fairly long to establish a good solid beat for dancing. On slower numbers it's best to get into the song much more quickly with the minimum of intro.

In most cases, you should try to establish an effective chord sequence in the intro and a figure on guitar or keyboards which can be used again during the number.

For most purposes your numbers should be about three minutes long. Anything over that becomes boring. Disco numbers, where your main concern is for dancing, can be longer but normally not more than four and a half minutes. There's no harm, however, in the occasional seven or eight minute item, provided it's good.

Instrumental sections can be featured in vocal numbers. Make sure you follow the basic rules of good recording arrangements and give the chorus plenty of exposure. This is the section that people will remember. You should finish on the chorus repeated several times.

Many current hits have 'fade-outs'. The volume at the end of the record is gradually reduced to total silence. This is not a satisfactory way of concluding a live presentation. You will have to look for a firm, positive, finish. Most fade-outs go round and round on the chorus. When arranging your proper finish, use this repeating chorus a few times then, if possible, put a strong chord on the end. If this doesn't work easily you may have to invent something yourself. Listen to the intro again, the bit at the beginning of the record, if there is one. Maybe you'll get some ideas here. Or maybe there's a phrase in the middle of the record that could be slightly altered to make a final sound. Don't, whatever happens, settle for a fade. Your audience will never know you've come to the end of the song, and you'll get a lukewarm response.

Work hard on one or two numbers to start with. Build your repertoire slowly. Improvement will be more noticeable if you take your time and don't try to rush yourselves. Even when you think you've mastered a song, keep playing it. It'll get even better.

3. WHAT TO WEAR

It obviously doesn't matter what you wear in rehearsal but there are some simple rules for your first appearances. Presuming that you've spent so much on equipment, you'll want to dress as cheaply as possible.

Here are a few ideas, but whatever you do, present yourselves looking *clean*. Dress very casually, if you like, but there's no excuse for a slovenly appearance. If it seems that *you* don't care then how can you expect your audience to care either. A slick turn-out goes a long way towards a slick performance.

Fellas: I feel there's something to be said for uniformity in some way. I think a group all dressed differently tend to give the impression that they are all playing something different as well. A bit of togetherness in dress style helps the musical togetherness.

You could simply go for different colour shirts of the same style with trousers all the same. (Vice versa looks a bit messy.) If you can afford suits, then fabulous, but don't spend a fortune. Same shirts,

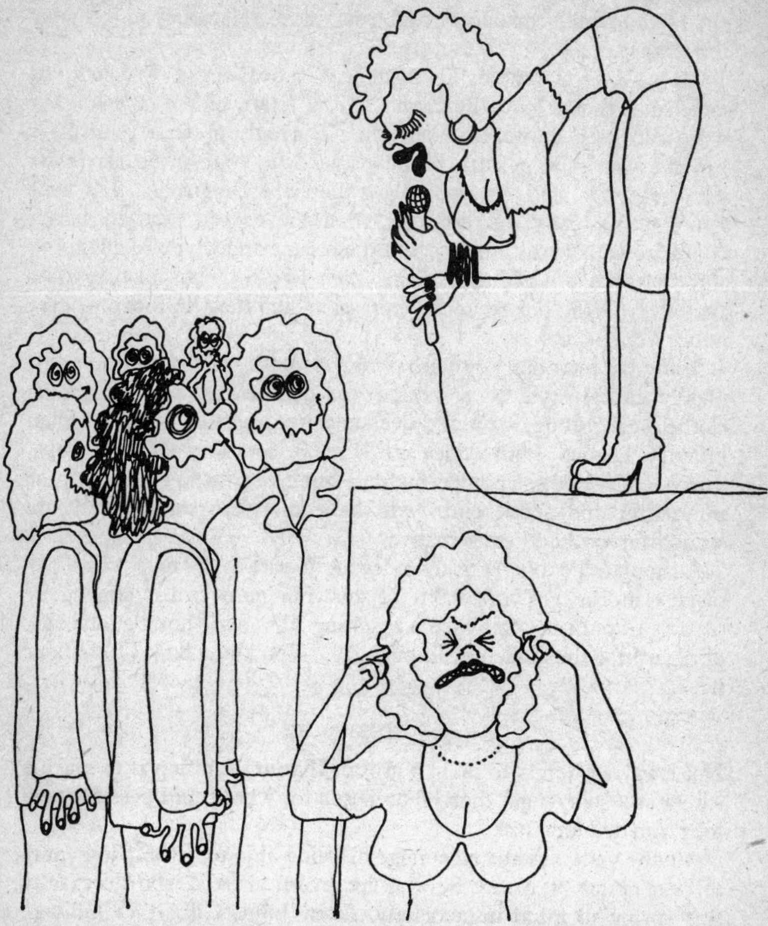

. . . if you're 38–24–36 and sing like a washing machine . . .

same trousers look very smart and can be part of your everyday wear.

Jackets look impressive but are often hot to work in.

Even if you decide (contrary to advice) to all dress differently, make sure you are individually smart. Nothing more is calculated to put off audience, managers and concert secretaries than a messy appearance.

Girls: Keep it simple. The danger is to over-dress. Try and find something that is complimentary to the fellas, either in colour or style, and keep it simple. Although I normally prefer a long dress I'm in favour of mini skirts or hot-pants if, (a) your musical style fits this dress style and, (b) you've got the right dimensions. It's your sound we're really interested in, so whatever you wear must not dominate your vocal prowess. On the other hand if you're 38–24–36 and sing like a washing machine then by all means display your attributes (if you'll pardon the expression) and they'll probably never notice your voice!

Many contemporary groups prefer to dress individually in completely casual style or sometimes in contrasting and outlandish clothes such as boiler suit and deerstalker or space-suit and German infantry helmet. Both styles are suitable for Top Of The Pops, discos, college dates and one-nighters but groups who plan to appear in cabaret and social clubs will have to select something more straightforward and conservative.

Although it's not entirely relevant to dress, I must voice my disgust at the growing habit of chewing gum whilst singing or playing in public. I think it's a revolting sight and shows a total lack of regard for the audience. Enough said. You know how I feel about it.

4. SOLO SINGERS

Not everyone wants to be in a group. If your ambition is to make a career as a solo singer then be prepared for what could possibly be a long and arduous task.

Maybe you have the advantage of being able to accompany yourself on guitar or piano. Several successful artistes who do exactly this spring to mind immediately. Elton John, Gilbert O'Sullivan, Lindsay de Paul, Carole King, all accompany themselves on piano. John Denver, Labi Siffre, Neil Diamond and Glen Campbell prefer the guitar. Of course, since fame came their way, they now appear with orchestras or are accompanied by their own groups. They all had to start somewhere, though, and at that time would have had nothing more than their own solo accompaniment.

You may be aware that all the above singers write their own songs and I shall be covering that aspect in a later chapter. Let's assume for the time being that you possess a reasonable voice, have a fair vocal technique but as far as song-writing goes haven't a clue. Select some songs that suit your vocal style and if you don't play piano or guitar find someone to accompany you at the piano.

Don't spurn the suggestion that you might take vocal lessons. Depending on the vocal style you wish to adopt, a teacher can be of great help. Some folks are born with a great voice and a natural ability to use it well. Others need a little technical help, especially with breathing. Knowing how to use the air in your lungs correctly is so important to a singer. This is more apparent in ballads than beat songs as the singer needs more control over the voice when singing slow and sometimes long phrases.

Of course, it is not absolutely necessary to take lessons if you're born with the natural gift of an attractive vocal sound and the ability to control it well and I would say that the majority of pop soloists have never taken a lesson in their lives. The more sophisticated or 'classy' your style, however, the more need there is to be a good technical singer and if you're in any doubt, a visit to a teacher is worth while.

You must find one, of course, who is sympathetic to modern singing and understands the necessities of the pop world. An operatic singing coach knows all the technical requirements for straight singing and can even help the pop singer to use his voice correctly. The opera singer, however, is trained especially to sing *without* a microphone and even when using a microphone stands several feet away from it.

The pop singer must develop a microphone technique, using the microphone sometimes only a few inches from the mouth, and this is where the two ideals tend to conflict.

As a solo singer you must get your music written down properly or be content with the key and arrangement of the sheet music. This is not very beneficial to girl singers, however, because their best singing range is normally lower than the written key. Although a girl with a soprano range would normally have no difficulty with the song copy key it has become increasingly apparent over the last twenty or thirty years that the majority of girls who become successful in the 'pop' world sing much lower than the soprano range. The boys fare much better in this connection. Having said that, it's also noticeable that boys are singing much higher nowadays, even using the falsetto range. Whatever your style, though, you must sing in the right key for you. A good pianist should be able to help you best in this direction.

Choose your songs carefully. Don't decide to perform a number simply because it's high in the charts. Furthermore, it's best to select songs which do not depend on a vocal group sound and which will come over well when sung simply by a solo singer.

Concerning the way you dress, the strict rules I like to see applied to groups will not apply to you, the solo singer. Just keep it simple and look presentable all the time.

5. DUOS AND VOCAL GROUPS

Whatever style you decide on, be it soul, rock, country or barber-shop, hard work is an important ingredient to success. A beat group accompanying themselves can get by with an inferior vocal sound by generating great atmosphere from the rhythm. Duos (even if one or more plays guitar) and anything from trios upwards are far more exposed vocally. Unless you're going to sing in unison continually (which is a waste of time if you're a vocal group) you need to work very hard on the harmony. Obviously, there will be occasions when you will want to sing something in unison and even that must be perfectly blended. Listen carefully to each other. When rehearsing watch each other's lips move until the timing of the phrases becomes second nature. Select songs which you can handle easily in the early stages and unless you have a fantastic sense of pitch don't attempt complicated harmonies. If you're arranging your own harmony try and make each part a melody line in its own right. Avoid difficult intervals between notes. They're hard to execute and if they don't work well they'll stick out like a sore thumb.

Listen to as many records as possible and sing along with them. Select your songs carefully.

If you don't accompany yourselves at all you must find a good pianist with lots of patience. Some vocal groups rehearse with one member playing guitar or piano. It's not so difficult with a guitar but whoever is on piano never gets a chance to stand up and sing 'in the line' (so to speak) with the others. I think it's important to rehearse in the same positions as you would want to use in public. In this way, in a trio, the middle member is used to hearing a sound either side of him. The outside members hear the one in the middle best, and each other not so well. You get used to what you hear and depend on this for your pitch.

Some smartypants will say: Okay when you've got mikes and sound systems you hear everything from in front of you, anyway.' Well, this is often not the case. The shape of a room or hall, the placing of the speakers and the acoustics must all be accounted for and very often, though the audience may hear you well, the practicalities decide that you won't hear so much.

Regarding your style of dress, uniformity is important, and so is the need to wear something that fits your vocal style. You've probably noticed that the more folky a group the more casually they dress, whereas the sophisticated soul groups like The Four Tops, Supremes, etc. dress very sharply. Study the scene and decide accordingly.

I'm very proud to be associated with Sweet Sensation through their recordings, and you may have noticed how stylishly they dress. We feel that's very much in keeping with their music plus the dress style of the youngsters today. Classy and smart.

6. ORIGINALITY

This is a subject that I might have enlarged upon in the introduction chapter but to fit into the jigsaw of success, it seems better placed here, and it applies to everyone.

It is very difficult to attain originality to start with. In your very early stages – and I'm directing these comments to beat groups, folk groups, vocal groups, duos and solo singers – you will copy and there's no escape from it. As you improve, however, your own style and personality will emerge and the tendency to copy will begin to lessen. Very soon, ideas of your own may begin to flourish.

I don't believe you can create total originality, something that's never existed previously, and it's not completely necessary in any case. What is important is to be something different from everything else around at the time. Am I making myself clear? . . . NO! Okay, I'll give you an example. Haven't you heard people say that Cilla Black is the present day Gracie Fields, or Tom Jones is to the middle 60s and 70s what Frankie Vaughan was to the public ten years before him. Tom Jones 'copies' don't stand a chance now and for several years to come but sooner or later, Tom will take it easier and a new funky, white, sexy soul singer will emerge.

The more original you are the more chance you have of making it, and enjoying sustained success. As I said before, you can't create total originality, because there's always s bit of someone or something else in the new image.

Even Gary Glitter, David Bowie and Alvin Stardust (who one might call original creations) owe some part of their image to their forerunners. What has been created is the new image itself and it is original in its time.

Paul Raven was an above-average singer of beat songs for years before he adopted the Glitter image. Shane Fenton nearly made the charts on several occasions then built up a good club act before he put on the leather and changed his name to Alvin Stardust.

David Bowie recorded for me in 1965. He was writing interesting songs at that time but was still not different enough to break through.

When he changed his visual, vocal and songwriting image, success came very quickly.

'You've gotta be different' is an important slogan and a theme which you should think about only after you've got your early experience. You can still earn a living with talent but you can achieve so much more with originality in your talent. The greater your originality, the longer you last.

As they stand at the moment, Glitter, Stardust and Bowie have a limited run ahead of them. (They should worry!)

I used to record the Searchers. They were good but not an innovation, so their days of success were unfortunately shortlived.

I wish you luck, then, in your search for that elusive ingredient... originality.

7. P.A. SYSTEMS

I don't think a few words of advice on this subject would be unwelcome.

Most clubs, discos and dance-halls have public address systems. They vary in standards and efficiency, however, and while the average system may be adequate for solo singers, duos and trios, it is rare to find a location with a sound system suitable for a beat group.

This is an area in which wise investment is of paramount importance. In the early stages of the formation of a group it seems that you do nothing else but spend money. Unfortunately like any business you do have to spend money if you want to make it, but overburdening yourself with financial committments is not a good policy.

There are P.A. systems which you can obtain for £200 and others costing £20,000. The £200 job will be more than adequate in your early days, not only for rehearsing but also for your first appearances. Admittedly it will be second or third hand but I recommend you take the advice of a reputable music shop. As your engagement book fills then you can think about a more efficient and more expensive system.

When using P.A. systems, whether they are yours or not, take care of the equipment. Don't drop the microphones, blow on them, bang the head or swing them by the cable and if you *must* throw them from hand to hand, Presley style, make sure you catch them safely.

One more word of advice. Many accidents have occurred when a guitarist has been in contact with his guitar at the same time as touching a microphone. Often earthing problems have caused the body to complete a circuit, thereby resulting in a sometimes lethal electric shock. Don't take any chances with equipment, whether its yours or not. Remember, never hold your guitar and touch a microphone at the same time. It could be the end of you.

. . . if you MUST throw the microphones from hand to hand . . .

CHAPTER TWO

GETTING HEARD

1. GROUPS

You may be lucky and be rehearsing at home when the entertainments secretary from a local social club pops in for a cup of tea and promptly books your group for a fifteen minute spot. He probably won't pay you anything and you'll be happy to do it for the experience.

If this doesn't happen, you'll have to go to him or a landlord at a pub which has music, presuming you're old enough to be on the premises. Apply for an audition or ask to do a 'turn'.

There are so many ways in which a group starts doing gigs (the business word for engagements). You may be a member of a youth club that's putting on a dance or rock evening. See if they'll have your group for a couple of short spots. Maybe you're a regular at a disco and you know the D.J. or manager and he'll let you do a spot. Most of these unpaid first gigs are like auditions so we'll treat them as the same thing, for similar rules apply.

Firstly, check if you need all your own P.A. system.

One or two numbers will be sufficient for an audition without an audience. Select them carefully. Make them varied. Rehearse them well beforehand. Arrive at the location well in advance of your allotted time with all your equipment suitably checked – leads, amps, instruments etc. Set up as quickly as possible. Ensure that everything is switched on and volume and tone controls are set correctly. Check tuning of instruments. Walk up to microphone. Announce your first number clearly and briefly and commence playing immediately, allowing no more time than for a count-in (1 2 3 4).

At the finish of that number, if you're not sent off with a flea in your ear or a firm offer, announce your second number and get into that quickly also. When you've completed both items, thank them for hearing you and disappear quietly. If they want to employ you they'll soon let you know, probably there and then. If not, no amount of pleading, hard sales talk, pounding the floor, pulling out hair, blaming each other or thumping the club steward will make any difference. Maybe you weren't good enough. Maybe you weren't what they were looking for. Maybe you'll get some helpful criticism, but I doubt it. Most employers haven't got the time.

On a trial engagement, the same rules apply, only you may well

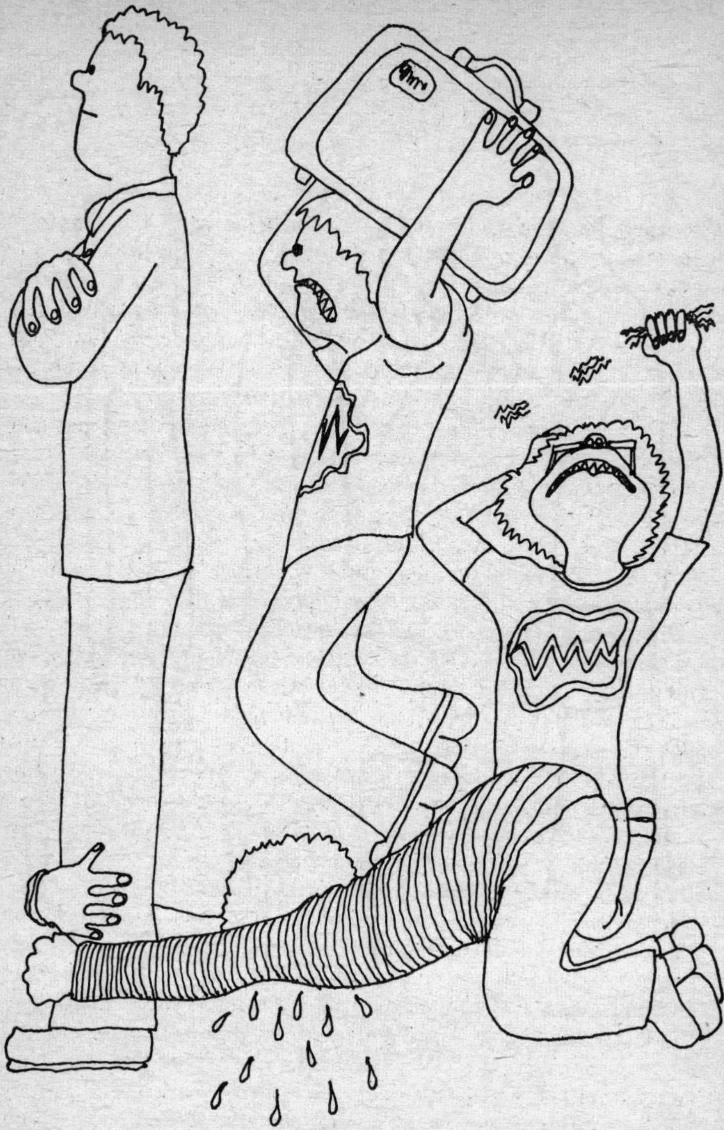

. . . if you fail the audition, try not to be bad losers . . .

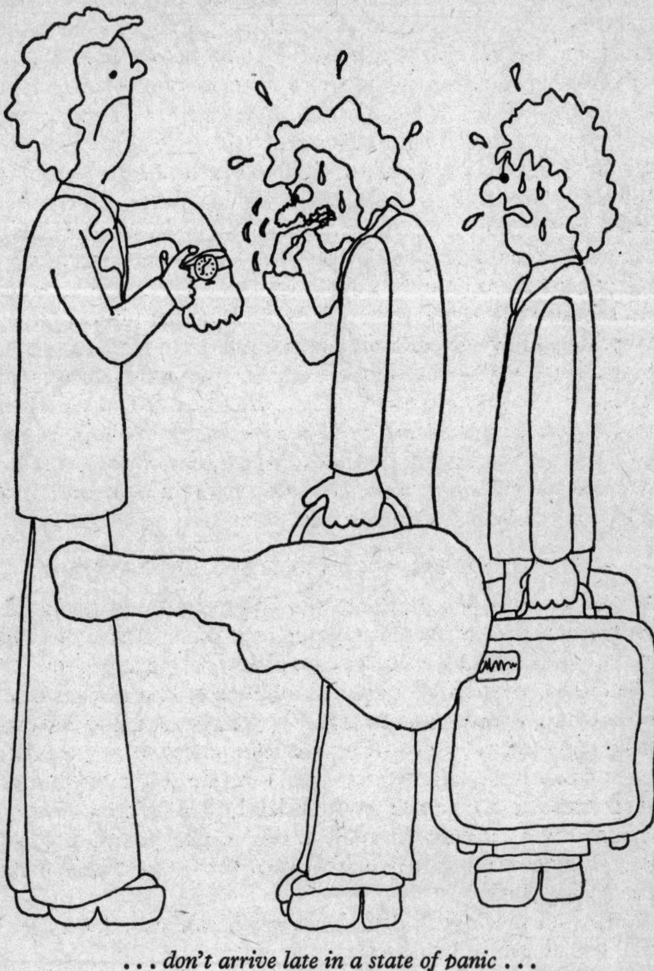

. . . don't arrive late in a state of panic . . .

perform a few more numbers. Don't agree to do longer than you can reasonably cope with and I'd say that's about fifteen to twenty-five minutes.

Treat your employer and the staff with courtesy. If you need help in setting up, a plug-board or another lead, there's normally an electrician, compere/stage manager or someone else to help you.

Remember, don't arrive late in a state of absolute panic. You'll learn pretty fast in this business that an employer will not accept any excuse for non-appearance or lateness save that of genuine illness. If your transport breaks down that's your problem. Jackie and I always try to set off for an engagement leaving plenty of time to spare, then if there's a breakdown, we have something in hand in order that we can hire a car or thumb a lift on a fish lorry if necessary.

When setting up, don't take all day about it. Plan your numbers and rehearse the announcements. Don't mumble incoherently. Put everything you've got into the performance even if there's only one person listening to you and remember that *every* engagement is important. *You* may not be enjoying it, but there are people out there who've paid to be entertained and deserve your best effort. Secondly, there could just possibly be another agent, club owner, etc. in the audience and a poor performance won't impress him. On the other hand, a good one may earn you more dates.

2. SOLO SINGERS, DUOS AND UNACCOMPANIED TRIOS

Most of the foregoing applies to you also so read it carefully. If you don't have the job of setting up equipment you will have the alternative task of rehearsing with the club pianist, organist or group.

Before you even embark upon an audition or first engagement you will have to get your music arranged for piano, bass guitar and drums. The best person to help you (for a small fee unless he's a great friend), is a club pianist or organist. He's best because he knows what a club group needs to accompany you efficiently. Not all the groups you encounter will necessarily be able to read or play your music to your iking, but the more clearly it is written, the better chance it stands of sounding good.

Keep your music in folders. That way it will last a lot longer and stand less chance of being lost.

Be courteous to the musicians and they'll co-operate with you. If a musician can't play something, point out the error and have it played several times until it's right. Don't smash him in the glasses or reduce him by insults to a quivering jelly. If he can't play it, then he can't play it and that's that. You'll just have to live with it.

Some time during your spot remember to introduce and thank

. . . thumb a lift on a fish lorry if necessary . . .

'the fabulous Tony Roy Group (or whatever) for their wonderful sound', even if they've played it all wrong. The audience won't be fooled but they'll appreciate your charity and *you'll* get the applause for being so decent about it.

If you hold the microphone, singers, don't obscure your face with it. We want to see you as well as hear you.

Unlike groups, unaccompanied singers can make stunning entrances and exits. Try and make your entrance over the introduction of your first number. If you have to walk two hundred yards then have the intro repeated until you're ready at the microphone.

See other acts in cabaret and learn what kind of music goes well with an audience. Visit the top clubs occasionally when a starring name is on the bill. Study the formula for success.

And all of you, when attending auditions, if you don't wear your actual stage outfits, at least appear looking presentable and fairly respectable.

3. FEES

As I've explained, you'll get little or nothing to start with and you're not in any position to argue unless you're sensational. The club manager will tell you what you'll get and for a while you must be satisfied. When someone else offers you more money then you've got a lever with which to negotiate.

4. RESIDENT GROUPS

If you have this kind of work in mind then you'll have to build a large repertoire of numbers. You'll probably be called upon to do at least four half-hour spots in an evening, and, without repeating yourselves, that's about thirty-two songs.

That's why the ability to read is so essential. For you can rehearse in the afternoon and introduce your version of a chart-climber the same evening. You may also be asked to accompany cabaret artistes, and if you can't read, you'll have all the problems I mentioned before.

5. MUSICIANS UNION AND EQUITY (THE ACTORS' UNION)

I strongly advise all musicians and cabaret performers to join one or both of the above unions depending on the kind of work in which you're involved as an entertainer.

Both unions are strong in the relationships with *your* employers.

The aim of the Musicians' Union is to negotiate fees and establish fair conditions of employment in places of entertainment. All musicians should join for their own united benefit. Contact your local branch. Fees are related to income.

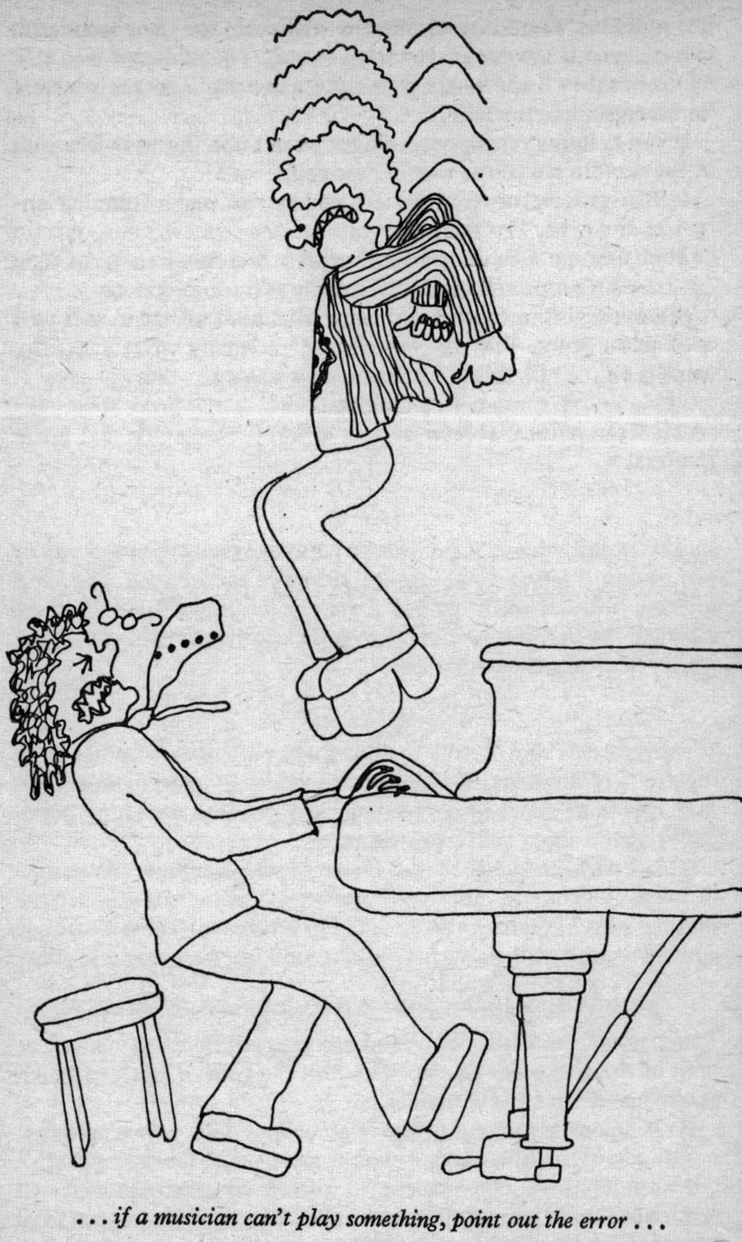

. . . if a musician can't play something, point out the error . . .

Equity represents actors, cabaret artistes, singers, etc. in the same manner as the Musicians' Union.

You may get away with not being a member of a union in a small social club in a remote village in Co. Durham but it is essential for television, theatre and major cabaret work to be in the right union. Apply for membership as soon as you start working.

Artistes who play musical instruments *and* sing in their cabaret acts normally join both unions.

If you are unable to locate your closest branch of the Musicians' Union then write for further information to the National Office at 29 Catherine Place, London SW1E 6EH. The Head Office of Equity is British Actors Equity Association, 8 Harley Street, London W1N 2AB.

CHAPTER THREE

YOUR OWN SONGS

1. SO YOU WANT TO BE A COMPOSER

The old saying used to be: 'Everybody wants to be a comic.' Now it seems that everybody wants to be a songwriter.

For every person with ambitions to record a hit song there must be another hundred who feel they could be just as *successful* writing those hit songs. This is because you don't need to be able to sing or have a good visual image, so it appeals to a far wider public.

The singer who composes his own successful songs also has a far greater advantage over the singer who relies upon others for his material, and the singer/songwriter trend is now fully established.

Since time began, singers have wanted to sing their own songs and all folk music was created that way. As far as contemporary trends go it really started with Lennon and McCartney, whose songs accounted for about 99·9% of the Beatles' repertoire. Many of the top groups and solo singers write their own songs and we think immediately of Elton John (with Bernie Taupin), Gilbert O'Sullivan, Carole King, Lindsay de Paul, Neil Diamond, Stevie Wonder, The Osmonds (to a certain extent) and Neil Sedaka.

Many writers have achieved success writing specifically for one or two acts. Nicky Chinn and Mike Chapman are renowned for their hits with Mud and Hot Chocolate; Bill Martin and Phil Coulter with The Bay City Rollers; Mitch Murray and Peter Callender with Paper Lace. I am also lucky enough to claim a four year run of success with Petula Clark who sang the songs written by Jackie Trent and me.

Most of the Tamla Motown hits are written by teams of professional songwriters who are constantly turning out ideas, making demos and experimenting with this vast stable of hit recording artistes signed to the record company.

A lot of songwriters are good record producers as well. This comes from many years in the business and a natural desire to see their work recorded exactly to their own requirements.

All of us had to start somewhere, however, and I can tell you that our early songs, while they may have shown promise, certainly fell a long way short of a standard necessary to get them recorded, let alone to become hits.

The first songs you write are normally pretty rough. They lack form, sound like someone else's work and are invariably one step behind the current trend, not one step ahead of it.

There are a few basic rules about songwriting and although they are sometimes broken I reckon that 90% of the hit songs you hear will stick to the rules under analysis.

I concede that a good song can be ruined by a lousy record and it happens frequently but our object is to provide the singer, record company or music publisher with the No. 1 we're *all* looking for and with luck the recording will derive great inspiration from the song itself, if there's something special about it.

On the other hand, a second-rate song can become a hit when someone makes a great record. This often happens with heavy rock records where the 'feel' of the rhythm and the excitement generated by the beat is the appealing element. Groups themselves can create this kind of record but it's very difficult for an individual to write and submit a song to a group.

2. FORM IN MUSIC

There are several natural forms for a song to take and they can best be explained as follows. (If I lose you on the way, don't worry, you can always come back to this chapter.)

AABA Sequence: Using the letters to represent a section, you have two repeated sections, a bridge (or linking sequence) and then the first part is repeated again. This form appears frequently in 'classy' songs. Examples: 'Lady Is A Tramp', 'Clair' (Gilbert O'Sullivan), 'We've Only Just Begun', 'Love Story', 'I Don't Know How To Love Him', 'Baby, I'm A Want You', 'Tara's Theme', 'Softly As I Leave You'.

In pop songs this form was used for nearly every successful song written from the twenties through to the late fifties. It's still very much in use, of course, sometimes gets into the hit parade, is invariably in film themes, always in Broadway musicals, but the least appealing to groups.

ABAC Sequence: Examples: 'A Certain Smile', 'An Affair To Remember', 'Joanna', 'Sing, (Sing A Song)' (Carpenters), 'I Left My Heart In San Francisco', 'The Shadow Of Your Smile'.

Not used so much in pop writing today as it reduces the frequency of repetition, one of the important ingredients of hit parade songs. The form was very popular in the fifties but with the exception of 'standard' type songs does not appear much in contemporary hit parade music.

JOANNA

BY TONY HATCH AND JACKIE TRENT.

[ANALYSIS OF FORM]

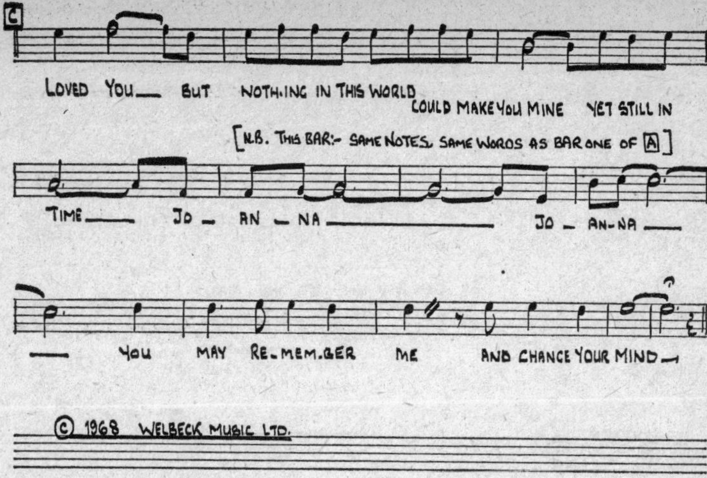

One section only: Probably one of the simplest and therefore most effective forms. Example: 'Gentle On My Mind'.

This form usually carries an exceptionally strong phrase at the beginning or, more often, at the end of the sequence. In this kind of song, it's *all* 'hook', as we say.

ABC (Verse, Link, Chorus songs): A variation on the straight verse/chorus song.

I used this sequence a great deal in the songs for Petula Clark. 'Downtown', in fact, had *three* sections before we got to the hook. 'Don't Sleep In The Subway' had two.

ABABAB etc. (Verse and Chorus Songs): Certainly the most popular form in use today for beat music because you can keep coming back to that chorus/hook and really hammer it home. Records normally fade out on the hook thereby making them stick in the mind even more.

Examples: 'Billy, Don't Be A Hero', 'Melting Pot', 'Tiger Feet', (Mud), 'Sugar, Sugar', 'I'm A Believer', 'Top Of The

World' (Carpenters), 'I Couldn't Live Without Your Love' (Pet Clark).

Sometimes the chorus comes first and then a verse, chorus, verse, chorus sequence follows. On other occasions it's best to save the chorus till after the first verse. The verse then has a building effect and makes the chorus stronger.

ABABCAB (Verse, Chorus, Verse, Chorus, Bridge, Verse, Chorus): A variation of the verse/chorus song. A sequence which combines the best of the AABC sequence with the AB (verse chorus) form.

Examples: 'Where Are You Now?' (Jackie Trent), 'Sad Sweet Dreamer' (Sweet Sensation), 'Call Me', 'Colour My World'.

A= VERSES
B= CHORUS
C= LINK OR BRIDGE

ME YOU'RE THE ONE GIRL
THOSE ENDLESS MAG-A-ZINES
BEEN THINKING A-BOUT YOU GIRL ALL NIGHT LONG
CAN'T HELP
B
SECOND CHORUS
SAD SWEET DREAMER — IT'S JUST
ONE OF THOSE THINGS YOU PUT DOWN TO EX- PER-I-ENCE
PER-I-ENCE
D.S. AL CODA
CODA
SAD SWEET DREAM- ER IT'S JUST ONE OF THOSE THINGS YOU PUT DOWN TO EX-
PER-I-ENCE
PER-I-ENCE
C
LINK OR BRIDGE
WAS SO HAPPY WHEN I
FOUND YOU
HOW WAS I TO KNOW
THAT YOU WOULD SET ME
WALK-ING — DOWN THAT ROAD
A
LAST VERSE
BEEN AN-OTH-ER HURT LOVE STO-RY —
BEEN AN-OTH-ER MAN THAT
THOUGHT THAT HE WAS OH SO STRONG
I'M STILL THINKING A-BOUT YOU GIRL ALL NIGHT LONG

There are sometimes slight variations of the above forms, but they do represent the basic construction of all songs.

No matter what form you use, the same basic rule always applies. The song must have a hook somewhere. As the term implies, it's that section of the song which hooks you, which gets on your brain. People will say a song is catchy which is the same thing, but it means they've been hooked by the hook! The hook can be a whole chorus in a verse/chorus song or just one fantastic phrase combining words and music in the A section of an AABA sequence.

My advice to all novice song writers is to go for the simplest form, the AB sequence of verse and chorus. If those two sections sound good one can always add a bridge and convert the song easily to an ABABCAB form.

And what is the 'bridge', you ask? It is the section that is different from the main verse/chorus section but which brings you back either to the verse or to the chorus again. In America they call it the 'release' which is just as it implies. It releases the song from the possibility of becoming too repetitious and boring, yet brings you back to one of the main sections. The bridge or release can be used one or more times either with the same words or something different.

Don't forget, work on the chorus, that's where the song succeeds or fails.

Songwriting *is* a science and the more you study it, the *more* you will understand it.

3. WHERE TO START

There are no hard and fast rules as to where you should start writing a song. Sometimes we (that's Jackie and I) start with a verse and struggle on the chorus. On other occasions it's round the other way. There's only one thing for certain, you can't start with the bridge because it must relate to the more important sections of the song, the verse and chorus.

The only important rule in verse/chorus construction is to try and create something really catchy in the chorus or hook.

Now this isn't just a matter of the right notes. You must attempt to marry the right words to these notes.

The title of the song should be repeated on the catchiest sequence of notes you can put together. Sometimes the title might appear several times on *different* notes in the chorus, but as long as you are establishing your title you are going in the right direction.

Many novices make the really basic mistake of writing just poetry – but there's a lot of difference between song lyrics and poetry, and while I admit that the odd song will always appear that doesn't repeat the title, these are rarities. This kind of song has to have an outstanding melody to carry it through and even hardened professional songwriters try to avoid it.

So it's the right marriage of words and music that helps to make a hit song. Something easy on the ear, something you can't get off the brain once you've heard it. Study every hit you can think of and you'll become aware of this plain simple fact that nearly all struggling songwriters fail to achieve. You'll notice that in every good song there are one or two lines you can *always* remember even if you forget the rest of the words and music. That's the hook, that's what you must aim for.

4. TITLES

For a start, take everyday phrases. See if they roll off the tongue easily. A clumsy sequence of words will make a clumsy sounding song. Try and find phrases that haven't been used too much. You've got to write a pretty fantastic song called 'I Love You' for anyone to be interested.

I can't say to you: 'Avoid all the well worn subjects like sun, moon, stars, loneliness, togetherness, sadness and happiness, love and hate', because they are all the stuff of which songs are built. It's how you put it together and how much originality in the marriage of words and music that really counts.

If you're writing beat songs go to a disco and see how everyone sings along with the hits. Watch the kids dancing opposite each other and note how they relate the words in a song to their own emotions.

It's not just the beat or the constant playing of a song that gets people involved. When we first completed 'Sad Sweet Dreamer' with Sweet Sensation we took the record to several discos a few weeks before it was released and we noticed that from only one play people were starting to sing along with it before the record had finished. And why? It's all in that catchy simple combination of words and music: 'Sad Sweet Dreamer, it's just one of those things you put down to experience.'

If you're writing sing-along songs or ballads, then pubs that feature music are a good measure to go by. Obviously, you get a lot

. . . audience reaction can be helpful . . .

of old songs in the repertoire but the kind of songs that Des O'Connor, Val Doonican and Ken Dodd sing will always be popular.

A songwriter must study his craft and I, for one, never stop listening to the radio, buying records or watching Top Of The Pops. You can learn so much by analysing other songwriters' work.

Simplicity is the key word. A sequence of notes with words that anyone can sing is the secret of a hit song.

5. LYRICS

The English language, like any language, has certain words which lend themselves better to rhyming schemes than others.

Use a rhyming dictionary if you so desire but always remember to keep your songs in everyday language. Some people say the words don't matter but good words with simple rhyming schemes are very important.

Obvious rhymes are: day, may, say, away;
me, be, free, agree, see;
more, before, sure;
then, when,
stronger, longer;
emotion, devotion;
tomorrow, sorrow, borrow;
you, do, through, new, few.

All basic, everyday words. When writing lyrics, we usually put the alphabet down on the first page for quick reference. Don't use words that are too long, because when they are split up over several notes they tend to sound clumsy.

Words like 'eventually' are difficult to scan and you can always find another way of saying it if you try hard enough.

Members of beat groups have the advantage over others because they can rehearse their songs with the group and even perform them. Audience reaction can be helpful to the development of a writer. If people comment favourably on the song, you're making progress. If they ignore it, ask yourself why.

If you don't feel capable of writing both words and music then find a partner with whom you can work – someone with the same musical tastes as yourself. Very often, two or three members of a group will write together and the collaboration can be very successful.

Don't send lyrics or music only to a singer, music publisher, record company or record producer. The chances of anyone doing anything with them are so remote that you're just wasting your time. It is better to team up with another writer to work on the songs. Words mean very little on their own, and although a good melody

. . . don't ramble on . . .

might inspire a music publisher to obtain a professionally written lyric, don't forget that he is also being sent dozens of complete songs which will attract his notice far more quickly, are easier to analyse and, if good, are ready for immediate exploitation.

6. SONGWRITER SERVICES

I don't recommend, furthermore, the services which some organisations offer. You send them either a lyric or music and they have the other half of the job done for you. This often costs *you* money. They will also offer a demonstration disc service which also costs you money. In addition they sometimes want you to assign the song to them for publication but may have little or no intention of actually exploiting it.

The weakness of the scheme is that it doesn't matter how bad your music or lyric is, as long as you are prepared to part with hard-earned cash they will make some kind of song out of your work, present you with a demo disc which looks pretty impressive (especially when you've paid for it) and you, the songwriter, get no real help at all.

I've also heard of another organisation which, for a fee, will analyse your song, giving marks for melody, lyrics, number of times the title is used, etc. It's no help at all to you to know that you got 8 out of 10 for your lyrics but still no-one wants to record it.

I'm willing to admit to being wrong but I don't know one song that ever became a hit through the services of one of these organisations.

I shall be dealing with music publishers and song contracts later in the book, meanwhile, hang on to your song and I'll tell you what to do with it.

7. MAKING A DEMO AT HOME

If your songs are receiving some kind of acclaim from the family then maybe you should set about making a demonstration tape. This is known, in short, as a 'demo' and hereafter will always be referred to as such. Demos are always more welcome than music and lyrics on their own. You may want to demonstrate your talent as a singer or vocal group. Home demos can be quite adequate if you approach the matter with some care.

The simplest form of demo is a cassette recording. Set up the recorder as per the manufacturer's instructions and, with an accompaniment of piano, guitar or organ, sing your song or songs as clearly as possible. Keep the accompanying sound well in the background.

Check the tape before you attempt to send it anywhere. Don't laugh, I've received countless blank tapes in my time.

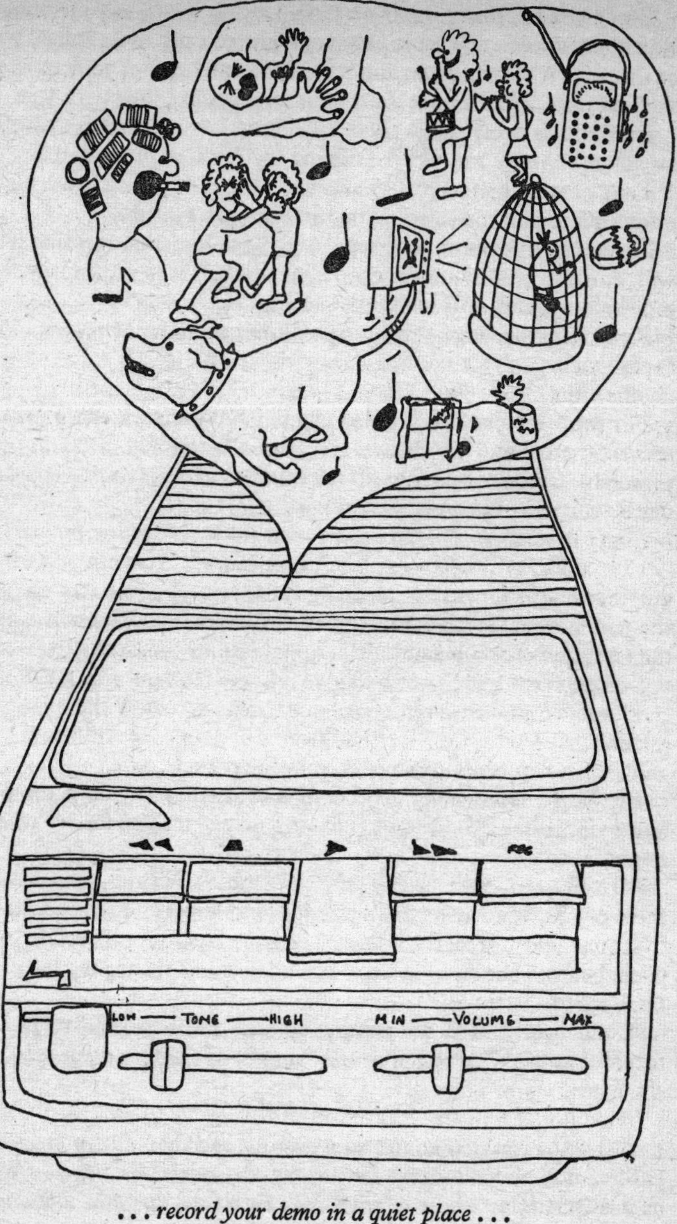

. . . record your demo in a quiet place . . .

Don't put too many songs on tape. Decide which is your best, or which you specifically want heard and record only those songs. Two or three is an absolute maximum for someone hearing your work for the first time. If he's impressed he'll soon get in touch with you.

Don't do as many songwriters insist on doing and that is to ramble on about the weather, when the song was written or apologising for the out of tune piano. Just get on and sing. Your song is all we are interested in, not the state of your grandfather's health.

If you can't perform your song well, have someone else sing it for you. A lousy rendition of a good song, even if it is accompanied by profuse apologies, will not do you any good.

Keep all birds, dogs, screaming children and telephones out of the room when you're recording. They don't add to the value of your demo at all.

For more advanced recording at home you can purchase reel-to-reel tape recorders which will give you a better sound quality and even have facilities building up the number of voices or accompanying instruments in consecutive stages.

Many manufacturers have their own trade names for this facility but it's normally known as: 'sound on sound'. You can record the guitar accompaniment first, then add solo voice, double-track it (sing it again so there's the equivalent of two voices) add some harmony then a little percussion and finish up with quite an interesting demo, with echo even, which helps to give it a less flat atmosphere.

The more sophisticated your equipment the better the quality of the finished sound. Consult your local hi-fi dealer, he will know what will best suit your requirements *and* your pocket.

I've heard some really good demos made this way on equipment that cost about £150 in 1975. This will give you some idea of what it might cost now.

All you need, once you've got the recorder, is time, patience and three hands, or an assistant to watch sound levels and twiddle knobs.

If your reel-to-reel recorder has no such facilities proceed to make your demo as the routine for a cassette demo. Always try to use 7½ i.p.s. speed.

When your demos are complete you'll want to send them to a record company, record producer, singer, or singer's manager.

8. SUBMITTING YOUR WORK

I must warn you that no matter who you send them to, you may well have to wait several weeks for a reply and in some cases you won't hear anything at all. It is advisable, therefore, to send a stamped, self-addressed envelope with your cassette or tape because it puts a

. . . all you need is time, patience and three hands . . .

greater responsibility on the person to whom you've sent it to listen to your work and return it if it's not suitable.

It is also advisable to keep a copy of your tape in the event of loss in the post or it being mislaid in someone's office.

The reason for the possibility of your tape not being heard at all and not returned is the vast amount of tapes, records and songs that are constantly submitted to singers, music publishers, record producers, artistes' managers and record companies. Many offices (such as ours) have an efficient system of booking-in the tape, etc. when it arrives.

Sometimes we are able to listen to it right away. On other occasions we have to let the pile build up for several weeks due to our own business commitments, then have a whole day going through the lot.

Letters are then sent to the senders, either accompanying the return of the material or asking to hear some more, giving advice, etc. When the tape is sent back this is also noted in our files in case of a future query.

9. PRESENTING YOUR WORK

If you have written the songs, label the tape container very clearly with the titles, running speed (if it's reel-to-reel), whether it's recorded on a four-track or two-track machine, your name, address and telephone number. Material is often mislaid in a busy office due to total lack of adequate labelling.

Include a clearly written or typed copy of the lyrics.

Although the melody line with words and chord symbols is welcome, it is not essential. Also put your name on the lyrics.

If you write an accompanying letter keep it very short and very legible, make sure your name and address and the date on which it is sent are all clearly indicated.

If you are presenting yourself as a singer/songwriter or group or any kind of act *always* include a recent photograph.

Don't send your work c/o a broadcasting organisation like ATV or the BBC. They've got enough mail coming in as it is without acting as a forwarding agent.

You can track down the name and address of the record company which releases the records of the artiste to whom you want to submit your work.

Most record companies have an Artiste and Repertoire Division sometimes called The Creative Department), and you can send your work to them for submission to the artiste.

Alternatively you can inquire the name and address of the manager of the artiste and send it direct to him.

You can obtain the names and addresses of record companies, artistes' managements and agents from the *Music Year Book* published by Macmillan and the *Melody Maker Yearbook.* Some useful addresses are in the appendix at the end of this book.

If artistes are in cabaret you can always leave your songs, etc. at the club where they are working but I don't advise trying to contact a big name on a one-night engagement . . . they just don't have time to see you.

If you prefer to send your songs to a music publisher you can generally find his name and address on a song copy. Mark your package for the attention of the Professional Manager.

Alternatively, if you look on the label of a record, the publisher's name is generally included in the information. A London telephone directory will usually provide the address.

Many music weeklies such as *New Musical Express, Disc, Melody Maker*, etc. carry adverts from record companies and music publishers. This is another source from which you may obtain an address.

10. COPYRIGHT

Don't worry about somebody stealing the ideas in your work. It rarely happens and the risks for those attempting such skulduggery are too great.

Many people ask how one can copyright a song without involving a music publisher. I am indebted to the Songwriters' Guild for allowing me to reprint the following extract from *Guild News* (June 1971) which explains the various methods available to all songwriters as concisely as anyone could wish.

> A musical work (and any associated lyrics) acquires copyright protection immediately it is committed to paper or fixed in some other material form, such as recording, and under the Copyright Act, 1956, no formal registration is necessary or called for. But the author and/or composer should always write at the bottom of the first page of the manuscript work the international copyright sign, THE SIGN IS IDENTIFIED THUS ©
>
> The author may then establish the existence of his work by registering this at Stationers' Hall. The registration fee of £2.00 together with a copy of the manuscript, should be send to the Registrar, Stationers' Hall, Stationers' Hall Court, Ludgate Hill, London, E.C.4.
>
> Before sending any manuscript, write to the Registrar, asking for an application form and enclosing 5p.

An alternative and cheaper method is for the auther/composer to: (a) purchase at the Post Office a printed official registered envelope (an ordinary envelope will not do) large enough to contain a copy of the work; (b) write on the OUTSIDE of the envelope the title of the work; (c) put the work in the envelope, AND SEAL IT; (d) address the envelope to yourself, and post it, being sure carefully to keep the Post Office receipt.

When the envelope is delivered by post, do NOT open it, but pin the receipt on it and put it somewhere where it can always be found. Then if any question arises as to when the work was created, the receipt, and the postmark, will provide incontrovertible evidence. But the envelope should be kept sealed and only opened in a Court of Law should there be any challenge as to date of origin.

As time goes on you may find you have quite a few sealed registered envelopes in your care, but you will know which contains what work if you have acted as indicated in (b) above.

A third possibility is to have the manuscript dated and signed by a solicitor, bank manager or other similar responsible person, but for this means to be effective that person would have to be prepared to give evidence or make a sworn statement.

In all three cases it must be realised that these precautions do no more than establish that your work existed on a particular date. This may be of vital importance; but it does not of itself afford a guarantee that the copyright in the work is yours. There is always a possibility that a similar work may have been created unknown to you elsewhere; and if the owner of this other work can prove that it existed before yours it might be held that your work is an infringement even though you were quite unaware of the other work's existence.

It is advised that no work should be sent or shown to anyone until one or other of the suggested precautions has been taken.

NOTE: Copyright in published works subsists during the life of the author and for fifty years after his or her death. In the case of joint authorship, the term is fifty years after the death of the surviving author.

Copyright in works unpublished before the death of the author subsists until the end of fifty years from the time when such works are or were first performed in public or broadcast, or offered to the public in the form of records.

© Songwriters' Guild of Great Britain, 52 Dean Street, London, W1V 5HJ 1971

You may worry that in the event of a dispute you won't be able to find the money to make a claim. In this case contact a solicitor who will advise you of your rights. It is almost certain that if your complaint is strong enough he will be able to obtain free legal aid for you.

CHAPTER FOUR

DEVELOPING AN ACT

I. GETTING STRAIGHT

The development of an act is the art of putting several songs together to produce a programme of music that is varied, entertaining and uses your talents to the fullest degree.

The act will depend on the type of music you perform and the kind of engagements you will undertake.

It can't be a specific length or number of songs because you may well be asked to perform for anything from fifteen minutes to an hour. As a supporting act you are more likely to be doing between twenty and forty minutes in your spot, so there is little point in planning for anything longer.

All performers, whether they have had hit records or not, must include many well-known songs in their acts. This does not apply so much to heavy rock or folk groups but you find that even they will include certain popular songs from their own particular field of music.

You can always try the occasional song that is little-known provided it is placed correctly in the act in relation to the well-known songs and, of course, provided it proves to be appealing to your audience.

The reason for the inclusion of popular songs in your repertoire is fundamental to the object of being as entertaining as possible. No matter who you are, from Tom Jones (world famous singing star from Wales) to Henry Tweedy (totally unknown singing failure from Chipping Sodbury) you cannot avoid including in your act songs which have already proved to have commercial appeal. Besides featuring these numbers as they were originally performed you can rearrange them to be slower or faster, however you wish. The popularity of the original song is still there, working in your favour. Think of 'My Way'. Nearly every solo singer in the country closes on this to deafening applause.

An act must have as much variety as possible. Slow numbers, fast ones, ballads, medium tempo, a bit of comedy, maybe an instrumental feature will all contribute to the whole programme.

The opening song should be up-tempo or maybe you could arrange a three-minute medley of bright numbers. This helps to win over your audience very quickly.

. . . Henry Tweedy, totally unknown singing star from Chipping Sodbury . . .

After your first number don't go into lengthy chat. Save it. Say: 'Hello, good evening, lovely to see you all,' and move on into a medium-paced item, not a slow ballad yet.

The more versatile you or the group are, the more variety can be featured in the act.

Each number should finish firmly and positively, preferably with a chord you can hold on to for a few seconds. This helps to let the audience know when you've finished. Also, the stronger the last chord, the greater will be the applause.

Unless you have a great line in gags or repartee don't waffle on aimlessly to your audience, or make in-jokes among yourselves, the band or the compere/D.J.

Some numbers you can do consecutively without stopping for announcements. This is called playing them 'segue' (pronounced segway). It often helps to give an act slickness or pace.

When you do make announcements or tell a joke, speak clearly, don't mumble into your bottom lip. You will lose the attention of your audience and have to fight twice as hard to win them back.

If you're a group, don't forget to introduce each other towards the beginning of the act.

If you're using the club's group for accompaniment don't forget to introduce and thank them towards the end of your performance.

When planning medleys (always popular) try to find a common idea to link them. It could be a medley of songs from one songwriter or songwriting team, or a selection of songs made famous by one singer. Consider such themes as a medley of songs all having rock in their titles, or about love, or on the subject of loneliness. These are just a few ideas but there are thousands.

Never turn your back to the audience. It's equal at least to ignoring them and at worst doing a Harvey Smith.

Balance your strong numbers with the weaker ones. You can't expect them all to be fantastic and some will appeal more to certain audiences than others.

You must open your act well and finish equally as strongly. After your last number, take your bows, acknowledge the audience's rapturous applause and exit promptly. Don't overstay your welcome.

Performances in ballrooms and discos are far less demanding than in cabaret rooms where the whole of the audience is normally seated and compelled to look at you whether they want to or not. Your presentation will have to be faster in ballrooms and in discos, where you'll probably be playing to a dancing crowd and you'll almost certainly do the whole act without any long gaps for announcements.

. . . never turn your back on the audience . . .

The more intimate or personal the room, the more opportunity you have to be intimate and personal with your audience (metaphorically speaking, that is).

Study the acts of several other groups, or singers. Compare the various approaches. You'll learn a lot this way.

2. BAND-CALLS

If you're a solo singer or unaccompanied group you will invariably need a band-call with the resident group. This is the show-biz term for a rehearsal. When you're booked for the engagement you will be asked if you need a band-call, then given a time to attend.

We've already covered much of this in earlier chapters. All I need to say is, don't be late and make sure your music is in good readable order.

Make sure your stage wear is clean and (if necessary) pressed.

At the band-call, be certain about your tempos. It will be too late during your performance to complain if something is too fast or too slow. If this does happen, speak to the leader or M.D. (musical director) after the show and he will, I'm sure, do his best to co-operate.

If you are the main or top act on a bill of several acts you are entitled to state which songs you want to perform and protocol demands that any act of lesser importance should omit any numbers you are performing. Since this is a progressive system, if you're bottom of the bill you may well find that two or three of your numbers are included in the other acts appearing after you.

When you arrive for band-call or an engagement you should give the compere or someone of similar position a running order for your act in order that it may be checked against the songs in any other acts.

If the club or ballroom, etc. has a decent lighting system your running order also assists the electrician to devise varied lighting to suit the changing moods of your songs.

Lastly, the list helps the compere, etc. to know when your act is coming to an end in order that he may lever himself into an upright position at the main bar and stagger to the stage in time to announce the next part of the programme.

One further piece of advice. Always abide by the 'house' rules, the rules of the club. If the management insists on ties and jackets being worn in the club then, when you have concluded your performance (the dress for which would not come under club rules) you should not go into the club unless you are prepared to adhere to these and any other rules.

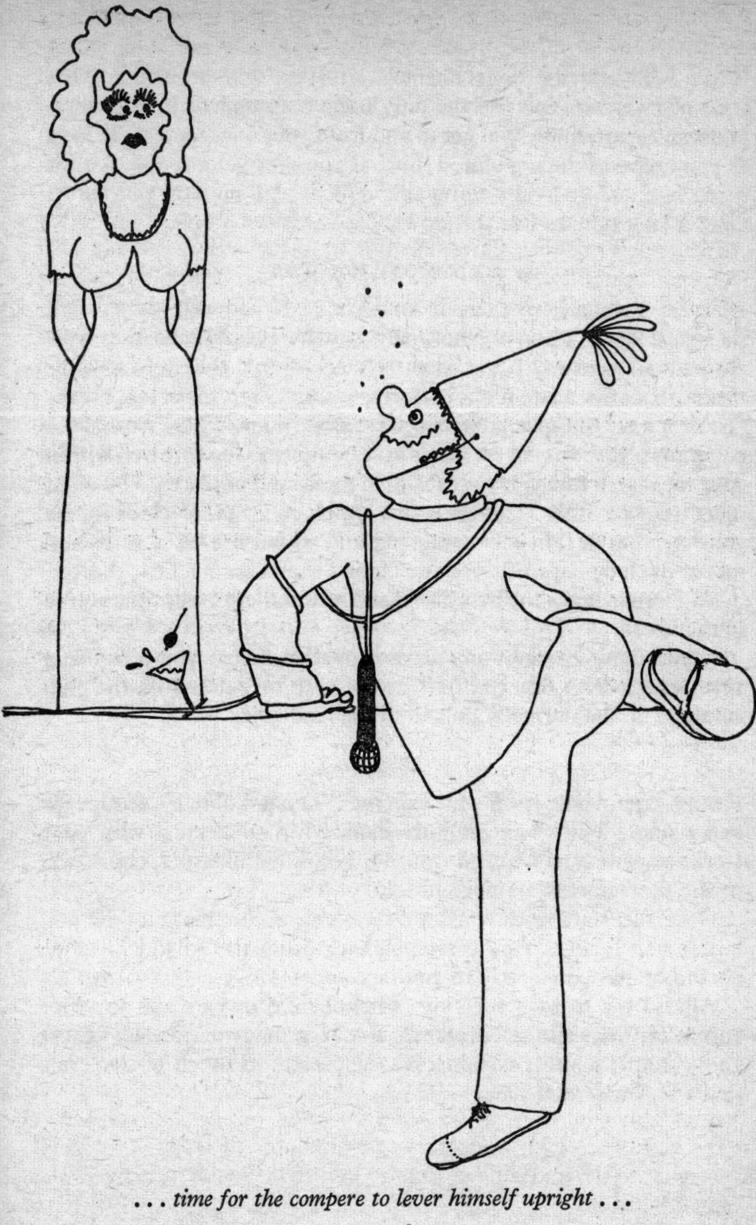

. . . time for the compere to lever himself upright . . .

3. TRAVEL

While realising that your financial situation will determine what style of transport you use the only basic requirement is reliability. It doesn't matter how you get to and from your engagements as long as you arrive at the appointed time. If you ever get a reputation for being late and generally unreliable nobody will employ you and it takes a long time to live this down.

4. ACCOMMODATION (DIGS)

In every town where there is entertainment you will always find theatrical digs. They are normally run by people who are sympathetic to artistes, being slightly stage-struck themselves. This means that after a late night performance they won't insist on breakfast at 7 a.m. but at a later, more realistic, hour. There's usually a communal T.V. Room, set meals at set times and the cost well within your means. Actually, it's great fun in these kind of places. You often meet a lot of other characters also appearing at other clubs in the area. A great deal of joke swapping and socialising takes place and makes the long days between the nightly shows seem a little shorter.

You'll soon know the best places and return there every time you're in that town.

If you don't know of any accommodation before you arrive in a town, check with other artistes at the club or better still, the club compere . . . he normally knows all the landladies!!

5. EXPENSES

Keep a careful note of *all* your expenses. Try and obtain a receipt for every single item of expenditure incurred in connection with your work: stagewear, travel and transport, digs, hairdressing, cosmetics, music, instruments, equipment, etc.

Once you start work contact a reputable accountant, and he will advise you further. Any correspondence from the Inland Revenue should be passed directly to your accountant.

Always try to save a certain amount of your earnings to cover future expenses and tax demands. I've seen many performers ignore these simple matters and involve themselves in much wasted time and worry at a later date.

CHAPTER FIVE

THE SMALL PRINT

1. MANAGERS AND AGENTS

These two terms and the activities they cover often confuse beginners in the world of showbusiness.

Strictly speaking, a manager is a personal manager who manages all affairs of the artiste he represents. This means advising on all aspects of the artiste's career, negotiating with agents, press, promotion and publicity, record companies and music publishers.

His activities might also include travel arrangements and accompanying the artiste to engagements, assisting with facilities at a club, keeping a watchful eye over the artistes at TV shows or coping with an over-enthusiastic fan at a stage door.

In general a manager does everything for his artiste except actually get up there and sing.

This is the theory of it, anyway. In practice many managers take as much as 40% of an artiste's earnings and hardly ever see them.

A good manager, however, is absolutely essential and many successful performers have almost been created by the right manager. They guide the uninitiated and protect the experienced with their own knowledge of the entertainment business.

Some manager/artiste relationships are like a business partnership, whilst others may have more in common with the employer and his employee. Some are like the blind leading the blind and that's where problems may occur.

If someone suggests they manage you, think carefully on what I've said before you commit yourself to an arrangement. Ask yourself if you really need management at this stage and if you can afford it.

Although it helps, experience in showbusiness itself is not essential. A good manager, however, should be an astute businessman, convincing salesman, and part-time psychologist to deal with the emotional problems attached to an existence in the entertainment world. He should also be honest and, though it may surprise you, most of them are.

An agent books you to appear at various engagements. He is not responsible in any way for organising your personal affairs.

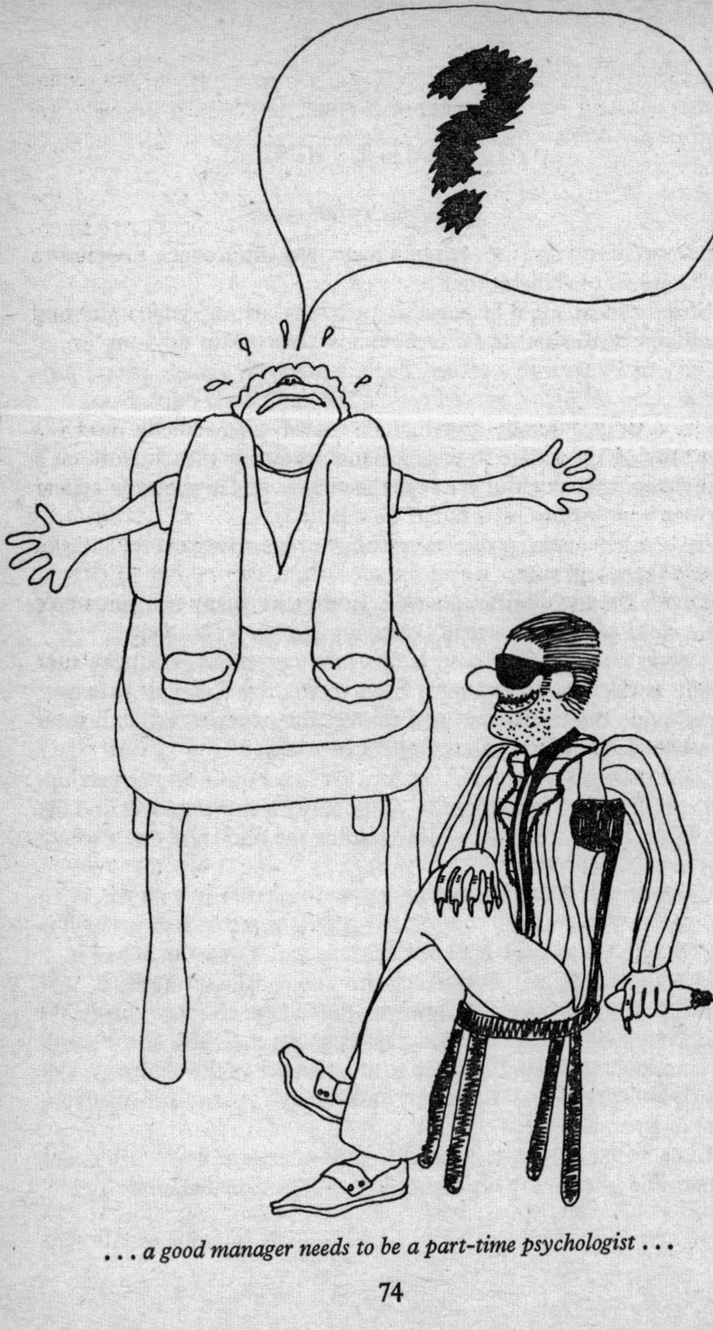

. . . a good manager needs to be a part-time psychologist . . .

2. COMMISSIONS

A manager or management company must not represent more than three acts and the commissions the acts pay to the manager are negotiable. Management commissions range from 10% to 40%. It just depends on how much you want to give away.

An agent may represent as many artistes as he wishes and the commission chargeable to the artiste is 10%. (In some cases where the agent negotiates with another agent the commission may rise to 15% and is divided between each agent.)

The same person who manages you may also be your agent and would be entitled to take commission separately for each service.

3. CONTRACTS WITH VENUES (CLUBS, ETC.)

In your early days as a performer you may not actually receive a contract. Many of the smaller social clubs are happy to work on a gentleman's agreement for an appearance, and as long as you appear on time and do your job well, you'll get paid and asked back again.

In time, however, you'll be asked to sign contracts and if you haven't got a personal manager you should know what to expect. Since we hope you'll be undertaking many engagements you won't want to go to a solicitor every time you receive a contract.

There is a standard contract for use in theatre clubs and cabaret engagements for all areas excluding the West End of London.

It shows your schedule of performances, the venue, rehearsal times, number of performances and times and, of course, your salary per performance.

There are often distance and time bars relative to your earning capacity. For example, artistes in receipt of salary of £200 or more per week or less than one week are barred from appearing at another venue within ten miles for a period covering six weeks before an engagement, during the engagement and two weeks after. The less money you earn, the less prohibitive are the barring clauses.

Very often you will be required to 'double' (do two engagements in one evening) or even treble, sometimes. Make certain you can get from one venue to another with all your equipment in adequate time. Some venues issue contracts for their own venue and lease you out to another venue the same evening at a different time. All these matters are well covered in the standard clauses.

Many venues use only one agent to book all their acts for them. If you are not represented by an agent or manager yourself you will be charged 10% commission by the agent acting for the club. If you are represented, then your agent may negotiate on your behalf with an agent representing a venue. The commission is then split between the two and with your agreement, 15% total commission may be deducted.

4. ILLNESS, INCAPACITY TO WORK

While the old motto 'The show must go on' always applies there will be occasions when through illness, loss of voice, broken limbs or death in the family you find that you just can't appear.

In these cases, make sure the venue is notified immediately. This can be difficult over weekends, etc. but you just have to keep trying. You can be excused on account of illness but never forgiven for having failed to notify the management at the venue of your condition.

A doctor's certificate must be produced as proof, even in cases of the death of a close relative where the emotional strain or domestic problems would prevent you from fulfilling your contract.

Obviously, if you're at the venue and the management is witness to the fact that a physical or emotional condition precludes your appearance then a certificate may not be necessary.

5. PHOTOGRAPHS

All artistes may be required to supply photographs to a venue for publicity purposes. You should always keep a small selection of 10″ × 8″ photographs available to cover this possibility.

A good photographer will advise what is best for you, but try and find one who is experienced in publicity photography. Very often your average wedding photographer is not the right man.

Solo singers need head-and-shoulders pictures as well as full length. Group photography needs a lot of attention when several heads and bodies need to be arranged in a suitable setting.

You can also select one of your pictures for reduction to postcard size for hand-outs and autograph purposes.

Don't order too many publicity or hand-out pictures at one time. The personnel of a group may change, and a solo singer may alter his or her image or hairstyle. If you're stuck with five thousand photographs you will be tempted to make do with them when you should be having a new photo session.

CHAPTER 6

HOW TO WRITE, READ AND ARRANGE SIMPLE RHYTHM PARTS

Presuming that you can now read and write a few chords and you have some musical knowledge, the following is a typical layout for a score (musical arrangement) for solo voice and rhythm section.

The arrangement is adapted from the song copy and the arranger would have listened to the record for guidance on the rhythm pattern. The song is 'Sad Sweet Dreamer'.

Remember that the bass sounds an octave lower than written. This also applies to the guitar where notes are actually indicated in preference to chord symbols.

The first point you will note is the economy of effort. This is because some instruments use the same musical notation as each other, and each part has to be copied separately for each musician anyway, so there is little point in unnecessary duplication on the score.

You will also notice that each part starts out to be quite well defined but once you've established a certain rhythm there's no point in wasting time detailing it in every bar. In addition, the musician will put more into the performance if he can do his own thing, the very crux of making music today.

The symbol for showing that one instrument shall be given the same musical notation as another is Col ↑ or Col ↓ or if the staves are not adjacent, Col Gtr or Col Bass Guitar, etc. (see left hand of piano). 'Col' is Italian for 'with'.

The symbol for indicating that a bar or several single consecutive bars shall be played as a previous bar is ⁒ (see Drum part). Where two bars are identical to two previous bars the symbol is written thus 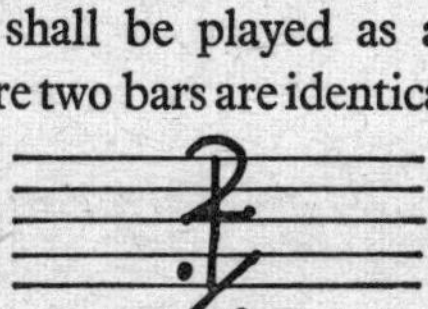 'Continue sim' means continue in similar style.

Abbreviations on drum parts are as follows:

H.H.	Hi-Hat	S.N.	Snare	CYM.	Cymbal
B.D.	Bass Drum	R.S.	Rim-Shot	T.T.	Tom Toms

SAD SWEET DREAMER. DES PARTON. M.+M. MUSIC.

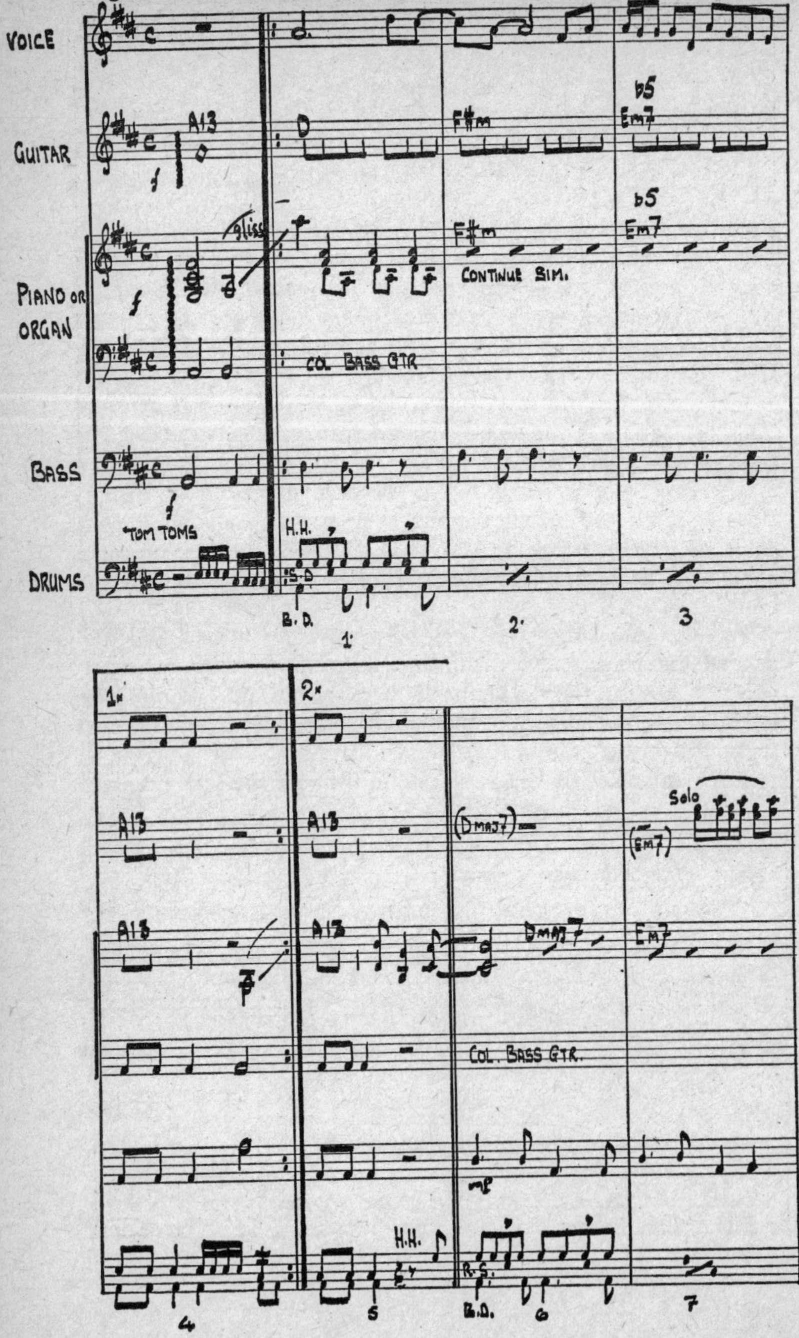

(Dmaj7)
(Em7)
Dmaj7
Em7/D
Dmaj7
Em7
Dmaj7
Em7/D
COL BASS GTR.
8
9
10
11
Dmaj7
Em7/D
Dmaj7
Em7/D
Em9 Gm D
Dmaj7
Em7/D
Dmaj7
Em7/D
Em9 Gm D
12
13
14
15

D
Gm
A
BAR 10
BAR 11
D
16
17
18
19
BAR 12
BAR 13
BAR 14
Em7
Em9
Gm
F#m7
COL GTR
COL BASS GTR
20
21
22
23

Bm7
Em9
A7
BAR 1
BAR 2
COL. GTR
COL BASS GTR
24
25
26
27
BAR 3
BAR 4
28
29
ETC.

The drum part is written as simply as possible and the drummer elaborates the rhythm pattern as he wishes.

We number each bar so that when a section appears that has the same accompaniment as a previous section and we don't want to put 'repeat' or Dal Segno (𝄋) signs we can simply refer to the previous section by its BAR number. These are called 'reference' bars.

If a section is the same as a previous section but up a semitone or any other change of key we can denote this by indicating 'Copy BARS 1–8 up semitone to E♭' or whatever the requirements may be.

We also number the bars for reference when checking wrong notes, making cuts or for any other alterations to the arrangement. All this saves valuable time when arranging, copying and playing music.

CHAPTER SEVEN

RECORDING STUDIOS AND DEMONSTRATION RECORDS

Having written a few songs or worked with a group for some time you will want to put some of your ideas down on tape in a recording studio.

At this stage you won't want to spend a fortune and it's not necessary in any case. The important factor to remember is, like anything you pay for, the more expensive the service the more sophisticated the facilities offered and, obviously, the more professional the finished product.

I won't say that records made in primitive conditions have never been hits because one or two have, but it's the exception to the rule.

The top recording studios in London charge around £36 an hour at the time of writing, in 1975, and many hours are spent in the production of a tape suitable for transfer to a record for sale to the public.

You wouldn't be looking for that kind of service and in most provincial cities you won't find it. But firstly, we must explain exactly what recording means, for whether it is highly sophisticated or very simple it is still basically the same.

As with your domestic tape recorder, recording is the transfer of sound waves created by a voice or instruments into electrical impulses, then imprinted on a piece of chemically treated tape.

At home, the microphone feeds straight into the tape recorder, the level of impulses is adjusted by a recording volume control (or automatically), then it is sent through amplifiers to the recording head which is in contact with the moving tape. A fairly unsophisticated system compared with a modern studio system.

In a recording studio the object is to take several sounds from the various microphones covering the voices or instruments, put them through a mixing desk which is equipped with devices to control and alter the sounds, *then* transfer them to tape.

The studio is acoustically treated to make the sounds as natural as possible at their source, and to separate them from each other in order that they may be more easily controlled. We'll explain this in more detail later.

You may have heard of the following terms. Here is what they signify.

Monaural recording: One track of sound images is recorded.

Stereo recording: Two parallel tracks of sound images are recorded.

Multi track recording: Anything from three to thirty-two parallel tracks of sound images are recorded on one piece of tape. These tracks must be mixed yet again through the control desk to arrive at a monaural or stereo tape.

The width of the tape for monaural and stereo recording is ¼″. Tape recorders designed for three or four tracks use ½″ tape. The next standard is a machine which can record up to eight tracks and it uses 1″ tape.

Following this comes a 16-track machine using 2″ tape and capable of recording anything from one to 16 parallel tracks. There are also 24- and 32-track machines.

Now what, I hear you ask, is the point of having a mixing desk which is capable of mixing the sounds from a recording studio down to two parallel tracks (STEREO) in the first place when we still record everything on to a multi-track recorder?

As I said before, most commercial records are made under very sophisticated conditions and multi-track recording offers the following benefits.

On a full orchestral and voice recording session, by placing various instruments and sections on different tracks one allows a far greater margin of selectivity over the final balance. Furthermore, by using say only fourteen of the sixteen tracks available at the time of recording you would leave two spare on which you could add two further instruments or a vocal group, etc.

Secondly, when mixing the multi-track tape down to two tracks (stereo) you can add echo, alter the sounds and add various gimmicks. All this at your leisure.

Thirdly, if you don't like your mix you can always come back and do it again till you're satisfied.

The track layout on an orchestral session initially recorded on a 16-track machine might look something like this.

Track	Instrument	Track	Instrument
1 –	Percussion	9 –	Vocal group
2 –	Guitar	10 –	Strings (in stereo)
3 –	Piano	11 –	
4 –	Drums (in stereo)	12 –	Woodwind
5 –		13 –	Trumpets
6 –	Bass guitar	14 –	Trombones
7 –	Organ	15 –	SPARE
8 –	Solo voice	16 –	SPARE

It is possible, of course, to only record the rhythm section first then add other sections, solo instruments or voices as you go along. Whether you initially record three or fourteen of your sixteen tracks the technique of adding is called 'overdubbing.'

Groups always record this way, recording the basic rhythm first then overdubbing the voices, solo guitars, or an organ maybe.

When making an overdub you must of course be able to hear what has previously been recorded in order to match perfectly the sounds to be added.

A multi-track recording machine is designed so that you can hear what you've previously recorded and only record on to any tracks that are selected without erasing the first recordings.

The balance of sounds previously recorded that you hear as a guide for your overdubbing is called 'foldback'. These are played to you on headphones (always called 'cans' in the studio) or over a loud speaker.

Echo is seldom added at the time of the original recording as it can never be taken off again once it's on tape. Sophisticated recording studios offer the facility, however, of being able to hear echo on the sounds you're recording without actually adding it to the sounds on tape. This is not just a luxury item but very necessary for trying to assess in the early stages how certain sounds might be assisted by the addition of echo.

Although echo is not added at the time of the initial recording, the producer attempts to make each sound as near to the sound he would like to hear on the finished record, and whether one is using all the tracks on a multi-track recorder or only two or three the aim for perfection is the same.

The placing of the microphones in relation to the sounds they are receiving is very critical. The sound of a voice or instrument can be altered quite substantially by a movement of only two or three inches of the microphone.

Altering the tonal quality of the sounds after they have left the instrument but before they are put on tape is a fundamental technique of modern recording. This is called equalisation and in simple terms can be likened to the bass and treble controls on any domestic amplifier. The equalisation systems in modern recording studios, however, have a far greater effective range than those manufactured for domestic amplifiers.

Limiters and compressors are used to control the dynamic range of a voice or instrument. If the loudest parts of a sound can be reduced and the softest parts made louder, then the overall sound will be more even and, when added to other sounds, won't sometimes stick out too much or at other times be lost altogether. You will be able to hear this particular individual sound clearly throughout. These devices are also used in the final balance.

The producer advises the musicians and singers as to how he wants them to perform. Getting the sound right is not just a technical matter, it has to be performed the right way as well.

Now we come to the mixing of all those sounds.

The basic aim of modern recording is to produce a clearly defined sound that is as compact as possible in dynamic range. This 'compactness' does not apply to classical recording but since we are dealing basically with pop recording it is an important requirement.

I always think of the complete sound as a total 100%, made up of other sounds in varying percentages (it's not important how loud you listen to the sound, it's always the same).

For example, a solo voice recorded without any echo would equal 100%. As soon as you add echo the percentage of true voice is reduced by the amount of echo added. Add instruments and the percentage of voice in the total sound is even lower.

Taking it to its logical conclusion one might get a mental picture of voice, guitar, bass, drums, piano as follows:

Voice	40%
Echo on Voice	5%
Guitar	10%
Echo on Guitar	5%
Bass	15%
Piano	10%
Drums	15%
	100%

The voice is loudest. Bass and drums are well up. Guitar a little back with some echo. Piano about the same. This is only arbitrary. You can have whatever balance you like.

The only reason I'm explaining it this way is because when you're mixing, be it from a multi-track recording or a straight stereo recording in the studio, you have to get your percentage factor right.

Many inexperienced producers make the common mistake of increasing the level of the voice because they can't hear all the words, then they bring up the bass guitar because the voice has started to cover it, but now the drums have lost their impact because the voice and bass guitar are too high so they increase the level of those also, but notice finally that the guitar has apparently disappeared altogether so they bring that up a bit.

We're now back where we started. I do this myself sometimes whilst producing a record until I remind myself there's only 100% of sound and everything I've got to balance has to go into it.

As at the time of recording we use equalisers and limiters and compressors to assist us while mixing, but there's no computer or electronic device to mix a record. The choice of balance is what your ears tell you is right.

I realise that I've covered the enormously complicated subject of recording rather sparingly at this stage. This is because a minimum of general knowledge is all you will need to get you by on your first recording ventures, presuming these are for the purpose of making demonstration records.

At least I think you will have grasped the fact that if your demo session is to be straight monaural or stereo recording (the cheapest) then you will get the work done more quickly but you will not have the benefits of multi-track recording followed by mixing.

Of course, even in monaural or stereo recording there is always the facility of recording a rhythm track on one tape machine and, providing a second machine is available, transferring the rhythm track to the second machine whilst adding a solo voice, or more voices or further instruments. This is not totally satisfactory, however, because the balance must be exactly right when you make the transfer and addition because the recording on your second machine is the finished master. Secondly, the quality deterioration is often greater this way then when using a multi-track recorder which is designed to defeat these problems.

Most small studios are now equipped with a 4-track recorder at least, and that's why I've gone into some detail about multi-track recording in general because it doesn't matter whether the tape recorder for your initial recording is 4-track or 16-track, the principles of multi-track recording equally apply.

You will still be faced with apparently foreign sounding terms like E.Q. (equalisation), foldback, overdub, compression, echo (or reverb) and master, so it's worth knowing something about them as soon as you embark upon your first recording session.

To help you along further, I think it's a good idea if we run through a mock recording session, the kind of session you might undertake yourself for the purpose of making a demonstration record.

You've written some songs, you and your group have rehearsed, you've booked Turtle Studios, a small set-up in North Haven for four hours one afternoon and you're starting at 2 p.m.

You arrive at the studios at about 1.30 to set up. Sessions are always expected to start promptly at the time booked and you're not charged for your setting up time.

You've already told the balance engineer what your group combination is and with this information he does a studio set-up plan in advance of the session. He has an assistant, the tape operator, who, armed with the plan is laying out mikes, screens and chairs as you arrive.

This is what his plan may look like:

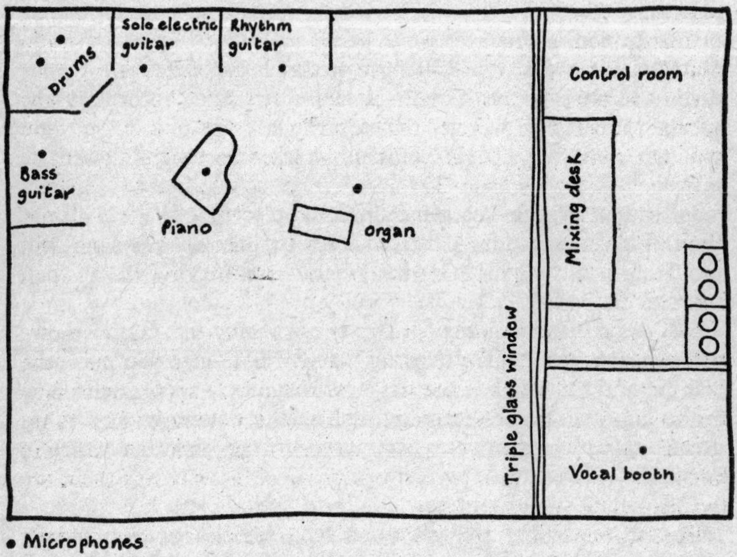

The dots refer to microphones.

Turtle Studio seats about fifteen people in comfort. One section is acoustically treated in favour of loud percussive sounds like rhythm sections. The other section is treated more in favour of sustained sounds, i.e. voices, woodwind, strings and brass. (After several months of experimenting the engineers found they obtained the best rhythm sounds with the above layout and so this set-up always follows the same pattern.) There are only five of you in the group so half the studio is empty.

The straight lines separating instruments denote screens and the drums, in fact, are actually in a sort of booth with a low roof over it. Once inside, the drummer is practically concealed.

To get the best sounds the engineer must also get them as separate as he can. He wants there to be as little of the drums as possible, for example, picking up on the piano mike. He wants to hear bass guitar on its own mike not picking up on everyone else's. In this way he has total control over each instrument.

Further perfection is achieved by choosing the right microphone for the instrument to be recorded and placing it in the correct position in relation to the instrument or group of instruments. It's an important point and although you won't need to know what type of microphone is covering what instrument it's useful to know what 'separation' means, and good separation is a fundamental of good recording.

Turtle Studios also has a vocal booth adjacent to the main studio should a client wish to record the vocals at the same time as the rhythm section. Because the human voice has such a relatively low output compared with the sounds of a rhythm section it is the worst sound to try to record in the studio at the same time as the rhythm. Everything else picks up on the vocal mike so a completely separate room with a loudspeaker or headphones is provided. You will not be using this room today. Since your group sings and plays you will first record the accompaniment (known as a backing track) then overdub the vocals.

Incidentally, whilst we're on this subject of vocals many singers still prefer to record *in* the studio at the same time as all the musicians because of the exciting atmosphere generated by a spontaneous performance. This is especially applicable to classy singers or to an out-of-tempo song that demands a vocalist to sing with an orchestra under the baton. I've recorded many times this way but there are two important considerations.

Firstly, one must achieve superb separation on the singer's microphone with no other instruments picking up on it; and secondly, one prays for the perfect performance from both singer and orchestra at the same time. Of course, you always have the advantage of being able to overdub the solo voice later if you feel that a better performance may be achieved by the singer, but this somewhat defeats the object of trying to obtain a magical spontaneous performance on the original recording session.

Although groups used to record everything at the same time (my first Searchers record 'Sweets For My Sweet' was a No. 1 in 1964 and made this way) it didn't take long for everyone to realise that far better results could be achieved with the all-playing, all-singing group if the all-playing section was done first and the all-singing bit put on afterwards. Hence, the Ampex Corporation of America devised a system whereby a tape recorder could replay something previously recorded on one or more tracks whilst further sounds were added to other tracks. Other manufacturers devised their own systems but the basic idea is the same and works as follows.

For each track on tape there is an erase head to eliminate all unwanted sounds and to provide a perfectly clean track. In sequence then follows a record head followed by a playback head.

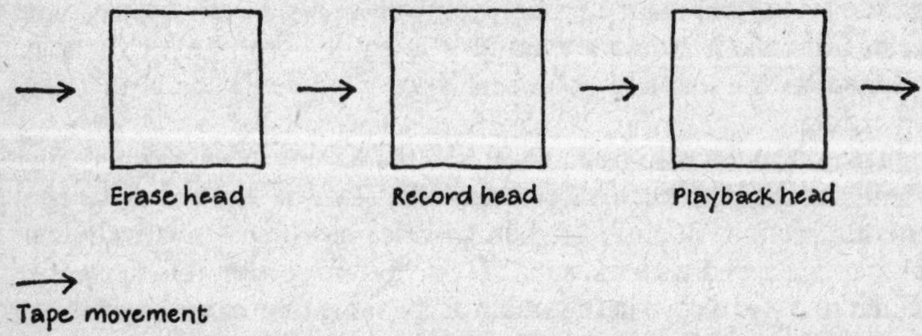

It will be noticed that there is a space between all the heads. When overdubbing, the playback head is not used to provide the accompaniment track to which one performs because the added sound *must* be recorded via the record head and the new sound would not be synchronised with the original. The record head on the previously recorded tracks is therefore switched to become a playback head and any new sounds recorded via other record heads on other tracks will inevitably be in a parallel position to the originally recorded sounds.

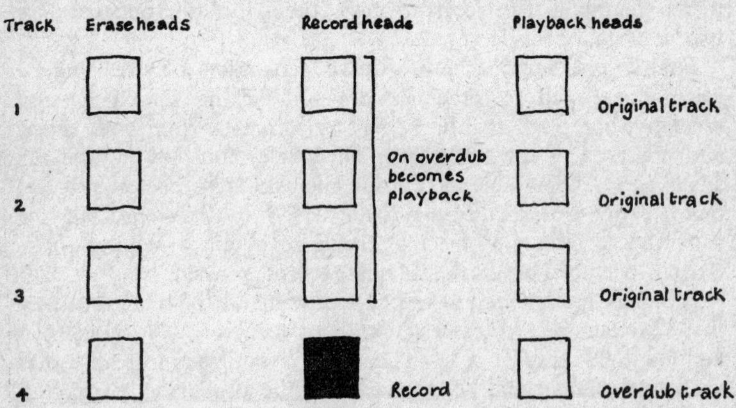

In the above example the record heads of tracks 1, 2 and 3 become the playback heads for the purpose of overdubbing and track 4 is recorded.

For playback after recording the recorder is switched to replay all sound via the playback heads and everything is synchronised.

Returning to your actual session, you have now set up your instruments and are ready to commence rehearsing.

This is necessary to allow the balance engineer time to sort out the various sounds coming to him via the microphones in the studio.

The leads from each microphone plug into wall sockets in the studio and are circuited to the control desk in the control room. For each microphone in the studio there is a volume control on the desk. This control is known as a 'fader'.

Modern studios use the slider fader but you may find in older set-ups a simple control knob.

We must assume that you're working in a fairly efficient studio, at least, so further explanation is necessary.

If you read that a studio has a 16-channel mixer then it has 16 faders on the desk. This doesn't imply one microphone into only one channel, although that's the way it generally works out. It is quite possible to have two microphones (say, on four trumpets) fed into one channel and controlled by one fader.

All studios will either have a system of switching various mike lines to various channels or a jack-board carefully marked out on which, using connecting leads, one can take the feed from mike line 1 and put it into channel 3 on the desk, for instance. Many studios have both systems to be completely flexible.

The jack-board is generally made up of rows of sockets and in very simple terms may look like this.

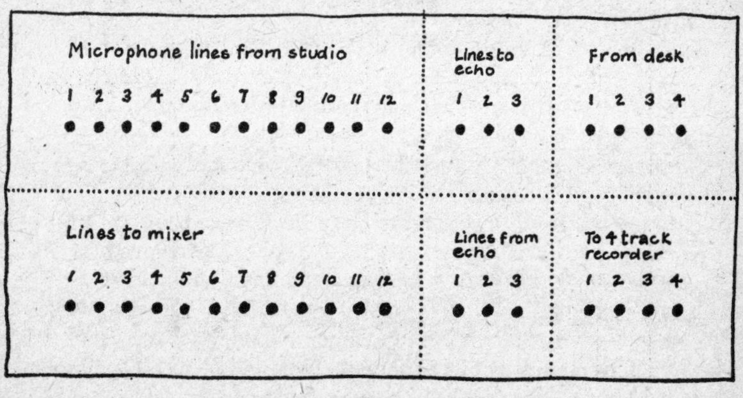

The above is very basic and I've omitted many lines but you can take it that just about every audio circuit involved in recording and playback will come up on this jack-board in order to give complete flexibility to the system.

As I have explained, every channel has a fader but also each channel has further systems incorporated.

The faders are arranged in parallel lines spread along the control desk. In circuit you may also find controls for adding echo, providing foldback to musicians or singers in the studio, equalisation, and track selection on the recorder. The diagram will help you sort out that lot.

Most studios use a modular system whereby a unit can be pulled out of the circuit if faulty and replaced by another. This normally applies to faders and equalisers rather than the other controls.

Working from bottom to top on one channel the various units do the following jobs:

Fader: Controls amount of sound.

Foldback: Whilst recording in the studio, musicians (especially the drummer in his booth) may not be able to hear too well what everyone else is doing. The sound from each channel can be selected, balanced with others and sent back to the studio where the musicians hear it through headphones (cans).

Echo Send Control: Used mainly when the control desk is used for mixing as echo put on when recording is on the tape permanently. Most producers prefer to add echo when mixing later. Several echo systems are used. The most popular is the echo plate, made of metal and suspended in a cabinet. Sound is fed to one end of the plate via a contact and picked up at the other by another contact. The whole unit is approximately 9ft × 5 ft × 1 ft, very compact and very flexible.

Echo chambers (empty rooms, apart from a microphone and loudspeaker) were the original echo system. Still in use but not so popular as control is less flexible and more space is required (one room might measure 10 ft × 8 ft × 6 ft).

Think of singing in a tiled bathroom or loo and you have some idea how an echo chamber works.

Another system is spring echo. Very small, very compact but not a popular sound as it appears very thin. Tape echo systems have also been tried but I don't know anyone using them now.

On the channel itself the signal is only sent to the echo device. Another control determines the amount coming back from the device. This control is placed separately on the mixer. The amount

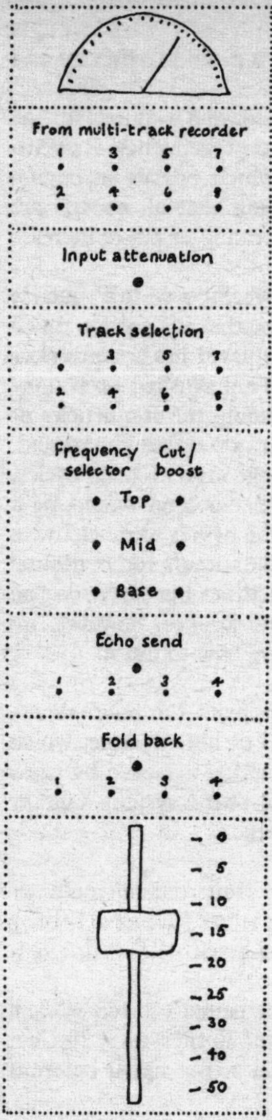

Meter

When mixing from multi-track recorder through desk this selects which track of recorder feeds into this channel

Controls level of input to channel

When recording on multi-track recorder selects track. When mixing, selects track to stereo or mono recorder

Equalisation. Alters tonal quality of sound in this channel by selection of frequency range and corresponding cutting or boosting in that range

Feeds off a signal to whichever echo device is selected and controls level going into it

Sends signal in channel back to studio for use by musicians when recording

Fader. Thumb controlled slider which controls volume of sound

(This diagram is not to scale and layout is not necessarily always like this)

of echo being returned is mixed with the pure signal from the fader then sent via equalisers, etc. to the tape.

Equalisation: This is in three sections – top, mid-frequency and bass.

For each section there is a frequency selector and a control for the amount of increase or decrease of sounds at that frequency. Remembering that sound is made up of waves which pulsate at certain frequencies (cycles per second) and realising that all sounds are made up of a wide range of frequencies, one can filter out or increase any sounds at a certain frequency.

Let's take the bass player's sound. It's covering a wide frequency range. You think it could be a harder sound, that it's got too much 'bottom' and needs more impact. The bass player has tried to alter it on his amplifier and guitar but you're still not satisfied, so you try equalising the sound. This may mean reducing the frequencies at 30 cycles per second and boosting at 100 or 200 cycles per second. You may even try something in the mid range around 3,000 cycles.

Top equalisation around 10,000 cycles per second would be a waste of time because your basic sound on the bass is so much lower than that. You use equalisers in relation to the sounds you're dealing with. All studios are equipped with these facilities but rarely do you find them exactly the same. The principle applies, however, no matter where you go and the engineer knows how to use it.

Track Selection: the sound is coming in from the microphone, going through the channel but one needs to be able to select which track on the recorder it's going to. This is either achieved by press buttons, a selector knob or using the jack-board system. One or more channels can be switched to a single track.

Attenuation Control: Signals coming in from the microphones may be at different levels. When the mixer is used for final mixing from multi-track the signal from the multi-track will be different again.

In order to eliminate overloading of a channel (or too weak a signal) and to permit the faders to be operated in their most efficient range there is a control for setting the level of the signal before it goes into the fader channel.

Selection from Multi-Track: When the desk is used for mixing one needs to be able to select a particular track from the multi-track recorder to be fed into the channel. Sometimes this selector is omitted and the jack-board used to link up the multi-track recorder to the channels on the desk.

Meter: This informs the engineer how much volume is going out of the channel and on to the tape. It's very important to get as much sound on tape as the recorder is capable of taking. The amount of background noise from the tape goes up in ratio to the amount that the signal goes down. This hiss (as you will know from domestic recording) is unwelcome. All sound is measured in decibels (known as Db's).

Monitoring: You listen to what you're recording through loud-speakers. The volume is separately controlled so that no matter what sound is coming off the tape you can listen at whatever level of sound you wish. Some studios have facilities for listening to the sound and adding echo. This doesn't affect what is going on tape. The monitoring channels provide a further foldback system used when overdubbing is in progress.

This is the basic set-up that will confront you when you first walk into a control room in a recording studio.

You are now satisfied that you are ready to record a backing track of your first title.

The engineer is happy that he's got a good sound, the red light goes on, and away you go. Having recorded it, you will now go into the control room and listen to it.

Assuming that the studio has a 4-track recorder the track layout may look like this.

Track	Instrument
1.	Drums, Bass Guitar, Rhythm Guitar and Piano
2.	Solo singer
3.	Spare
4.	Spare

Although there are three microphones on the drums, two on the top kit and one on the bass drum, going into three separate channels on the mixer, all these have been selected along with bass guitar, rhythm guitar and piano to go on track 1 of the recorder.

The solo guitar will need special effects later so you put this on its own track.

Track 3 is left spare to overdub the organ because you only have one keyboard player, and track 4 is for the vocals.

Because of the above flexibility if the guitar appears too loud it doesn't matter, because it's on its own track and the volume can be raised or lowered at will.

If, however, one of the sounds on track 1 is not to your liking, bass guitar too loud or not enough drums maybe, you will have to do another take (the term for recording) and attempt to get it right.

Now you can see why larger multi-track machines are so popular because with another four or twelve tracks you could have spread your rhythm section out on several other tracks and if it was simply a matter of volume of a certain instrument then this could be adjusted when you came to do the final mix.

For reasons of economy, however, you're on 4-track and so another take may be necessary.

This take is now completed and you listen again. In the control room you decide that the basic rhythm is good but the solo guitarist must have had a mental block in the middle of a section. Now you can either overdub the whole section again, keeping the original rhythm on track 1, or only record the particular section that went wrong. Maybe your guitarist isn't confident he can do the whole thing again so you decide to 'drop in', as we say.

You locate that section that wasn't very good from the guitarist but there has to be a space between the last good section and where you want to start recording. This is to give the engineer just enough time to push the record button on track 2. When the section is recorded he stops the tape and anything already on track 2 from that point onwards will not be erased.

The sounds on track 1 are fed to the guitarist via the foldback system incorporated into the monitoring channels.

He sits in the studio, guitar in hand, cans on, and listens to the track. Just before the point where he needs to start playing, in the brief pause, the engineer selects record position on track 2 and the guitarist starts playing. Having completed the section the tape is stopped.

When the tape is replayed and both tracks 1 and 2 are heard the whole piece is continuous.

Now that tracks 1 and 2 are recorded it only leaves the organ to be added to track 3.

Normally, any further backing tracks for songs are completed before the vocals are added. Assuming that all backing tracks for songs are complete it only leaves the voices to be added.

This is achieved in exactly the same manner as any other over-dubbing.

If the studio used an 8-track recorder it might also have been

'Mr. and Mrs. Music' ... Tony Hatch and Jackie Trent.

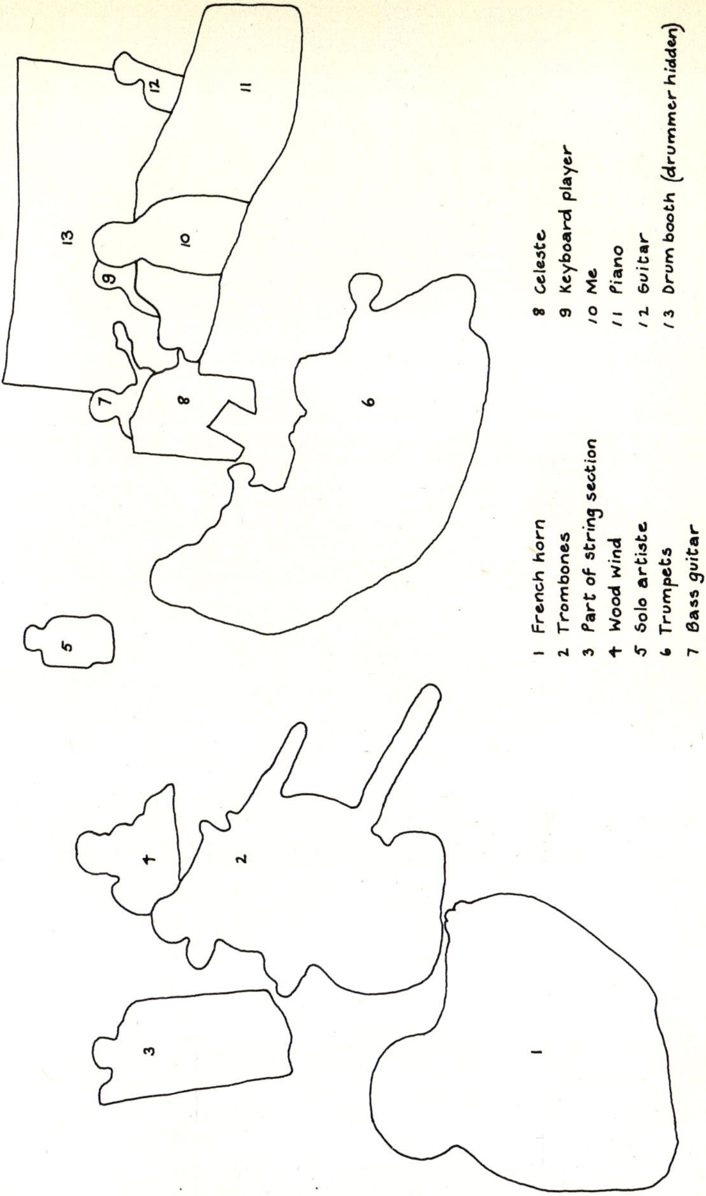

A recording session in full swing. Tony has keyed the sketch above to explain who's who.

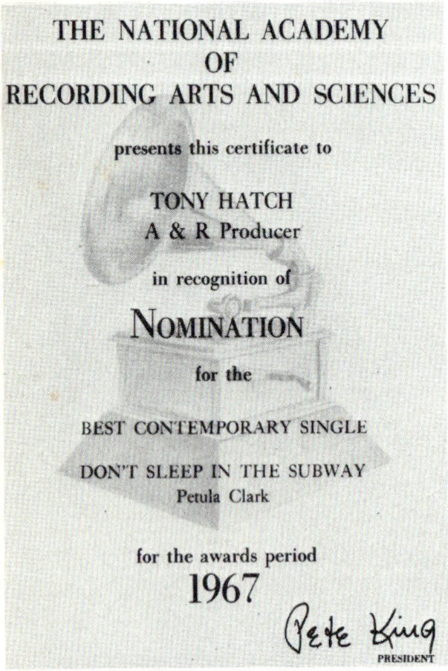

Top left: A gold disc from Pye for *Downtown*. Top right: The Ivor Novello Award for *Sad Sweet Dreamer*. Centre left: The National Academy of Recording Arts and Sciences nomination for *Don't Sleep in the Subway*. Centre right: Jackie Trent's silver disc for *Where Are You Now?* which was written by Jackie and Tony. Bottom left: An award from Nashville for a country song—*Look at Mine*.

possible to put your voices on twice. This is called 'double-tracking' and involves singing the identical part once more on another track. Slow numbers are far harder to double-track than brighter ones since the margin of error will be greater, making it more difficult to achieve a perfectly matched double. You can use further tracks to add vocal backings, 'oohs' and 'ahs', etc. and even double-track these for better effect. Listen to the Carpenters as the prime example of lead vocals double-tracked plus double-tracked backing voices. A very warm sound.

A further facility available on multi-track machines is known as 'track-jumping'. Provided there is a spare unrecorded track, any number of previously recorded tracks can be put through the mixer, mixed together and re-recorded on the spare track.

This is particularly useful when you find yourself running out of available tracks and feel you need to add more voices or instruments.

In your demo session you could have mixed tracks 2 and 3 together and put them on track 4. Your track layout would then look like this:

Track	Instrument
1.	Rhythm
2.	now available for recording on
3.	now available for recording on
4.	A mix of organ and solo guitar

You would then be able to use tracks 2 and 3 for further work. Of course, the sounds on track 4 can never be separated again and will always be together in the final mix.

Mixing: The various tracks are re-plugged through the mixer like the microphones were and come up on the various channels.

The mixer is re-plugged so that the output is either stereo or monaural and feeds the stereo or monaural machine instead of the 4-track.

So now, instead of mike lines into mixer channels into 4-track, it's 4-track into mixer into stereo or mono recorder.

You listen to the sounds, and if necessary add echo or equalise each of them and balance them together into your final mix.

The way we set up the 4-track recording in the first place would not produce such a great stereo mix but it could be done like this.

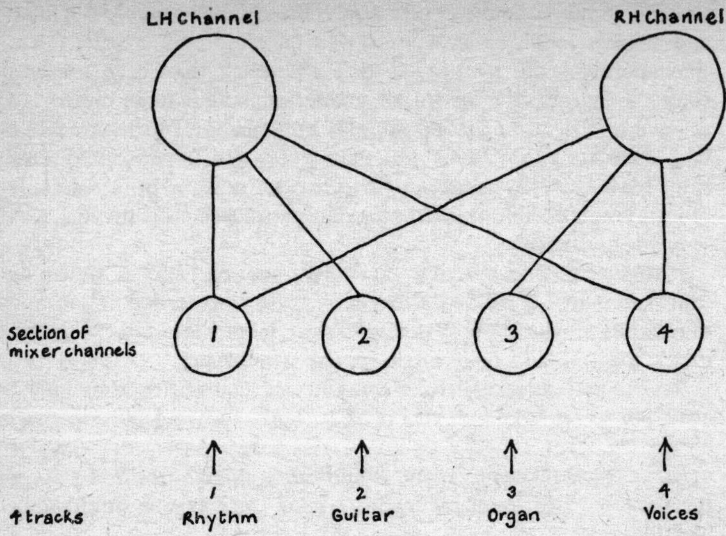

Track 1 (the rhythm) is split between L.H. channel and R.H. channel. Because it is equally divided between both channels it will appear in the centre.
Track 2 Solo guitar on left only.
Track 3 Organ on right only.
Track 4 The vocals are treated as the rhythm, to appear in the centre.

You will see that the more tracks available in the first place the more flexible your placing of various instruments and voices in the stereo picture when you come to mixing.

1. Bass goes left and right – appears centre.
2. Drums go left and right – appear centre.
3. Rhythm guitar goes left.
4. Piano goes left.
5. Solo guitar goes right.
6. Organ goes right.
7. } Voices go left and right and appear centre.
8. }

If slightly more sound is put either one side or the other it will swing the sound off-centre and this is often used to give the effect

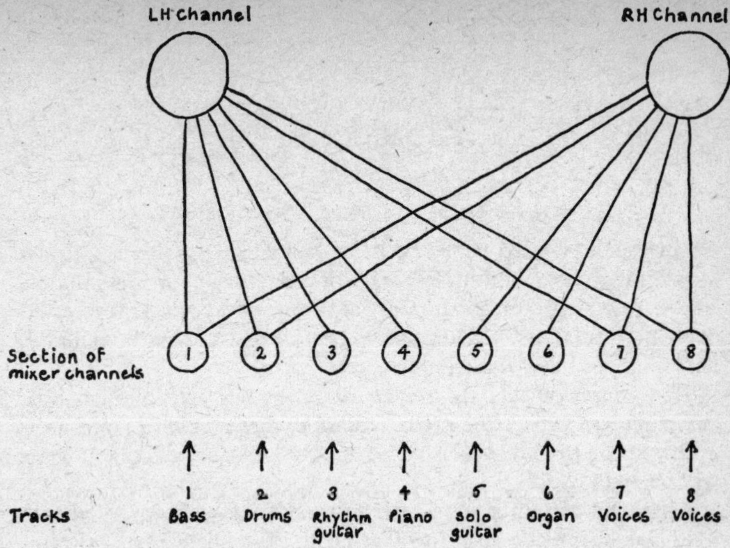

of even more of 'spread' sound rather than three defined spots, left, centre and right. You can have sounds exactly mid-way between left and centre or right and centre. The control for this is known as a 'pan fader'.

Most finished tapes, even demos, are in stereo so the above information is valuable.

The finished mix will be in stereo at 15 i.p.s. (inches per second). It is advisable to have 7½ i.p.s. copies made for sending to record companies, artistes and managers.

CHAPTER EIGHT

THE BIG TIME

1. FURTHER DEVELOPMENT OF STAGE ACT

No matter how long you've been in show business, there is always something to learn and further ways of improving your presentation.

The solo singer or group must always continue to better yesterday's performance by additional rehearsal and the introduction of new songs and new ideas into the act.

The longer you keep the act the same, obviously, the more natural and confident will be the presentation but there comes a point when even you will become bored by the same old routine, and the audience will begin to notice.

There are certain items which you must always keep. Maybe it's a number that really goes down well with the audience every time or, if you've had a hit record, even a small one, it's a song you're expected to perform without fail.

It doesn't matter whether you're a solo singer, beat group, vocal group or folk trio, as you develop, the polish on the act must be seen to shine brightly. Even if you prefer an intimate, casual approach, it must always have a feeling of confident continuity about it. The audience wants to feel respected by you and if you appear not to care then you will lose their attention.

Sometimes it's pretty tough in some of the clubs and discos where two hundred of the six hundred people present may be propping up a bar and talking nineteen to the dozen entirely oblivious of your efforts and spoiling the evening for everyone.

In these cases you have to be extremely patient, cut down on your chat, keep the music going and smile all the way through it.

Under these circumstances it also helps to use your most 'sing-along' type songs and cut down on the slow, soft ballads.

You should always be prepared to try out new songs and fresh ideas. Never try to change too much of the act at one time. You'll never remember all the changes and your tentative approach (you can't help it) will show through. It's best to rehearse one new number at a time and make sure you know it well.

Put it in the act when you're confident that you know the new routine thoroughly, and place it in a safe spot. By that I mean precede and follow the new item with songs or routines that you can guaran-

. . . it's pretty tough in some of the clubs . . .

tee will always work well and can save the day if you make a mess of the new routine or if you've over-estimated the potential popularity of it.

This has happened to us on several occasions in our cabaret work. Jackie and I have persevered for hours on a new routine. Having rehearsed it at the piano, I then arrange the music for the orchestra, get the parts copied, take them to the band-call, rehearse it again *with* the orchestra, put it in the act on Sunday night and take it out on Monday (and for evermore) simply because we realised at the time of performing it for the first time that it just wasn't right and never could be.

Sometimes, of course, it may simply need moving to another place in the act, or taking at a brighter tempo or altering in some other way and *then* it works. You have to experiment all the time, but it's a great thrill when a new routine or number is a success the first time you introduce it or at least shows some promise.

One of the most important aspects of live performance is contact with your audience. It's difficult to describe this contact but it really means that the personality of a solo singer or accumulated personalities of a group are warm and strong enough to compel a roomful of strangers to become involved and let their minds become totally devoted to the performance which is being given.

You don't have to be Danny Kaye or Shirley Bassey to make contact with the audience and it's not simply a matter of having a sensational visual and musically brilliant act. If the audience feels you're really glad they are there in front of you, you're half way home.

Part of this contact is achieved by simply being yourself. An audience (though they wouldn't be aware of it) can spot a phoney a mile away. You've probably heard of 'cold' or 'friendly' audiences. Well, that's normally a consequence of the performer or performers being either cold or friendly.

You know how it is when you walk into a room and you're introduced to someone for the first time. You either feel warm towards the person immediately or absolutely disinterested.

It's the same when you walk on stage. You have to positively exude personality to your audience and they will feel you care about them.

I don't believe this ideology of the remote, distant, untouchable, star personality. Even some of the greatest characters in the pop business, David Bowie, Roy Wood and Mick Jagger have that marvellous ability of appearing to have total disregard for the public but their audiences love that very image which they project and if the power of personality didn't exist would soon lose all interest.

A stage act must be developed to embody all the facets of the performer's personality within the dimensions of the music.

There is no point in using a song unless you can really put something into it.

There are so many styles of performer that to try and categorise them all here would serve little purpose, but the following examples should help prove the point.

As middle-of-the-road family entertainers, Jackie and I use songs which project this image. Our opening sequence has always been based on the 'Together' theme.

Currently we have a medley containing 'Two Can Make It Together', 'Everlasting Love' and 'United We Stand'. To push the point that we are a musical duo, a little later in the act we have a medley consisting of 'Sing' (Carpenters), 'A Song For You' (the Leon Russell number) and Kiki Dee's 'I Got The Music'.

Back on the marriage lines we up-dated the old song 'Together' and use a warm treatment of 'You are the Sunshine Of My Life'. 'Little Green Apples' has always been popular in our show and, of course, we couldn't ever omit 'The Two Of Us'.

All this helps to project a certain image.

Showaddywaddy have a sensational stage act and the whole image is based on the Rock and Roll craze of the fifties and sixties. In particular this act has worked very carefully on its opening sequence, its medleys, the way it introduces musically each member of the outfit and a tremendous finish which leaves everyone breathless. The most important point is that every musical item is carefully tailored to their own image.

Sweet Sensation are a British act based on the style of the American black vocal groups. Besides their own hits, they use songs made famous by their American idols like the Four Tops. In the act they only use songs which they can really move to because this is their style of performance and a song which didn't project this visual image would be useless to them.

I do like to see sufficient variety built into an act so that many sides to the performer's personality are presented.

If you're a singer and play a little guitar then work on it and introduce a number where you can feature it.

If you've developed the ability to impersonate another singer, and it's a good impression, there's no harm in using it carefully in the act. With groups I love to see a musical sequence which introduces the various members. It's so much more interesting than just saying: 'Now we'd like you to meet Charlie Burns on the drums,' etc.

Rhythm has become so important in our lives that no act can afford

. . . the beat has something to do with our primitive instincts . . .

to overlook its importance. Music with a beat somehow makes people feel happy. It's got something to do with our primitive instincts, I think. I always remember the sensational opening of Diana Ross and the Supremes stage act. There seemed to be about three minutes of steadily increasing mind-blowing rhythm before they actually appeared on stage, and by the time they did, the rhythm had built the excitement in the room to such a fever pitch that the audience was already well and truly hooked.

An act is not simply going on stage, singing a few pleasant songs, introducing the band and walking off.

You've got to carefully plan your entrance and opening number, work out all your links and announcements and any little jokes or comedy sections, all your songs must be balanced with each other, you've got to finish well, take your bows and leave the audience wanting more.

You've got to know where you're going, and exactly what you're doing through every minute that you're on stage. Every detail must be planned with care, and the more of you on stage the more necessary this becomes.

An act that finishes a number, waffles incoherently to each other, can't remember what the next song is, tunes up incessantly during long boring announcements and is generally disorganised is a pain in the neck.

It's once of the hardest tasks in the world to achieve a brilliant stage act but it only comes with time and experience and learning from other successful people in the business.

2. TV TALENT SHOWS

Despite the controversy that surrounds TV talent shows I am totally in favour of any programme that gives newcomers a chance.

It's hard enough for established performers to get television exposure these days so any format that presents complete unknowns to the general public, agents, record producers and clubs must be valuable.

If only the critics knew the mad scramble that exists between competitive record companies and agencies to sign up successful contestants they would not be so ready to stand in biased judgement.

Both the current talent shows, Opportunity Knocks and New Faces, have been responsible for the discovery of some extremely talented people and put them on the road to success.

Those that win on the programmes but don't find consequent success were either plain lucky at the time (maybe the competition wasn't too great) or they really don't have what it takes to turn their opportunity into a stairway of success. If you've got the talent, then a break on one of these shows will undoubtedly put you on the bottom step. From then onwards it's up to you and your advisers to make the climb.

You have to apply in the first place for an audition. Write to the television company concerned and send brief details of your act, your ages, a recent picture and outline your experience. You will be granted an audition in due course. These are often held in various parts of the country.

Don't forget that hundreds of others are also waiting for an audition but the producers do try to see everybody, so be patient. Don't bombard the office with irate telephone calls and threatening letters, or stick pins in wax effigies of Hughie Green and Les Cocks. It won't do you any good and will probably end all chance of opportunity knocking for you for ever more.

Having taken an audition you will still have to wait some time to find out if you've passed. Even when you've passed, further time may elapse before you are given a programme date. Once again, patience is a great virtue.

Once you know that you're booked to appear then you must carefully select a number to perform on the show. Unless the producers ask for a particular number (maybe your audition piece) then the song which you use must display your talent to the full. You'll only have about three minutes but those three minutes could be the most important in your life.

Choose the number that is absolutely right for you and which suits your style perfectly. That's half the battle. The TV company will arrange for an orchestration to be made if necessary.

If you're a group and you're given the okay to perform the number of your choice start rehearsing right away, no matter how many times you may have done it before.

I can't emphasise too much how important this opportunity can be for you, so you must work on polishing that three minutes right up until the very moment you perform.

These guide-lines will apply to any short TV spot that you may be lucky enough to be offered. Even a small regional station may have a local programme where local talent is featured. All you have to remember is that television reaches a lot of people and you must make the most of it.

Take care over your appearance. You've got to look good as well as sound great.

. . . don't stick pins in wax effigies of Hughie Green . . .

Maybe, one day, there will come a moment when an agent, manager, or record company will make an approach to represent you or to offer a record contract.

Taking agents and managers first, if you have no representation at all, then you are free to talk business. If you already have an agent, then unless you can mutually terminate your agreement you are not in a position to talk about new representation. Likewise if a potential manager approaches whilst you already have a management contract you would not be free for other negotiations.

If you have a manager, and an agent approaching you, then, provided you are happy with your manager you should refer all inquiries to him for his advice.

If you have an agent but no management you would normally be free to appoint anyone you like to manage you, but check any contract you have with your agent, just to make sure there's nothing in small print which precludes this.

Supposing you're really unhappy with your present agency or management or record company and want to get out of any existing agreements in order to make new arrangements. Before anything else, you must inform those approaching you of any contracts you may have already signed. If you sign a new agreement whilst an old one is still in force you alone will be responsible for the consequences which may ensue, because when you sign a contract you guarantee that you are free to do so.

When the person approaching you knows the situation he may offer to advise you, but in the end, no one can help you better than a solicitor. He will tell you where you stand legally and I think it's worth paying his fees to have that information before you take action. Of course, you may be able to sever a contract amicably with a manager, agent or record company and if this is so, then all the better for your reputation and your pocket. If there's any doubt, however, consult a legal adviser. It's safer to *know* your rights than *assume* them.

Now, presuming you have no existing contracts or you are able to terminate any existing agreements we can deal with the approaches.

Very few managers, agents or record companies will promise you anything substantial.

A manager may promise to use his best endeavours to promote your career. An agent may promise you several weeks work. A record company may promise you a three year contract with an album and two singles each year and a five hundred pound advance, but don't let anyone fool you by promising you'll be the greatest discovery of the year. Until it actually happens, nobody can tell.

I'm only drawing attention to this because you must treat any approach with a completely level head. Don't be carried away with the excitement of it all. Many performers have lived to regret the day they put their signatures to a contract without really studying all the implications of it.

4. AGENTS

As I've explained before, an agent fixes work for you. He takes a commission from the fee which he secures for you for each engagement. This commission will be no less than 10% and sometimes 15% of your fee if he is splitting the commission with another agent with whom he is dealing.

He is not responsible for looking after your personal affairs relating to your work.

You can be represented exclusively by one agent and in that case you must not deal with anyone else. If another agent approaches you, refer him to your own agent or your personal manager if you have one.

Many agents, when offering their services to you, may guarantee work in the first year to the value of, say, £5,000. Many will refuse to be committed but it's worth trying to get a guarantee. It all depends on the reputation of the agent. If he's well known in the business and handles other acts who never seem to be out of work then it's possibly unnecessary to insist on a guarantee. If you believe the organisation will be good for you then there's no point in pushing the matter.

An agent may want to sign an exclusive agreement for anything from one to ten years. I think two or three years is quite long enough for an exclusive agreement. If you're a success at the end of those three years due to the efforts of the agent then you'll want to stay with him anyway.

You can always ask an agent who approaches you if it is possible to have a six or twelve month trial period with an option in *his* favour to extend for a longer period.

Obviously he will not want to help create a success in the final twelve months only to lose it in the following year.

Remember that until you actually sign a contract everything is negotiable and it's worth asking the questions and being satisfied before you enter into an agreement.

You may have had high hopes of someone at the time of signing with them only to find out after a few months that nothing much is happening. It doesn't matter whose fault this is and it is best to try and negotiate an amicable parting of the ways.

Some agents, unfortunately, will know they have a potential star on their hands but have no ability themselves to promote the artiste. They just hang on, hoping that something will happen, then they'll be able to ride along with the success. As I've intimated, it's so easy to put your name on the bottom of a contract but often very difficult to terminate that agreement when you're dissatisfied with your representation.

Most agents will keep regular contact with their clients, the artistes. They make sure of seeing them in the venues into which the artiste is booked. I would be disappointed with an agent who never bothered to look at the product he was promoting.

No agent can work miracles but a good one has many contacts, has a lot of experience in show business and should be a great hustler for his artistes.

5. MANAGERS

A manager's job is to guide and advise the artiste in all aspects of his career. The commission is negotiable. No manager may handle more than three acts.

If you have a manager he will negotiate all contracts for you whether it be with agents, record companies, TV companies or clubs. A manager may be your agent as well.

Once again, I don't believe an initial contract should be too long even if your manager is your brother. Three years is quite long enough to find out if you can create a good relationship.

A good manager will never stop trying for his artiste. He's the tough front, often the awkward guy who prevents the artiste from being pushed around and takes the pressure in difficult situations. It's no use having a weak manager. If you, the artiste, end up doing your own negotiations and your manager is afraid to speak up for you then he's not the right person. On the other hand, you have to be careful that your manager is not so despised and disliked by everyone that his bad reputation affects *your* name. Your manager needs to be respected, and that, plus good judgement in matters relating to your career will work in your favour.

A management contract must be checked very carefully. It will normally state that all advice and decisions must be handled by the manager. The manager will be entitled to take commissions on *everything* you earn unless it's specifically stated that certain areas of earnings are excluded.

If you're a singer and after a while you start writing songs which become successful then the manager is entitled to commission on your songwriting earnings, and I think this is fair because it's all part of your show-business activities. If you don't agree make sure songwriting is excluded from your contract.

A management agreement normally only states that the manager will use his best endeavours to procure work for the artiste, and no manager in his right mind will commit himself further.

Very often, a manager will advance finance to the artiste in the early days to help with the purchase of clothes, music arranging, equipment, photos, etc. If the manager doesn't have the cash available for these items he may be able to arrange financial help from a record company or agency, provided that the artiste can suitably impress the executives that he or she is a worthwhile investment.

He may also deduct from your earnings any expenses he may incur whilst working on your behalf, e.g. travel and accommodation expenses, etc. He is not entitled to deduct the expenses of running his office.

I've seen some good and some bad management contracts but I've never seen two the same. I've seen simple agreements on two pages and others covering five or six.

Here are some points to watch out for.

I don't believe a manager should take money twice over, i.e. if he's your record producer as well then he should receive a royalty from the record company or a percentage from the income if he's made a master tape deal (see Record Companies). To take 20% for personal management plus an additional percentage for production (all from the artiste's own royalty) *and* to take production royalties from the record company or have a financial interest in the label or production company for which the artiste records is, to my mind, simply cheating.

Secondly, the manager may be a director of the music publishing company which publishes his artiste's compositions. He may want to take 20% of the songwriter's earnings *and* benefit from the profits of the music publishing company. Once again, I don't think it's fair.

Of course, if he negotiates a good deal for the artiste with any company that he doesn't have an interest in then he's perfectly entitled to whatever percentage is agreed in the management agreement.

If the manager is handling all your money make sure you get regular statements of your financial position.

Watch out for clauses that give the manager the right to assign the benefit of the agreement to another party. In the first place you, the artiste, appointed the manager and you may not agree with his choice of successor. It's up to you to dispute such a clause.

Watch out for endless options to extend agreements wrapped up in complicated legal jargon. Check exactly what they mean in terms of the total possible period that you could be committed to. You might have a three-year agreement with options in the manager's favour to extend for a further seven consecutive years. This would make ten years if all the options were exercised.

Be concerned about clauses that state, in general, that the manager is not committed to spending all his time managing your affairs. This might be innocent if he is managing two other acts but it also might be covering the fact that he's a professional wrestler, for instance, with a pretty heavy schedule of commitments himself.

Watch out for the clause which states that the manager is not responsible for your travel arrangements. That's not so bad when you're undertaking engagements on home territory but it could get complicated if you're fixed for a tour in Rhodesia.

Make sure that 'artiste's expenses' and 'manager's expenses' are clearly defined and make certain you have right of approval of the appointment of a road manager. You might end up with a right so-and-so.

Try to get some say in what is to be spent on your behalf like photos, equipment, clothes, etc.

It's too late when it's done and you're not happy.

Whatever happens, a manager, record company or agency will only provide initial finance as an advance. Once you start earning good money it will be deducted from your salaries. If it's a record company advance you'll have to earn all of that advance in record sales before you see a penny more.

Surprisingly, money only seems to be really needed when success is actually knocking on the door. It's strange how the same old guitars, drums, amplification equipment and stage wear will suffice whilst you're struggling but a little taste of success and you have to spend a small fortune just to keep up with other artistes in the public eye.

As I've said before, don't believe in promises. The manager who puts an arm round your shoulder, blows Havana cigar smoke in your face and says soothingly: 'Don't worry about a thing, I'll make you a star by the end of the year,' can be taken with a pinch of salt.

Not only that, it's more than likely he's seen too many fictional show-biz films.

Management is a very difficult job no matter how much potential an artiste may have and it's a great shame that there are a few man-

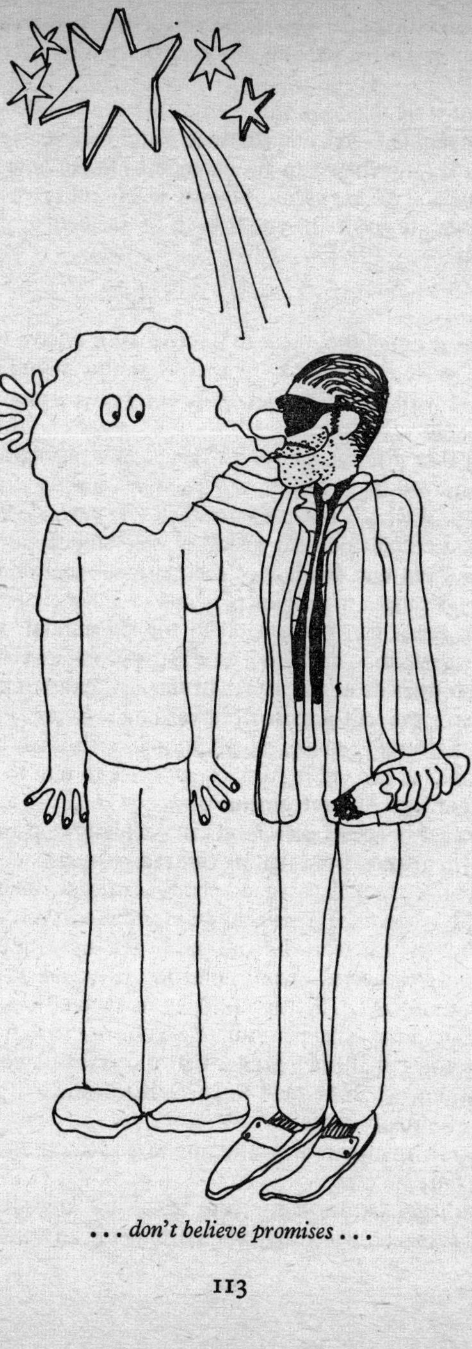

. . . don't believe promises . . .

agers who haven't a clue about the real issues involved in guiding a career and can only see the job as a quick way of making easy money.

Make sure your manager will really work for you before you sign a long and possibly restrictive contract. I still believe a trial period is the best answer, maybe six or twelve months to see how things work out. If, at the end of this period, you are still friends, trust each other and have enough goodwill, you'll both be pleased to continue the arrangement.

6. TERMINATION OF AGREEMENTS

This is a most difficult subject to discuss since I have to generalise but it's just as well that you know the procedure should you become totally fed up with your manager or agent for any number of reasons, either personal or business.

Realising that it is the artiste who engages a manager or agent to represent him you may wonder why you can't simply sack him if you feel that way. Well, it's not as easy as that. Okay, you have read in the papers that a certain popular group or solo singer has dismissed a manager or agent and the fact of the matter is that one party can't enforce an agreement to provide personal services. But the dismissed manager or agent can make a claim for substantial damages and financial compensation and this is where the problems start. Although the law is on the side of the artiste in this matter stating, in general, that you can't prevent a man from earning a living, a manager or agent with a strong legal agreement with an artiste which is repudiated is entitled to take all legal steps available to him to substantiate his claim or enforce the agreement.

The manager or agent, therefore, can't actually stop an artiste with whom he is in dispute from signing contracts to work or make records or whatever – but he'll have a good try. He can apply for an injunction to be issued against the artiste in an attempt to prevent him from signing other contracts or he can apply for an injunction against another manager, agent, record company or venue to prevent the artiste being employed. He is not likely to succeed however, as the legal view is that the artiste is entitled to continue to earn a living and normally a court will only decree that a certain percentage of the artiste's earnings shall be held to cover the dismissed party's claim when it is eventually settled.

A dismissed manager may attempt to sue another manager for enticing his artiste away.

All these legal battles can create havoc for any artiste concentrating on his career. Secondly, when dismissing an agent or manager one has to consider the effect it may have on future engagements and dealings with the record company etc. Obtaining legal advice and taking defensive action is also costly and time-consuming so the artiste must carefully consider all these aspects before attempting to repudiate any contract.

If the manager or agent has power of attorney (the artistes' authority for the manager etc. to sign contracts or any other documents on his behalf) then any engagements accepted by the manager or agent on behalf of the artiste before the notification of dismissal must be completed otherwise the artiste is in breach of contract.

The manager or agent should not continue to accept engagements once he has been notified of dismissal since he may not be able to provide the services of the artiste.

Some managers will even have written into agreements with artistes that they (the managers) cannot be dismissed. I'm afraid the strength of such a clause is very much in doubt in view of the inability of anyone to enforce an agreement for personal services. I don't think this one has ever been tested in court.

My final advice for any artiste contemplating the dismissal of an agent or manager is that he should consult a solicitor before any action is taken at all.

I personally believe that in the event of any dispute an amicable settlement is the best answer. It can save a lot of time, money and mud-slinging.

Finally, I must declare that the advice given in this book on any matters relating to legal documents or artiste, manager, agent relationships is given without prejudice to any actual situations that may arise and that I am in no way responsible for any actions that may occur from the use of this advice.

7. RECORD COMPANIES

I don't believe any artiste or act should sign a contract with a record company without the guidance of a manager or agent or someone with sufficient experience of record company contracts. I'm not suggesting that record companies are out to 'con' an unsuspecting singer or group. Far from it. The majority of record companies have been established long enough and value their reputations sufficiently not to become involved in unethical dealings. They are commercial concerns, however, and if they are fortunate enough to sign an act that becomes an international smash hit for a long period at a low royalty then they'll be very happy.

This normally results in the artiste being dissatisfied, then a new manager stepping in and getting tough with the record company.

Consequently, bad feeling is established that could easily have been averted.

Far better to arrange matters correctly from the outset.

Record company contracts come in various forms.

Direct Contract: The artiste signs directly with the record company for the purpose of making records. The record company pays all the recording costs and pays the artiste an appropriate royalty on the records sold. The record company appoints a producer or agrees to the artiste's choice.

Period: This is normally for one year with options in the record company's favour to extend for further periods. These options could be for a second year with a further option for a third year. Provided all the options were taken up this would result in three years with that company. The company may ask for one year with four optional annual extensions, making five years in all. The period is, therefore, negotiable. Some companies go for a straight two or three year period but the one year with options is more usual.

The options are in the company's favour because it would certainly be bad commercial practice to help create a hit recording artiste only to have the artiste free to leave the company after only one year. If the artiste fails to find success then the company would normally not take up the option unless they had great faith that fortunes may change for the better in the second year.

Royalties: These are formulated in percentages which is a far safer way than the old system which was in pennies for if the price of a record goes up, then so does the royalty.

The royalty depends a great deal on the artiste's potential and the negotiating power of the management or the artiste himself if he's smart enough.

Most companies base their royalties on the recommended retail selling price less sales tax based on 85% or 90% of sales. Few companies base it on 85%, most on 90%. Record companies have valid reasons for not basing it on 100% of sales, and the deduction is to cover promotional records and records damaged or lost in transit.

Taking this as our formula, a typical commencing royalty could be 4½% for the United Kingdom. This royalty could rise by a ½% or maybe 1% in each option period. The overseas royalty will be lower than the U.K. royalty as most companies will be licencing the sale of the record to other companies in territories outside the U.K. The overseas company may be a subsidiary of the U.K. company or simply a licensee, an independent company unconnected with the U.K. company but licensed to sell the U.K. company's product. Some overseas sales are by direct export from the country of origin.

A royalty structure may look like this:

	U.K.	*Overseas*
1st year	4%	2½%
2nd year	5%	3½%
3rd year	6%	4½%

All royalties are negotiable, and the above is only an example.

A deduction in percentage form is normally made if a 45 r.p.m. single is distributed in a special bag and not the standard bag of the label. Further deductions are made for sleeves and containers in respect of albums.

Royalties on reel-to-reel tapes, cartridges and cassettes are lower than records due to the materials involved in the manufacture.

In addition there are different royalty structures for composite albums (several artistes on one album) and budget or low-price re-issues.

I can't give specific details of royalties as each company has its own system but the above principles are invariably observed by the majority of record companies.

Some companies deduct the cost of the recording session from royalties earned and only pay the balance after the deduction. I don't like this system. Since the artiste has probably had no say at all in how much was spent in the first place I don't think it's fair that he should be expected to offset what should be the company's responsibility. Some companies make it, say, a £200 limit. In other words, even if the session costs £350 they can't deduct more than £200 from your royalties.

All such conditions are negotiable and if you don't approve, don't sign.

If you are fantastically successful, a company will probably agree to increase your royalty beyond that agreed in the initial contract. They will do this out of goodwill and trust that you may re-sign at the end of the present term.

A company may even suggest an extension of the present agreement tied in with an increase of royalties.

Commitment: A record company will normally only agree to *make* two sides of a 45 r.p.m. record (in the first year), not even to release it if they don't like the results of the first recording session.

Even with such a small commitment the company may feel that, although the first session was a failure, the artiste has promise, and more records should be made. They may release the product from the first session and although it fails even to get a single spin on Radio One, still feel the artiste has potential and agree to another session.

Although one can get a record company to agree to a minimum commitment of, for example, three singles and an album in each year of the contract, it doesn't help very much. Unless you are specifically an album artiste you won't want to release an album until you have a hit single behind you. And if you get one hit single then you can bet your life that the record company will want you to make an album and more singles anyway.

The worry that some artistes have of being unsuccessful and tied for three or five years to a record company is also unfounded.

If the company can't make any money with you then they'll be the first to call a halt to expensive recording sessions and won't want to hold you to the contract.

Every time they take up an option they are at least committed to spending money on the minimum of one recording session and there is little point in doing this unless they have real faith in the artiste. A reputable company won't even hold an artiste for the remainder of the year if the session took place in the second month (for example) and they have no plans to make any more records.

The reason why most companies commit themselves only to *make* a record is because the cost of releasing and promoting a record is so great that to release a record they don't want would be a total waste of good money. (With something like a hundred singles being released every week by companies in the U.K. who wants a bad record released anyway?)

If the first session is a real failure it always gives the record company the opportunity of terminating the agreement early and saving further expenditure.

Some companies work on a sliding scale system for royalty payment, whereby one starts on a basic royalty and then this is increased in ratio to the number of records sold.

e.g. U.K. Royalty:

On records sold up to 50,000	3%
On records sold between 50,000 & 100,000	4%
On records sold between 200,000 & 300,000	5%
On records sold between 300,000 & upwards	6%

These are only examples, no precedents are established.

Territories: A record company will want to sign an artiste for the world and only the most successful artistes are in any position to argue on this point.

Lease Tape Deals: These work two ways.

An independent record producer may sign an artiste to a recording deal. He would negotiate a contract similar to the one that a record company would offer, but the producer pays all the costs of recording and leases the master tape to a record company at a royalty that could be anything from 6% to 12½% of the retail selling price less purchase tax. (Some highly successful artistes on lease tape deals can command even more than 12½% from a record company.)

The artiste royalty is paid out of the royalties received by the producer.

The type of contract that a record company issues to an independent producer is similar to one issued directly to an artiste with options, increasing or sliding scale royalties and commitments.

Alternatively, an artiste may finance (or the artiste's management provide finance for) an independent production which is leased direct to a record company in the same manner as any other independent production.

In a few cases a record company will allow an artiste to make his own records with the record company carrying all the costs. The record company will, in this event, undoubtedly pay an extra royalty to cover production costs but will want a lot of say in how the money is spent. Only successful artistes with reputable management control could hope to secure such a deal.

Costs: Record production is an expensive business. At the time of writing this book the following costs can be expected.

Studio: £36 per hour (approximately) plus 25% between 6 p.m. and midnight and another 33⅓% on top for weekend recording. This is for 16-track recording. One reel of 2″ tape for 16-track recording is approximately £30.

Then you need mixing time. This will cost approximately £25 an hour plus 25% between 6 p.m. and midnight and 33⅓% for weekends. One reel of ¼″ tape (for the master) is approximately £7.

Musicians: £22·50 per musician basic per three hours recording (15-minute break compulsory).

To play two instruments (called doubling) is basic fee plus 25% of basic fee.

To play three instruments, basic fee plus 50% of basic fee.

On top of this certain instruments qualify for porterage fees of

£1·50 to £3·00 depending on the size of the equipment or instrument.

Orchestras are normally booked by recognised orchestral management, whose fees are around 10% of the total cost of the orchestra.

Arrangers: If you're recording a solo artiste you may need an arranger/conductor for the session. One arrangement could cost you anything between £30 and £100 depending on the size of the orchestra and the reputation of the arranger.

Each arrangement must be copied by a music copyist so that each musician has his own part from which to play. This can cost from £10 to £30 depending on the size of orchestra and length of arrangement.

If the arranger also conducts the orchestra on the session you can expect to pay him between £30 and £60 just for this job.

I don't believe that a brand new unknown singer or group should push too hard on the royalty question in the first year. Bearing in mind how expensive recording can be – and it may mean two or three sessions before the big break arrives – I recommend that the artiste should give the record company the benefit of recouping the investment by accepting a low royalty to start with. That's why I also like the sliding scale system because the company can earn back its investment during the lower sales whilst the artiste can reap huge rewards when the volume of sales is at its greatest.

Hit records can bring overall success to artistes who otherwise might have remained for ever in obscurity.

Many people criticise the record business. On several occasions, especially on New Faces, I've had to defend the philosophy that for many acts the only way to success is through the hit record.

I can name hundreds of artistes that would still be languishing in frustrating obscurity had it not been for one, just one, hit single.

Tom Jones' No. 1 smash, 'It's Not Unusual' brought him international fame. 'Release Me' did the same for Engelbert Humperdinck. 'Love Me Do' launched the Beatles. 'Just Loving You' did for Anita Harris what 'Where Are You Now' did for my Missus, Jackie Trent. Petula Clark's international career only really happened as a result of 'Downtown'. Although Pet was a success in Europe, her records in England were failing dismally in 1964 until I was suddenly inspired with the words and music of a song which eventually changed her life. (Even at that time, before the record was released, neither of us could imagine its ultimate success.)

People say a hit record isn't everything, but ninety-nine times out of a hundred it is. They try to draw comparisons with artistes of the twenties, thirties and forties when record sales were much lower, and music-hall and radio were the media for promoting talent. But if you recognise the fact that a hit record associated with a singer or group in the mid-seventies is only the same as a hit song associated with a music-hall and radio star of the thirites, then any argument against the power of a contemporary hit record is defeated.

Ask the older folks what they remember most about Marie Lloyd, Harry Lauder, Jack Buchanan, Gracie Fields and Jessie Matthews and you are told it's the songs that are associated with these performers. Every time they went on stage they would be expected to sing the songs they had made famous.

Would Vera Lynn have become the Forces' sweetheart if she hadn't sung 'We'll Meet Again' and 'White Cliffs Of Dover'? I don't see any difference between Vera Lynn singing those songs and a singer today finding great success through a hit record, the song on which stays with the singer for ever.

Even Barbra Streisand first came to the public's attention through her marvellous albums, developing thereafter as an actress.

I'll concede a couple of points. One is that there are some performers who can make it without a hit record – but they've really got to have something special going for them.

Liza Minelli is a good example (but I bet that you mention Liza Minelli and think of 'Money, Money, Money' from the musical 'Cabaret', so even there the song has power which you can't deny).

The other point is that sometimes, just one hit record or near hit or album track can bring a singer the success which he or she deserves and from then onwards the career blossoms without the aid of further hit singles.

On the whole, though, the majority of successful artistes owe that success to the songs with which they are associated. It's very easy for people actually in showbusiness to forget this, but the public sees it that way.

Go to a Petula Clark concert and note that the songs which really grab the audience are the songs from the hit records. If she omitted to sing a few of the songs people remember her for, the audience would feel badly let down.

The same applies to the heavy groups, beat groups, folk-rooted singers – in fact, every act that makes live appearances. Can you imagine an Osmonds concert without 'Crazy Horses', 'Too Young', 'Why' or any other songs from their hit repertoire?

Many people wonder where the songs come from. Well, there are people like me and Jackie Trent, professional songwriters with contacts throughout the music business.

Sometimes we're asked to write specifically for a singer or group.

On other occasions we write a song and submit it direct to the artiste, their management or record producer. Frequently our songs are heard on albums and a record producer or singer will get an idea to make that title as a single.

That's how my song 'Call Me' became famous. It was first recorded by Petula Clark just as an album track. Then our music publishing company in America played it to a record producer with A & M Records in California. The result was that he recorded it with Chris Montez and the song went to No. 4 in the American charts. Lulu recorded it first as a single in the United Kingdom but although it made the lower end of the charts it wasn't the smash we hoped for. Since then it has become a standard song with many album versions, translations and a value as a 'performance' song unequalled by anything else we've written.

Many writers, including us, sign up groups or singers so that we can write for them specifically and produce their records.

Mitch Murray and Peter Callender worked this way with Paper Lace. Nicky Chinn and Mike Chapman had the same scene with Mud and Hot Chocolate.

Many groups tend to write only for themselves (with great success, I might add) and this is especially advantageous since they can rely in the future on their own source of material.

Music publishers are also responsible for putting together teams of songwriter, artiste and producer. Wearing my music publisher's hat I was lucky enough to be introduced to a songwriter called Des Parton. He introduced me to Sweet Sensation and I arranged their recording contract with Pye Records. Des writes the songs, rehearses the group and together we make the rhythm tracks. Des supervises the addition of vocals, I arrange, conduct and supervise the addition of the orchestra to the rhythm tracks and together we produce the final mix.

Behind the release of most records there is a tremendous amount of activity and a lot of expense involved in production and promotion. Over a hundred singles are released every week – more around Christmas – and the competition between record companies is enormous.

Occasionally a record company with great faith in an artiste will invest heavily in the production and promotion of the artiste. David Essex is a prime example. Fortunately, David Essex had the talent and image to match the investment.

Sometimes a record will literally escape, rather than be released and can still be a smash hit. Very often, only one play on a peak hour radio programme can 'break' a record.

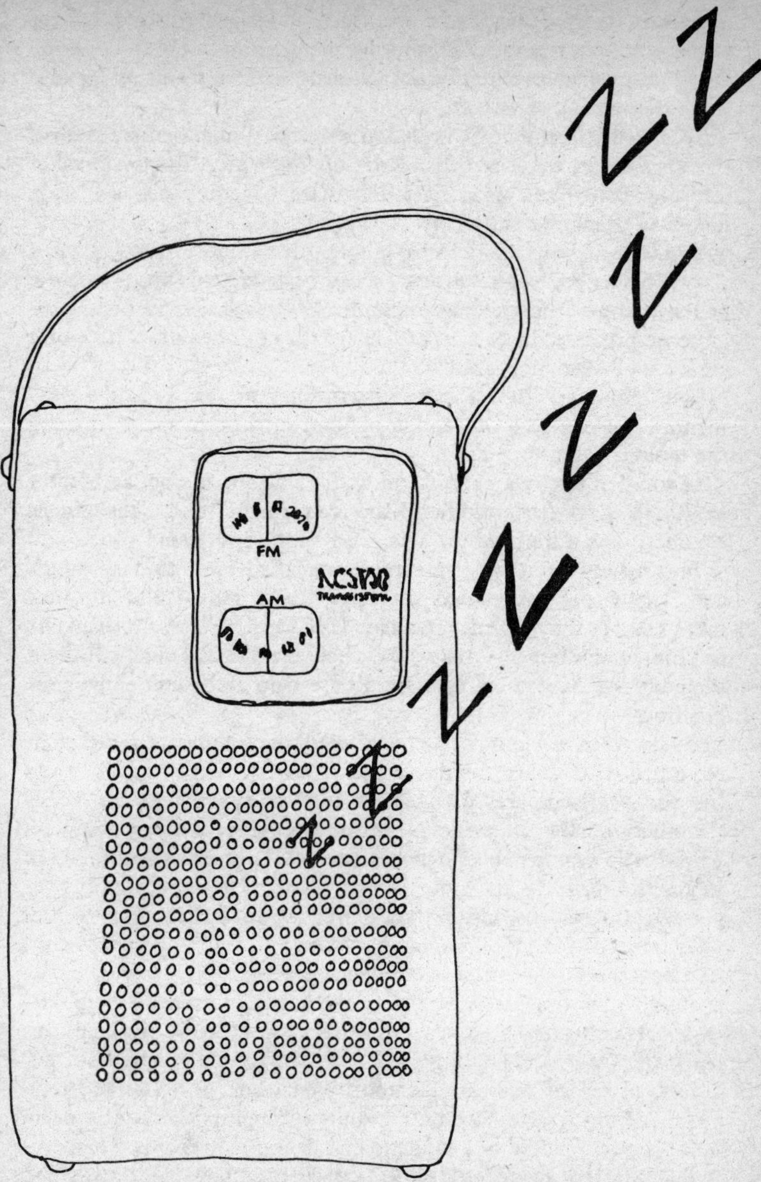

... records that take months to get into the charts are called 'sleepers' ...

Records that take weeks or even months from the date of release to the point of gaining sufficient sales momentum to put them in the charts are called 'sleepers'. (Sometimes they are so 'asleep' you'd think they were dead!)

Most record companies prefer to have good management behind the artistes on their records. Back-up promotion in the form of television and live appearances and newspaper publicity can go a long way to making hit records.

Radio is an important factor in the promotion of records. If a record gets enough spins then sales can be generated simply because of the brain-washing effect. Sometimes every disc-jockey and programme producer loves a record, plays it to death, but it still won't sell. This is known as a turntable hit.

The problem with our radio system for years has been the BBC monopoly with Radio One and its out and out Top 40 image covering the nation.

If you don't get your record on Radio One and it's not acceptable to Radio Two (the middle-of-the-road mums' and dads' music channel) then a tremendous area of promotion is denied you.

Fortunately we now have local commercial radio stations which are largely pop orientated although there is a limit to how many records they can play in a day. BBC local radio is also available for the promotion of artistes and their records although much of their output consists of network Radio One and Radio Two programmes.

Radio Luxembourg has contributed enormously to the promotion of pop music for many years and has helped create many hits that would otherwise have been completely ignored.

Sometimes the system of selecting pop records for playing on BBC Radio One has been heavily criticised but since I can't think of a better formula (and since I wouldn't want to prejudice my own position anyway) I won't get more involved than that.

The record producer has just got to make a really playable record and hope his opinion is shared by everyone else.

A television show such as Top of the Pops can make all the difference between a hit and a near miss. When a record is breaking, this show can push sales sky-high.

Not all record sales are created by exposure on radio and television. Many singles have become hits through constant playing in discotheques. There is a demand for danceable records which are more attractive to *disco* devotees and D.J.'s than *radio* D.J.'s and producers.

These records may often be overlooked even by record companies

. . . no wonder we're all wealthy nervous wrecks . . .

themselves. It may be a deleted single that is picked up by the discos, it gets played, word spreads, disco fans want to hear the record in other discos which they frequent and a demand is created.

Several record companies specialise in recording and promoting acts only recognised on the folk-club circuit and huge sales have developed. The university circuit has also proved a great market for heavy bands and other specialised non-Top 40 material. The record company uses the social events organisations within the university community to discover, record and promote groups and singers that are favourites with the student fraternity. Some of these acts may never be heard of by the wider general public but have an enormous band of devoted followers.

Whatever field one is in, the competition is so great and the odds against getting a best-selling record with a new act are so stacked against you that when you do finally hit the jackpot it's like winning the pools.

Then your problems really start.

Soon you've got to try to follow it with another success.

(No wonder we're all wealthy nervous wrecks.)

When considering which record company to approach, although this is a matter which is best handled by a reputable manager or independent record producer the following points should be assessed.

Many record companies maintain the policy of keeping the artistes and their management at a discreet distance from the top executives. It's obviously impossible for me to draw comparisons between various companies but I personally like to have contact with all levels of management in the record companies with which I deal, from managing director, through finance, contracts, sales, artist and repertoire and promotion. Accessibility to all departments is important and you get a feeling about this as soon as you walk into a record company to negotiate a contract.

When problems occur or an artiste becomes dissatisfied on some matter related to his recording contract it's a comfort to know that he can talk to the right people on the label. Lack of communication is the biggest single contributory factor to misunderstandings between artistes and their labels.

I suppose most people associate my name with Pye Records and I'm certainly not ashamed of that, having spent ten successful years with them. Even though I'm no longer a direct employee of the company I still work on an independent basis for them and can vouch for their 'accessibility' factor.

I know of many occasions when managements or artistes have

. . . certain producers find a magic formula . . .

resolved their grievances through negotiation with top level executives. At least three acts to my personal knowledge re-negotiated their contracts for higher royalties before the initial contracts had expired and were surprised at the response to their requests.

When considering record producers and record companies and their various offers it's also worth analysing the track record of the people concerned. Certain producers find a magic formula or chemistry which only seems to work with one record company and they can boast a long chain of consistent hit-making.

Sometimes an artiste is immensely successful with one record producer for three years, switches record labels for a better deal, then somehow fails even with the same formula as before to find similar success. This can also work in reverse with an unsuccessful but promising artiste switching labels and finding the chemistry for instant chart-form.

Before diving headlong into any record contract try to study the form of the organisation. It's good to be with a winning team.

One must never forget also the by-products of making hit records. These are personal appearances, concerts, clubs and television dates. A record company may carry all the initial risks in the making of records but ultimately, it's the artiste that can reap enormous rewards.

CHAPTER NINE

MUSIC PUBLISHING

I. PUBLISHERS

Though the role of the music publisher has changed dramatically over the last twenty years he nevertheless plays an important part in today's music business.

Many years ago the only place where you could find a new song was in the office of a top music publisher. Although writers and publishers were still anxious to get a big name to record their songs, the records were not as important as the use of the song in music-halls and radio broadcasting. Music publishers were as active then as they are today but in a totally different way.

A songwriter would take his song to the music publisher and actually play it to him on the piano. Just think of that. And more incredible still, every music publisher could play the piano as well so that when a bandleader or singer visited his office looking for a new song, the manuscript would be brought out and the listener would be treated to a *live* performance . . . Please forgive the irony, which is a little unfair, because today, although the guitar and demo disc (or tape) has taken over from the live demonstration at the piano there are still many music publishers and writers who can sell a song to a singer by accompanying themselves at the piano.

If a song-writer writes at the piano or is a handy pianist his song-writing style sounds acceptable just with a piano.

Writers like Elton John, Gilbert O'Sullivan, Lindsey de Paul, Carole King and Neil Sedaka obviously use the piano a lot when composing because it is their instrument, and I'm quite sure, listening to their records and live appearances, that they wouldn't need any additional instruments in order to demonstrate a song to a group or singer.

I've made very few demos over the fifteen years I've been writing. I experiment with melodies and chords at the piano, maybe get an idea for the hook and a few lines of the verse then consult my writing partner, Jackie, on the lyrics.

When the song is finished I'm then able to play it over at the piano to the singer or group.

Incidentally, whilst we're talking about piano-playing composers, you'll probably notice that most of the records they make have strong piano intros and a continuous piano rhythm throughout. I don't believe this is simply to tie in with their style of performance. When you write a song at the piano it seems to demand the inclusion of a piano sound when the rest of the instruments are added for the record.

Song-writers who play guitar and use it when composing have greater difficulty in demonstrating their songs with the guitar alone unless they are folk-rooted songs. That's why the demonstration disc is the ideal answer. Piano, other guitars, bass and drums, organ maybe and even brass and strings can be added to dress up the appearance of the song and thereby make it easier to sell than just voice and guitar.

This isn't the only reason, however, for the innovation of the demo disc or tape. Even piano-playing composers make demos.

The demonstration disc makes the business of promoting new songs much easier for the writers, artistes and, especially, the music publishers.

Song-writing nowadays isn't always the sole object of putting words and music together. Often the whole concept of a finished sound is imagined by the composer and the demo disc is the only way of getting somewhere near this.

If you want to try to get your song recorded by Elvis Presley then the best thing is to find a recording session singer who does a good imitation, book a studio and musicians and try to make for Presley a demo that will instantly sound good for his style. If there's a particular guitar figure that sounds great for the song you make sure that is on the demo as well. You can get the tempo right, the feel and the overall sound.

Copies of a demo disc or tape can be made, sent to any part of the world and left with an artiste or record producer for any length of time in order that the fullest opportunity may be given to the consideration of the song for recording.

And that's where the music publisher comes in. Although many writers and singer/songwriters send their own songs to other artistes, this is mostly done by the music publishers.

A singer/songwriter may be well-occupied with his own TV, live appearances or recording work. Other songwriters may have the time but not the contacts.

The good music publisher discovers writers, encourages them, points them in the right direction, invests in demos and uses his contacts to secure records on the songs.

Some music publishers even make master tapes for record companies to release as commercial records. It's all designed to

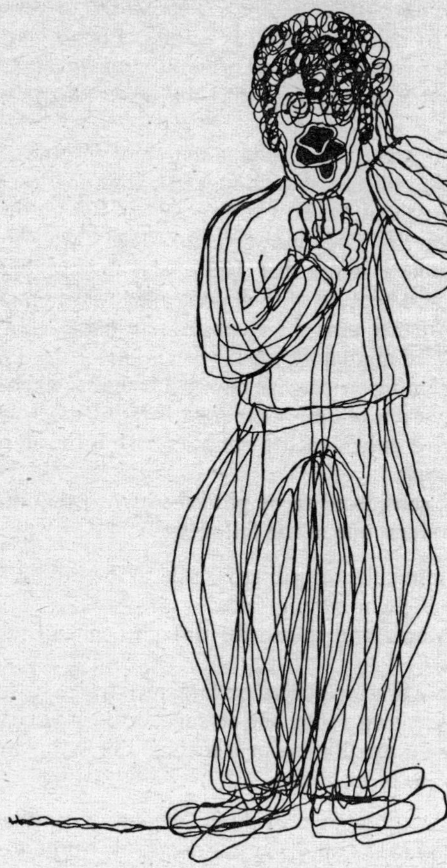

. . . making a demo for Presley . . .

make the songwriter successful and generate income for the music publishing company.

Many music publishing companies acquire songs from territories outside the U.K. Many American music publishers either have their own companies here in Britain or have agreements for British companies to promote their material. This works in reverse also, with a great deal of British material going in the opposite direction.

Like any commodity there is a thriving import/export business (for want of a better description) with the whole of the world involved.

Current hit songs are not the only source of income. Standard songs in the music publisher's catalogue can continue to earn good money for years without the cost of promotion. 'Downtown', 'Call Me', 'Don't Sleep In The Subway' and 'The Two Of Us' are amongst the standard songs that Jackie and I have been lucky enough to write, and because of their continued usage on radio, TV and in live performance plus the recordings available, they provide us with a guaranteed annual income.

Many up and coming writers ask me what it means when a song is 'published'. They even tell me their song is 'published' when they really mean they've only signed a contract with a music publisher to publish their song.

A song is only considered to be published when the music publisher has done at least one of the following:

(a) Secured a commercial recording for sale to the public. This can be a 45 rpm single or album track.
(b) Printed the words and music for distribution and sale to the public.
(c) Promoted the work for public performance, radio or television. A publisher may own a song and arrange for its use in connection with a television programme as a theme. The song would then be considered to be published.

Most publishing contracts provide for the entire copyright in the song to be assigned to the publisher for the whole world, except that where the writer is a member of the Performing Right Society certain parts of the copyright are automatically assigned to the Society. In exchange for this transfer of rights the publisher undertakes to pay the writer a specified percentage of all royalites earned on the song. The normal percentages are 50% of recording royalties and 10% on sales of sheet music; royalties on performances and broadcasts are dealt with later.

The contract is often worded in such a way that unless the

publisher secures an 'A' side of a record within, say, six months of acquiring the song, then the copyright will return to the writer.

Being the copyright owner the publisher is in a position to license other publishers ('sub-publishers') in different countries to publish the song and to have foreign lyrics written if necessary.

If a publisher takes several songs from a writer at any one time he may issue only one contract naming all the songs. In his files, however, the documentation for copyright information and accounting will be individual.

A writer may have a service agreement with one music publisher whereby the publisher has the exclusive right to acquire all the writer's songs. A service agreement can be for a certain period of time. The publisher must, however, provide a consideration in return for the exclusivity. This is legal jargon for a retainer or monthly salary or a lump sum paid to the writer. These can either be in the form of a non-returnable inducement payment or an advance against future royalties or sometimes an amalgamation of both.

Even with a service agreement the writer must still assign each song to the publisher. There is no form of blanket agreement and in any case, by assigning each song as it is written, valuable information for copyright purposes is documented.

A publisher, unless specified otherwise in the contract, acquires the copyright in a song for the life of the copyright.

The life of a copyright is from the date the song was first registered as a copyright work to fifty years after the death of the composer (or, in the case of two or more co-writers, the death of the last survivor). This is intended mainly to protect the heirs of composers or other beneficiaries but the publisher also benefits, and rightly so, for he is there to administer the collection of royalties which continue to be passed on to the writer's successors.

The main sources from which the writer of a successful song can expect an income are as follows.

1. Public performances and broadcasting (radio and television).
2. Sales of sheet music and publication of the song in magazines, etc. (usually lyrics).
3. Recording. Apart from records made for retail sale recordings may be made for all sorts of specific purposes. For example, the song might be featured in a film or a television play, or used for advertising purposes (think of 'Up, Up and Away' and TWA or 'Yellow River' and the Post Office Yellow Pages). The Bell Telephone Company of America paid a large sum of money to

record my song 'Call Me' for a radio advertising campaign in the U.S.A.

Royalties on records sold in the shops in the British Isles are calculated at a minimum of $6\frac{1}{4}\%$ of the recommended selling price (that is just for the songs; royalties paid to the performers are quite separate). For records exported the rate is normally 8%. In the case of a 45 rpm single this $6\frac{1}{4}\%$ is divided between the publishers of the song on each side, and the publisher normally contracts to pay 50% of his share to the writer. Note that the 'B' side (which is seldom heard) makes as much as the hit. Obviously if both sides of the record have songs by the same publisher and/or writer(s) they receive the entire royalty between them.

On albums (whether in the form of LP records, cartridges or cassettes) the royalty is divided by the number of copyright works included and distributed among the respective copyright owners.

Recording royalties are usually known in the music business as 'mechanicals'.

On budget-line albums where a large number of tracks are used in relation to a low-price structure the record company negotiates on the royalty with the various publishers because, for example, 24 into $6\frac{1}{4}\%$ of £1 would be a very low royalty and not acceptable.

The writer's share from the sale of sheet music is normally 10% of the marked selling price of a single song copy or a proportionate royalty in the case of song books where several writers' works may be included in one edition. The writer does not receive a fee from the use of lyrics only in newspapers or periodicals.

From any other sources outside mechanicals, performance and sheet music, the writer receives 50% of all monies received by the publisher. For example, if the publisher makes a special agreement with an advertising agency for the use of the song the writer would be entitled to half the fees or royalties thereby derived.

A writer may ask for and may receive an advance against the royalties he could receive. This could be anything from twenty-five to a thousand pounds for one song depending on several conditions. The publisher would consider how good the song is, or, if it's already recorded before the songwriting contract is signed, how much chance the record has of selling in large quantities.

Throughout the world each country has its own copyright laws relating to mechanicals or the sale of records.

The British publisher often assigns to an overseas publisher the right to publish the song in a foreign territory. The British publisher will get the best deal possible.

Sometimes the foreign publisher takes 50% of what is sent to him by the record companies in his territory and forwards 50% to the British publisher. Very often the deal is 60/40 in the British publisher's favour and can be even better depending on the negotiating power of the company concerned. But whatever the British publisher receives from overseas (be it fourpence or four thousand pounds), he then gives 50% of *his* share to the writer. In some cases a British publisher will use an established collecting society to collect the royalties in overseas territories. The percentage that a society deducts is anything from 10 to 15% which means more money for writer and publisher but no promotional effort.

2. PERFORMING RIGHTS

Whenever a song is performed in public or broadcast on radio or TV the writer and publisher must be paid.

Each country has a society of composers, authors and publishers which is responsible for granting licences to establishments and broadcasting organisations giving them permission to authorise performances of musical works, the rights of which are administered by the society.

They collect royalties and fees from the various establishments and broadcasting organisations, etc. and – after deducting a percentage for administration expenses – distribute the income to their own members in their own country (the writers and publishers) and where applicable to other societies in other countries with whom they have reciprocal arrangements so that the foreign society may then distribute the proceeds (after deduction of expenses) to its own members, the writers and publishers.

Let's simplify this by using the United Kingdom as an example. In this country we have the Performing Right Society (usually known as the PRS), a society of composers, authors and music publishers.

PRS controls the performing rights in millions of copyrights not only from British writers and publishers – it looks after the interests of similar foreign societies with whom it has reciprocal arrangements. Foreign societies collect on behalf of the PRS and account periodically to the PRS.

The PRS does not license performers nor does it license performances on a song-by-song basis. What it does is to issue a blanket licence; to broadcasting organisations on the one hand, and to establishments where music is performed in public on the other. For example, its licencees range in size from the BBC through concert halls, hotels, nightclubs, dance halls, cinemas and factories, etc., right down to small barber's shops and dentist's waiting rooms.

The amount of money paid for a licence depends on the size and nature of the premises, and is fixed according to tariffs which are normally negotiated with national music users' organisations. For example, the tariffs for hotels and restaurants are agreed by the Society with the British Hotels, Restaurants & Caterers Association. Of course, the users want to pay as little as possible and the Society wants to charge as much as reasonably possible. If agreement cannot be reached by negotiation the Society's charges can be referred by the users to a special tribunal (called 'The Performing Right Tribunal') which decides whether or not they are reasonable.

Wherever possible the royalty is fixed as a percentage of the music user's receipts. For example, the cinema tariff is based on a percentage of the box office take, and the BBC pays a percentage of its income from broadcasting receiving licences. Commercial radio stations pay a percentage of their advertising revenue, but the commercial television stations pay a lump-sum adjusted at regular intervals to reflect changes in the cost-of-living. In theory all the Society's licencees are obliged to make returns to the PRS with lists of the songs and other musical works performed, showing the number of times they have been played. In practice smaller premises are excused this chore, and the returns from the larger establishments are used by the Society to allocate all its revenue among the writers and publishers it represents. The broadcasting organisations do make complete returns.

When the Society has allocated the income it collects among the songs and other works performed (using a rather complicated points system) they then have to be divided among the composers, lyric writers, and publishers interested in each title. This is often complex, especially in the case of foreign works, and for this and many other purposes the Society uses its own computer.

Under the PRS rules the standard division of royalties is two-thirds to the writer(s) and one-third to the publisher, but this is allowed to be varied by agreement provided that the publisher can never get more than 50%, and in practice PRS royalties are usually split between writer(s) and publisher on a 50/50 basis. All the revenue collected by the Society is distributed to the composers, songwriters and publishers (British and foreign) which it represents, except for its necessary administration expenses which average out overall at about 13% of the gross income.

The Society's affairs are managed under the direction of a General Council consisting of 12 writers (composers and/or lyric writers) and 12 music publishers who are elected by the members at the Annual General Meeting, which is held in London each year. The

Society's policy is laid down by this Council and by various Sub-Committees, and the day-to-day work is under the control of a General Manager and a staff of about 500 people, most of whom are based at the Society's Headquarters in the West End of London; the Society also has throughout the country a team of Licensing Representatives each of whom lives in his own territory and works from his home.

Nowadays it is very easy for a songwriter to become a member of the Society; he needs only to show that he has one song which has been either published, commercially recorded or otherwise used in a way which might give rise to public performances or broadcasts. There are three grades of membership: provisional associate, associate and full membership. Promotion from one to the other is governed by seniority and the level of the member's earnings from performances and broadcasts. Only full members (who are in the main full-time professional composers or lyricists and substantial publishing companies) have the right to attend and vote at Annual General Meetings, and to stand for election to the Council. I am honoured to be a member of the Council and, of course, my special area of concern is for matters relating to the younger popular music writers.

The PRS makes four basic distributions of royalties per year. These cover Broadcasting Fees in the British Isles, General Fees in the British Isles, Broadcasting Fees from overseas and General Fees from overseas.

When a writer or publisher becomes a PRS member he agrees to assign to the Society the right of performance which the Society administers on his behalf. A writer or publisher may remain a member for the whole of his life and his copyrights will continue to be controlled by the Society for fifty years after his death.

Since a writer should be classified for tax purposes as a self-employed person no tax is deducted by the PRS or music publishers and all fees, therefore, are paid in full.

Enquiries about membership of the Society should be addressed to The Registrar, The Performing Rights Society Ltd., 29/33 Berners Street London W1P 4AA.

3. THE SONGWRITERS' GUILD OF GREAT BRITAIN

All songwriters are eligible for membership of the Guild. It's like a professional association although you don't have to be a full-time songwriter to join. It represents the interests of its members, the songwriters and campaigns if necessary on their behalf to secure improved rates of royalties or eliminate unfair conditions from contracts.

Its main concern in recent years has been the campaign to improve the royalties due to writers from the sale of records. A valuable advisory service is available to novice songwriter members whose experience of contracts may be very limited.

The Guild also devised and, along with the PRS sponsorship now, organises the PRS Ivor Novello Awards, which are made annually to British songwriters.

The address of the Songwriters' Guild is: 52 Dean Street, London W1.

4. COPYRIGHT

As explained in an earlier chapter of this book a song is copyright from the moment it is first written. You've got to be able to prove it, though, in the event of a dispute. I've already explained how this can be done if you are a novice songwriter without a music publisher interested in your song or if you are not a PRS member.

If a publisher is interested in your work, however, and you are planning to assign the copyright to him then he will register the song for copyright purposes and you are fully protected.

If you are a member (at any status) of PRS then it's worth notifying them of each song you write, especially if you're not planning to assign the publishing rights to a music publisher.

A song may not be recorded without the copyright owner's permission, but, more important, the first recorded version of a song may not be issued for sale to the public without the copyright owner's permission. In other words, there's not much one can do to stop the first recording taking place if the words and music are available to those making the record but if no other versions of the song have ever been authorised, then permission must be obtained from the copyright owner before the record maker can issue his product.

Once one version has been authorised and permission granted for its issue then anyone may record and issue other versions of the song in the territory of the first issue.

This principle is accepted in each country and the music publisher will license other publishers in overseas territories to exercise the same control.

Sometimes, when a recording company wishes to issue a record of a copyright work and no music publisher or copyright owner can be ascertained in a certain territory, although every effort has been made to establish the rightful owner, the record company may issue the record under Copyright Control. This means that any royalties will be held by the record company until someone makes a claim with proof of ownership.

Often a record company is given permission by an overseas publisher to release a record although the overseas publisher does not wish to assign any publishing rights to a music publisher in the same territory as the record company.

The record company will either pay any royalties direct to the overseas music publishing company or they may be collected on behalf of the music publisher by an authorised collecting agency who will deduct a percentage for the work of collection and distribution.

In this case the words Copyright Control and the initials of the collecting society or agency may be found where the publisher's information normally appears on a record. In such circumstances, however, there is no music publisher in the territory of issue to help promote the record or print sheet music.

5. PLAGIARISM

This is the posh word for stealing someone else's ideas and calling them your own. You may not have even realised that your song is a pinch from another. You don't need to have even heard the other song but provided it can be proved that the other song was written before yours then you are guilty of infringement of copyright.

If someone contacts you direct, claiming you have stolen their song, then get in touch with a solicitor immediately. Don't try to defend yourself. Copyright law is complex and not for the uninitiated to try to unravel.

If you believe that someone has infringed your copyright then take the same course of action but make sure you can prove the date on which you wrote your song.

Many songwriters are reluctant to send their songs to managers, artistes and record companies fearing that the work may be used, no credit given to the true writer and someone else taking the credit *and* the royalties.

This rarely ever happens in our business because it's extremely difficult to get away with it. If it *should* happen to you then a solicitor will handle the matter for you. Don't attempt to deal with it yourself.

When you are accused of plagiarising another work the normal course of action is to attempt to prove that the work you are accused of copying is not itself original. It is obviously advantageous to find another earlier work that is no longer in copyright but in the public domain. (Remember we said a work is copyright for the life of the composer plus fifty years after his death after which it reverts to the public domain.)

If you establish that a certain theme was written in 1837 which is substantially similar to yours and the work you're accused of copying

. . . plagiarism is the posh word for stealing ideas . . .

then there is no case to answer. If you've wittingly or unwittingly copied a lyric idea as well then you haven't much hope of defending yourself.

The law states in principle that there must be a reasonable similarity between a certain sequence of notes for plagiarism to be established in the case of the musical content and a reasonable similarity between the words if the lyrics are included in the plaintiff's plea.

Normally it's only the music that is deemed an infringement of copyright and I can't recall a case where the lyrics were also cited.

Very few actions for alleged infringement of copyright ever actually get into court. Firstly, it's a very expensive type of case to fight; and secondly, the judgement is totally in the hands (or ears really) of one man, the judge, who must decide himself whether or not one tune is reasonably similar to another. Even though you may be absolutely convinced one way or another, depending which side you're on, the judge may not hear the alleged plagiarism in the same way. He has no precedents to go by since the permutations of sequences of musical notes are endless and two sequences may appear quite different to one person whereas another won't be able to tell them apart.

The normal course of action is for the parties to settle out of court especially if no earlier work can be established that is similar to the song that one is accused of stealing from. The defendants (those accused of the infringement) will pay the plaintiffs (those accusing) an agreed percentage of royalties earned by the infringing work.

I don't think it would be correct for me to cite names and places from my own experiences in alleged cases of infringement but I can mention the following facts in loose terms.

(1) I was accused of stealing the notes of a well-known TV jingle and using them in an instrumental composition. I did my own research on this one (don't try it yourself, I've got more experience) and found a few notes written by Dvorak which were identical to the the TV jingle thereby proving that the jingle wasn't original itself. The case never went any further.

(2) The administrators of the estate of a well-known American composer (no longer living, or course) claimed I had infringed the copyright in one of his works through one of my compositions for Petula Clark. In this event we retained the services of a music researcher who worked for us to find another piece of music written before the one I was alleged to have copied.

He came up with the following facts. When the American composer was writing the work I was alleged to have copied, he did some research in the Deep South of America and based this theme (and many others) on Traditional Negro folk songs. Our researcher was able to identify the actual folk song which was used, and these facts were brought to the notice of the estate administrators who took no further action against me.

In both the above cases I had to agree that there was a similarity between my work and the others that I was accused of copying but I was also certain that it could be proved that those songs were not even the original themselves and you can't have an infringement of an infringement.

(3) Jackie and I wrote a song and it was recorded and became a smash hit. A writer with no successes to his credit claimed he had written a similar tune at an earlier date, that we had stolen the song and used it as the basis for our hit song. I'd never even heard of this writer let alone his song but we asked him to send us a copy for comparison. Well, sure enough, the similarity was incredible and, believe me, totally accidental. Not just a few notes but about eight bars of the music. But worse than that, the copyright date was about five months earlier than ours. Ironically (contrary to all the advice I've given), we had actually written our song *six* months before we'd got around to registering it for copyright purposes. I had no way of proving it, however, whereas the other writer had conclusive evidence of his copyright date. No matter how much we pleaded that no writers with our successes, reputation and standing in the music business would need to steal other people's songs it made no difference. There was no point in going to court. We would have had to wait for a hearing and even if we had won it still would have cost us time and money to fight it out. To this date and evermore a percentage of that song has been and always will be paid to the other writer.

I have never myself taken any action against anyone else even though there have been several instances when I've felt that the copyright in our songs has been infringed by another party. Reason? We've been too busy writing more songs!!

Finally, when the writer assigns the copyright to a publisher he indemnifies the publisher against all allegations of infringement by guaranteeing that it's his own work. If there is an action over alleged infringement most publishers, however, will stand up and fight for the song because it's in their interests as well to do so and they realise that most writers wouldn't know where to begin a defence. If your song is infringed by someone else then your publisher will undoubtedly take steps to ensure that the correct course of action is motivated for the protection of your copyright.

CHAPTER TEN

ARRANGING FOR ADDITIONAL INSTRUMENTS

This chapter is not intended to be a full treatise on scoring for the orchestra. The ambitious music student will either be attending music college, taking private lessons or studying from the many excellent books which are totally devoted to the subject.

My aim is to help the novice arranger understand the instruments at his disposal, what they can do and how to use them in conjunction with writing for the pop record or cabaret arrangement.

I've already explained and illustrated the layout for a rhythm section score and many of the principles contained therein are also applied to scores for larger combinations of instruments.

The addition of certain instruments can doubtless enhance the presentation of a song on record or in cabaret and even a limited knowledge of the subject can help a keen musician to make an adequate start.

In music one learns a great deal from practical experience. Musicians playing your first arrangements will be only too willing to help you if you're willing to listen. Musicians can't tolerate 'buskers', not the street-musicians but other musicians who pretend they know what they're talking about and attempt to bluff their way through their ignorance.

If it's any help to up-and-coming arrangers then I should tell you that I've never had an arranging lesson in my life. I was lucky to get a thorough grounding in the theory of music and learnt to play piano at school but my knowledge of scoring for the orchestra was acquired by (a) reading books on the subject, Cecil Forsythe especially, (b) writing small arrangements (at first) and trying them out on dance-bands with whom I worked, (c) listening to records and analysing the arrangements, and (d) studying other experienced arrangers' scores whilst I worked with them in recording studios.

I must say I found the last way the most helpful, but I realise, of course, that many up-and-coming arrangers won't have the good fortune as I did of working in the recording world from an early age.

The first three ways of learning, therefore are the most useful if the student is not attending music college.

The basic requisite for the music arranger is to have a good 'ear'. If you can't 'hear' the sound of the instruments, whether they're individual or collective, then arranging is going to be a great problem for you.

Working at the piano whilst scoring does not imply lack of competence. It's a lot slower, but if you can't work out chords and instrumental figures or counterpoint lines without the aid of the piano, then don't worry. Many arrangers work this way, and you'll find after a few years that the necessity to refer to the piano will diminish as your experience grows. Even now, before I score a new arrangement, I generally run it over on the piano to get the tempo right and work out a few figures for the intro or the end, etc. And even whilst I'm actually putting it all down on paper I often refer to the piano if a chord is difficult to voice or a little theme needs trying out.

In the following examples I've only attempted to explain how to use instruments in the simplest way. Voicing four trumpets, four trombones and five saxophones (the big band sound), is a complicated business.

The various instruments can be placed in the make-up of a chord in so many ways that I have not gone into great detail on that sound.

Secondly, the big band sound is not used too often in writing for pop records. What I have shown you will be sufficient for you to make your first efforts very reasonable and you can experiment from there. Please note that the range or compass of each instrument illustrated is not necessarily the total range, but that which is most practical for orchestrating pop music.

I. THE STRINGS

Violins: One of the most popular sounds on pop records. Need to be used in fairly large numbers to get a reasonably full sound unless you're using a single fiddle for a country or folk rooted record. Can

play sustained lines or rhythmic figures and have a huge range. Anything less than four violins sounds pretty thin and even with four you have to be careful how you write them. The fewer violins available the more unison you should use and don't write them too high. If you've got twelve good players then dividing them into harmony parts or scoring them very high works well. The violin is a non-transposing instrument: the notes written sound in concert.

Violas: Slightly larger than the violin with a lower range and a more mellow tone. Seldom used on their own in pop records except for special solo gimmicks but often used with cellos to give solid support

to the violins. You need far fewer violas than violins in an overall string section as they produce a fuller sound.

The viola generally uses the alto clef although all players read in treble clef when required.

Cellos: Everyone knows a cello by sight and it produces a rare and beautiful sound either as a solo instrument or when used with the other strings. Like the viola you need fewer of them in a string section

to produce a full sound. The cello is a non-transposing instrument written in the bass clef.

The strings can be used as follows:

Unison Either all strings on the same note where the range of the melody permits or in octaves. Good for figures.

N.B. VIOLINS COULD BE USED ONE OR TWO OCTAVES HIGHER.
VIOLAS COULD BE USED ONE OCTAVE UP OR DOWN.
CELLOS COULD BE USED ONE OCTAVE LOWER.

2-*Part Harmony* Good for moving counter-themes. Either all violins on one line and all lower strings on another or divide the violins A and B and have the lower strings an octave or two below the B's.

3-*Part Harmony* Violins in unison, violas on the second part, cellos on the third part. Very warm for sustained backings when used in mid piano range.

4-*Part Harmony* Violins divided A and B (2 parts), violas on third part, cellos on fourth part playing roots of chords or same as violin A octave lower.

5-*Part Harmony* Several ways of doing this.

Ex. 1. Violins divided A and B (2 parts), violas unison on third part, cellos divided A and B (4th and 5th parts).

Ex 2. Violins divided A and B (2 parts), violas divided A and B (3rd and 4th part), cellos unison on 5th part.

Ex 3. Violins in unison (1st part), violas divided A and B (2nd and 3rd parts), cellos divided A and B (4th and 5th parts).

Violins can be divided in Ex 3 to produce 6-part harmony very effectively.

All the above examples of voicing can be used by the strings in fast moving or slow moving passages.

The violins can be used playing figures whilst the lower strings (violas and cellos) can sustain.

All the strings can be used to play rhythm patterns. These can be played with the heel of the bow.

They can play marvellous runs in consecutive fast moving notes

or chromatically.

They can trill

or tremelo the note

either bowed or fingered.

On the violins the lowest string (G string) produces rich warm tones.

In unison with violas or cellos, even stronger.

Because of the construction of the instruments the strings can jump quickly from high to low sounds, and vice-versa.

The sequence of notes shown presents no problem to string players.

The violins and violas can be muted but the cellos, although they *may* be muted, normally are only requested to play softer to match the mellow sound of the strings above them.

The strings are not phrased as for the piano or wind instruments. The phrasing marks seen above string passages are bowing marks. A continuous line denotes that the passage will be played in one movement of the bow.

The 'down' bow is indicated with a symbol like the lower half of a capital H; the 'up' bow is marked with a symbol like a capital V.

Don't worry about these yet. Write something for strings and see how the players execute the passage. If you do not put in bowing marks the leader of the strings will do it for you.

Strings can also be written PIZZICATO (PIZZ for short) and the string will be plucked by the fingers.

A brief pause must be given both going into and coming out of a PIZZICATO passage for the player to change the position of the bow in his hand.

The following are typical combinations of strings generally used in recording.

4 violins; 1 viola; 1 cello.
5 violins; 1 viola; 1 cello. (When dividing A and B, 3 violins up and 2 down.)
6 violins; 1 viola; 1 cello.
6 violins; 2 violas; 1 cello.
8 violins; 2 violas; 2 cellos.
10 violins; 2 violas; 2 cellos.
12 violins; 3 violas; 3 cellos.

Also illustrated are parts of the recording arrangements of Sweet Sensation's 'Sad Sweet Dreamer' and 'Purely By Coincidence'. You'll note that in the original score for 'Sad Sweet Dreamer' I used 4 cellos instead of 2 violas and 2 cellos. Listen to the records and compare them with the scores. Some sounds are not intended to be heard loudly but simply as a warm back-drop to the vocal and rhythm sound. You may not be able to identify all the notes but their presence is felt.

SAD SWEET DREAMER
© M+M. MUSIC
Vocal
Choir
ALTO SAX. [IN PITCH]
ALTO SAX [IN PITCH]
Saxophones
Trumpets
Horns
Trombones
Violins
AS VLN A
Viola
Cello
Percussion
CONGAS
DRUMKIT
FILL
Guitars
A13 9
Em7 A
+WAH WAH
D
F#m
Em7 b5 Bb
AS GTR 1
A13
Bass/Gtr.
Piano
Harp
1.
2
3
4

Vocal
Choir
Saxophones
Trumpets
Horns
Trombones
Violins
Viola
Cello
Percussion
Guitars
Bass/Gtr.
Piano
Harp
5
7
8
CONGAS
SOLO
Dmaj7
Em7
A139

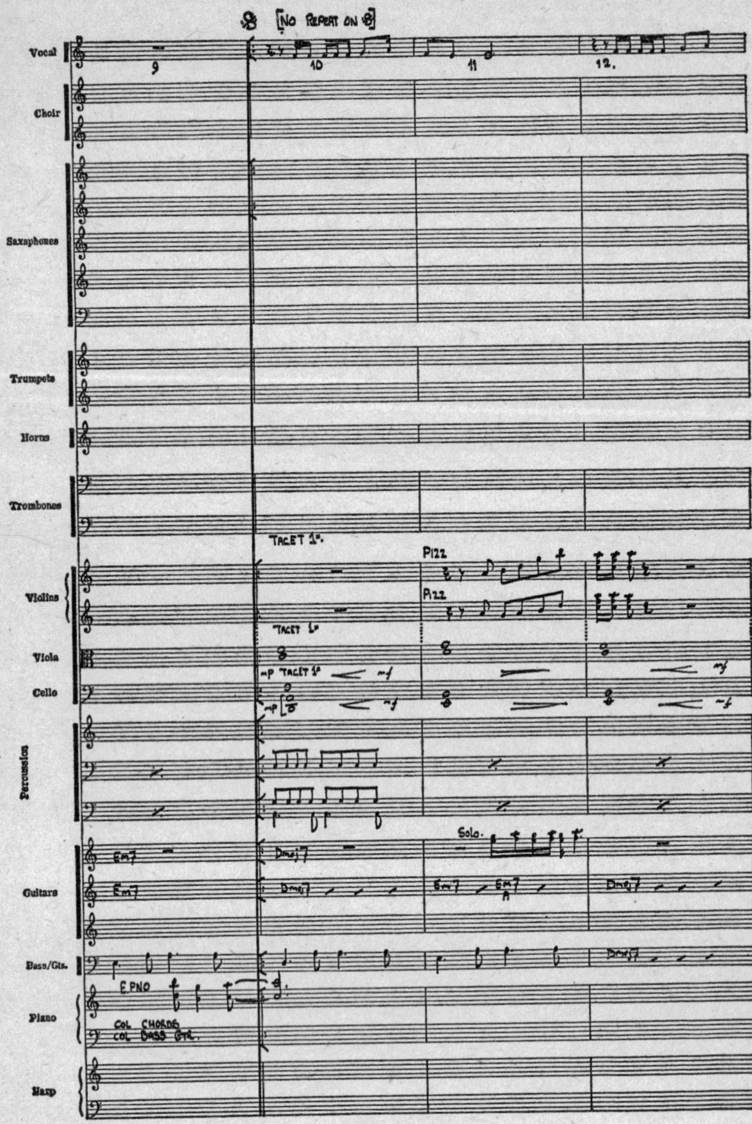
[NO REPEAT ON 𝄋]
Vocal
Choir
Saxophones
Trumpets
Horns
Trombones
Violins
Viola
Cello
Percussion
Guitars
Bass/Gts.
Piano
Harp
9
10
11
12.
TACET 1°
PIZZ
mp
mf
Solo.
Em7
Dmaj7
E.PNO
COL CHORDS
COL BASS GTR.

Vocal
Choir
Saxaphones
Trumpets
Horns
Trombones
Violins
Viola
Cello
Percussion
Guitars
Bass/Gtr.
Piano
Harp
Em7
Dmaj7
COL CHORDS
E.PNO
COL BASS
GTR

Vocal
Choir
Saxophones
Trumpets
Horns
Trombones
Violins
Viola
Cello
Percussion
Guitars
Bass/Gtr.
Piano
Harp
2x
17
18
19
20
Solo
ARCO
DIV
UNIS
Em7
Bm7
Em9
COL CHORDS
COL BASS GTR.

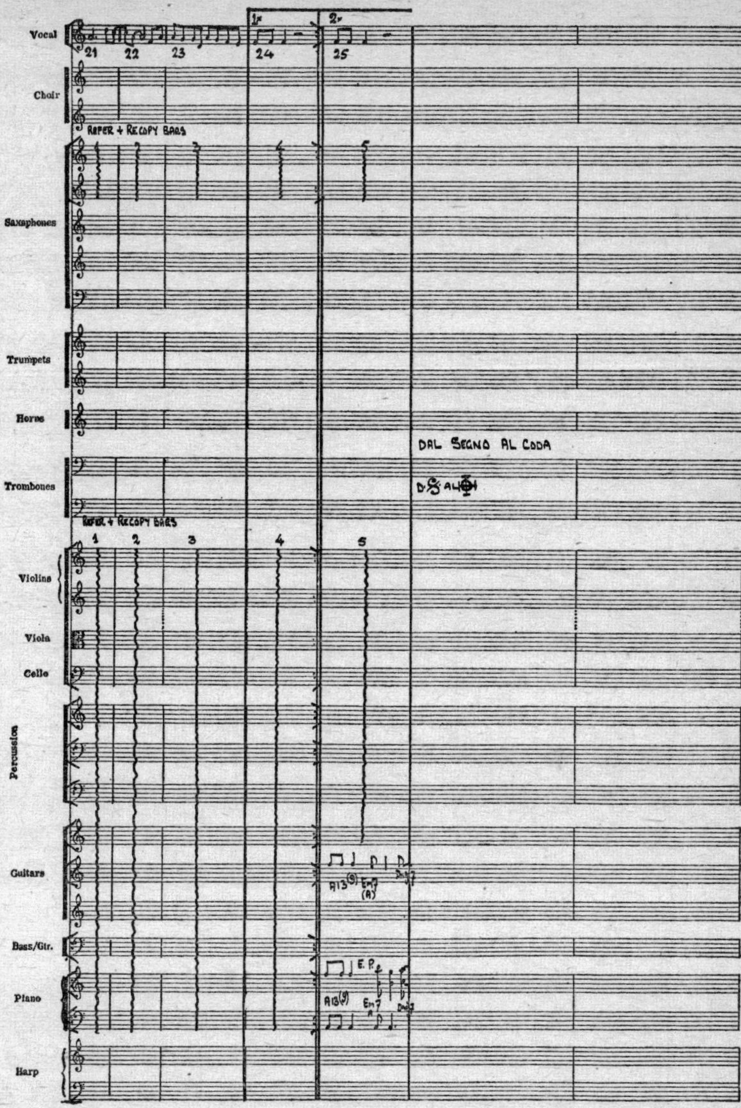
Vocal
Choir
Saxophones
Trumpets
Horns
Trombones
Violins
Viola
Cello
Percussion
Guitars
Bass/Gtr.
Piano
Harp
DAL SEGNO AL CODA
A13(9)
Em7
(A)

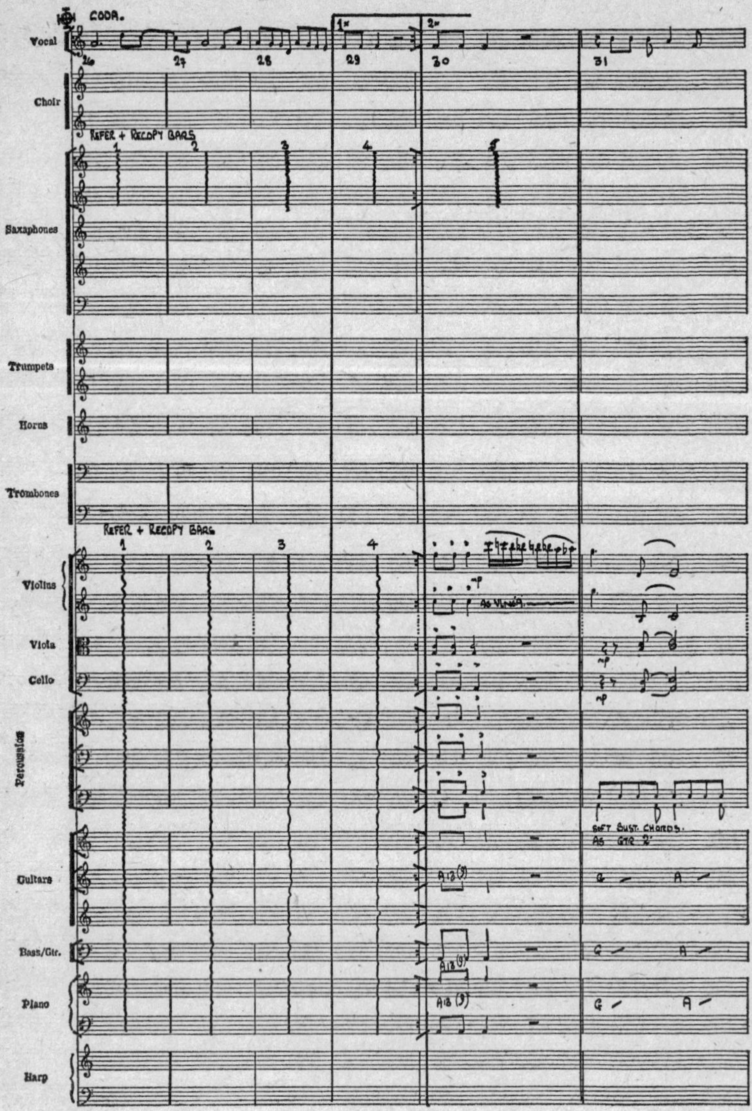
CODA.
Vocal
Choir
REFER + RECOPY BARS
Saxaphones
Trumpets
Horns
Trombones
REFER + RECOPY BARS
Violins
Viola
Cello
Percussion
SOFT SUST. CHORDS.
AS GTR 2
Guitars
Bass/Gtr.
Piano
Harp

Vocal
32.
33.
34
35
Choir
Saxaphones
Trumpets
Horns
Trombones
Violins
(DIV)
Viola
Cello
Percussion
Guitars
F#M
C
G
D
G
Bass/Gtr.
CHORDS
Piano
CHORDS
Harp

Vocal
36
37
38
39
Choir
Saxaphones
Trumpets
Horns
Trombones
TREM
Violins
Viola
Cello
Percussion
Guitars
Bass/Gtr.
CHORDS
E. PNO
Piano
Harp

Vocal
Choir
Saxaphones
Trumpets
Horns
Trombones
Violins
Viola
Cello
Percussion
Guitars
Bass/Gtr.
Piano
Harp
40
41
42
43
REFER + RECOPY BARS
10
11
12.

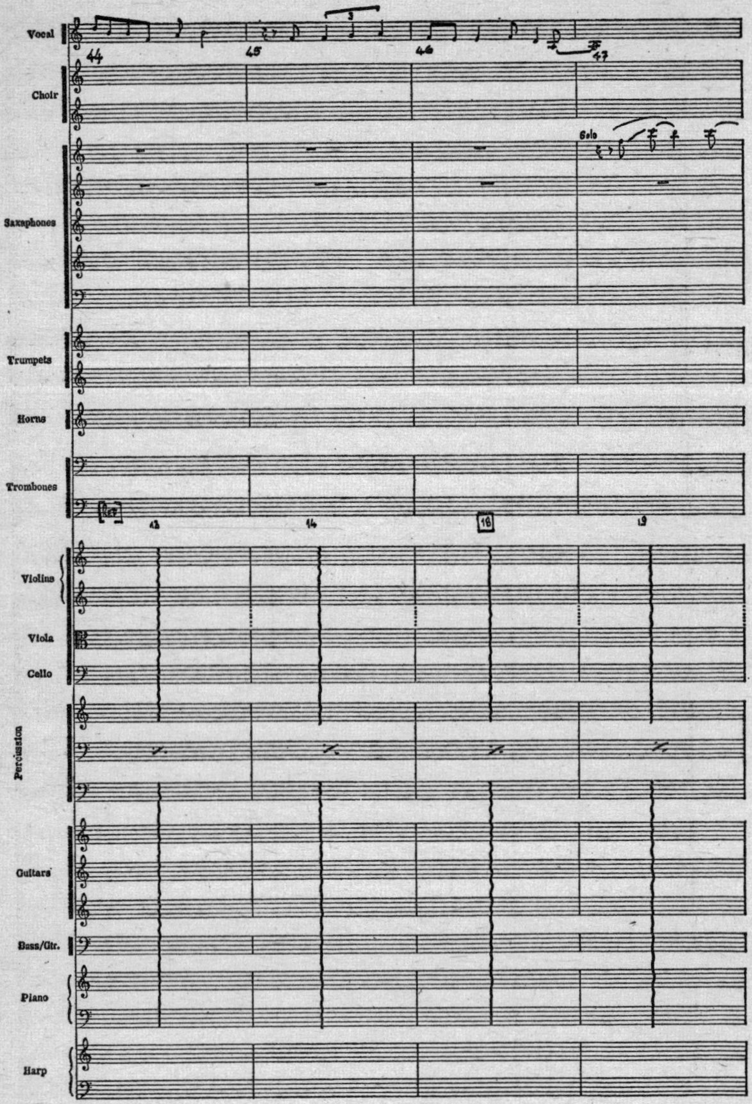
Vocal
Choir
Solo
Saxaphones
Trumpets
Horns
Trombones
Violins
Viola
Cello
Percussion
Guitars
Bass/Gtr.
Piano
Harp

REPEAT FOR FADE FINISH
Vocal
Choir
Saxophones
Trumpets
Horns
Trombones
REFER + RECOPY BARS
UP ONE SEMITONE [TO Eb]
Violins
AS VLN I
Viola
Cello
Percussion
CHORDS
Guitars
Bass/Gtr.
CHORDS.
Piano
CHORDS
AS BASS GTR
Harp

PURELY BY COINCIDENCE
© M.+M. MUSIC.
Vocal
Choir
ALTO
TWO
Saxophones
[IN PITCH]
Trumpets
FLÜGEL
Horns
Trombones
Violins
UNIS COL 'A'
DIV.
Viola
Cello
Percussion
SHAKER
CONGAS.
FREELY.
DRUMKIT
T.T.
BD
ELEC
ELEC. + WOW WOW
Guitars
ACC.
AS GTR 1.
Bass/Gtr.
FAIRLY FREELY.
Piano
ELEC.
CHORDS
AS BASS GTR.
AS. BASS GTR.
Harp
A13
Em7
D Dmaj7
E7
1
2
3
4
5

Vocal
Choir
Saxophones
Trumpets
Horns
6
7
8
9
Trombones
Violins
COL 'A'
Viola
Cello
Percussion
LIGHT FILL
D– Em9 A13
D– Dma7
E7 (D)
b5
Em7 A13
AS 1
Guitars
Bass/Gtr.
AS GTR
AS B.GTR.
Piano
Harp

Vocal
Solo
HARMONY
Choir
Saxophones
Trumpets
Horns
10
11
12
13.
Trombones
ARCO
Violins
PIZZ
Viola
Cello
Percussion
H.H.
Guitars
D
DMAJ7
Gm6
(E)
A7
Am
(ELEC. TACET.)
AS GTR 1.
B7
Bass/Gtr.
Piano
AS GTR 1.
AS BASS GTR.
Harp

Vocal
Choir
Saxophones
Trumpets
Horns
14
15
16
17
Trombones
Violins
Viola
Cello
mp.
Percussion
Guitars
EM G
b5
EM7 A7
AM
B7
Bass/Gtr.
Piano
EM G
b5
EM7 A7
AM
B7
AS BASS GTR
Harp

Vocal
Choir
Saxophones
Trumpets
Horns
Trombones
Violins
Viola
Cello
Percussion
Guitars
Bass/Gtr.
Piano
Harp

Vocal
Choir
Saxophones
Trumpets
Horns
Trombones
Violins
Viola
Cello
Percussion
Guitars
Bass/Gtr.
Piano
Harp
22
23
24
25
DIV
AS. VLN A.
mp
LIGHT FILL
Em7 b5
A13
D
Em9
F9
A7
Am
AS GTRS.
AS BASS GTR.

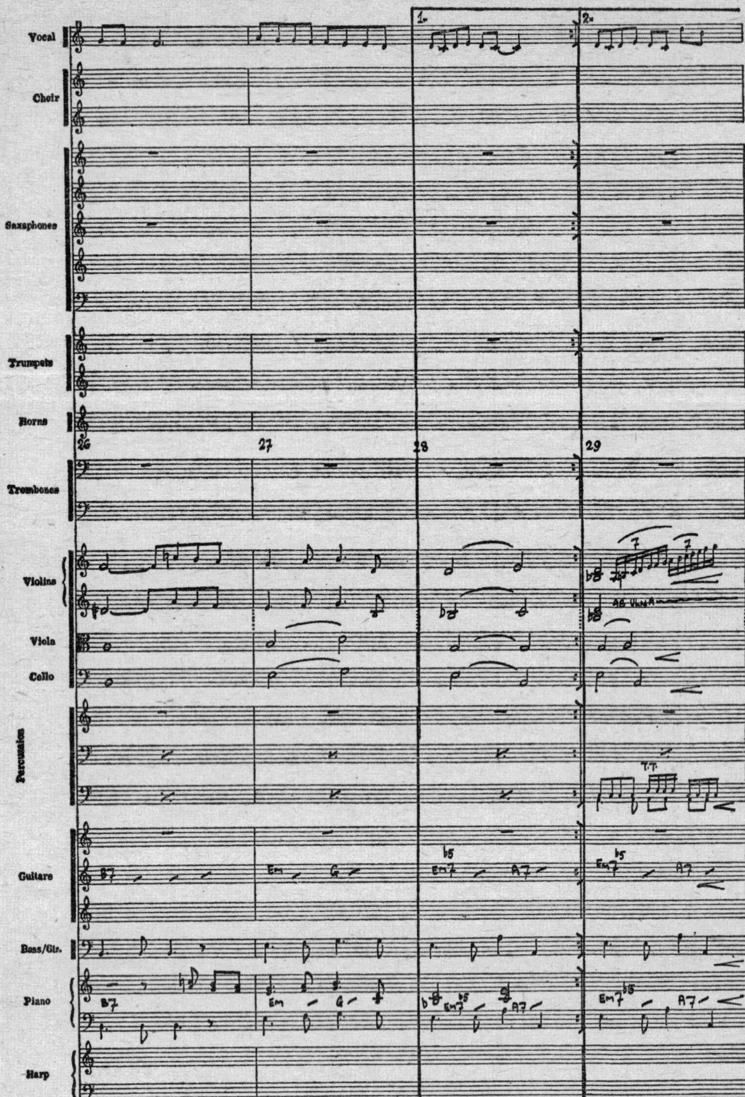
Vocal
Choir
Saxophones
Trumpets
Horns
Trombones
Violins
Viola
Cello
Percussion
Guitars
Bass/Gtr.
Piano
Harp
1.
2.
26
27
28
29
B7
Em
G
Em7 b5
A7

Vocal
Choir
Saxophones
Trumpets
Horns
Trombones
Violins
Viola
Cello
Percussion
Guitars
Bass/Gtr.
Piano
Harp
30
31
32
33
LIGHT FILL
ELEC + WOW WOW
D Dmaj7
E7
Em7 A13
D Em9 A13
AS. GTR1
AS. BASS GTR

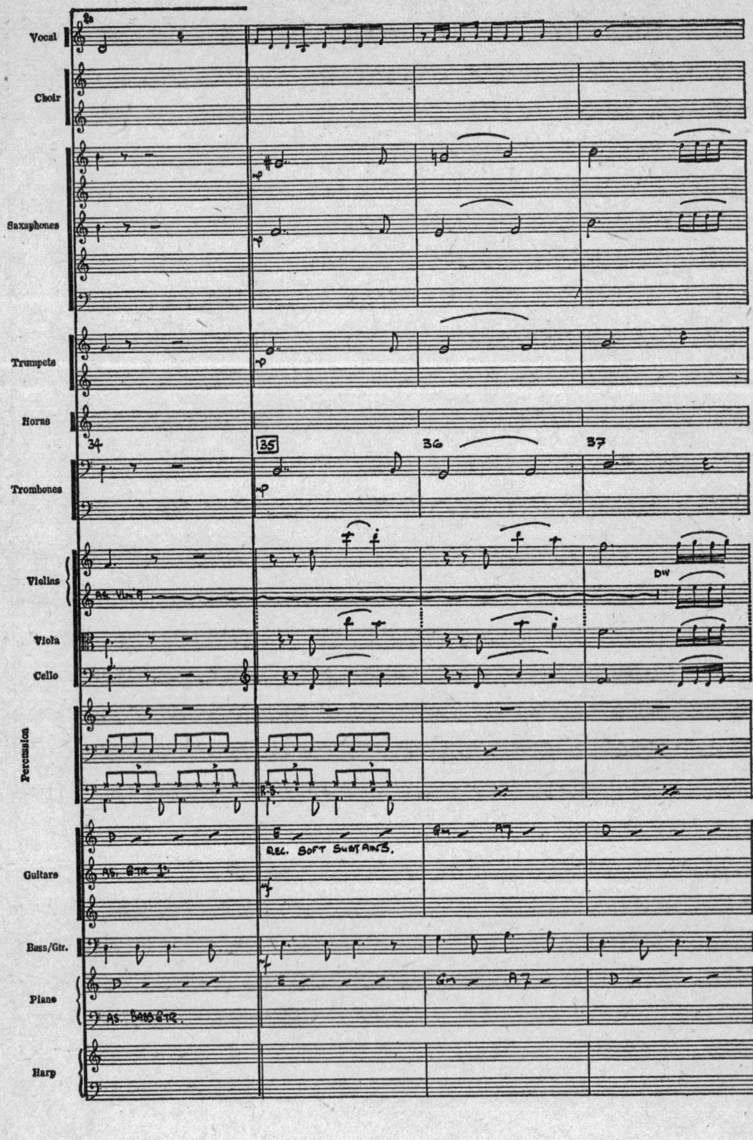
Vocal
Choir
Saxophones
Trumpets
Horns
34
35
36
37
Trombones
Violins
DW
AS. VLN A
Viola
Cello
Percussion
R.S.
Guitars
D
E
REC. SOFT SUSTAINS.
Gm
A7
D
AS. GTR 1.
Bass/Gtr.
Piano
D
E
Gm
A7
D
AS. BASS GTR.
Harp

Vocal
Choir
Saxophones
Trumpets
Horns
Trombones
Violins
Viola
Cello
Percussion
Guitars
Bass/Gtr.
Piano
Harp
38
39
40
41
AS VLN 'A'
ELEC. SOFT SUSTAINS.
D
E
EM7 (A)
A7
Am
AS GTR 1
AS BASS GTR.

Vocal
Choir
Saxophones
Solo
Trumpets
Horns
42
43
44
45
Trombones
Violins
AS VLN A
Viola
Cello
Percussion
Guitars
B7
Em
G
Em7
b5
A7
Fm7
Bb7
AS GTR 1
Bass/Gtr.
Piano
Harp

[REPEAT FOR FADE FINISH.]
Vocal
Choir
Saxophones
Trumpets
Horns
46
47
48
49
Trombones
Violins
AS VLN A
DIV
Viola
Cello
Percussion
S.D.
FILL
Eb
F7
(Eb)
b5
Fm7
Bb13
Eb
Fm7
Bb
Guitars
AS GTR 1
Bass/Gtr.
Piano
AS. BASS GTR
Harp

The Harp: The harp is a very versatile instrument capable of playing light figures, chords, arpeggios and glissandos. It's normally used in conjunction with the strings but works equally well with woodwind or guitars. It's even been used with brass and sax line-ups. It's system of notation is the same as the piano. The player uses pedals to tune the strings to certain pitches. When writing chords that shift quickly from key to key or consecutive glissandos in different keys, one must make sure the player has time to pedal the change. Most competent players read chord symbols so when writing glissandos one only indicates the starting and finishing note and the notes of the chord to be covered and the player selects his own notes. For glissandos involving all the notes in a scale one may indicate all the notes to be played.

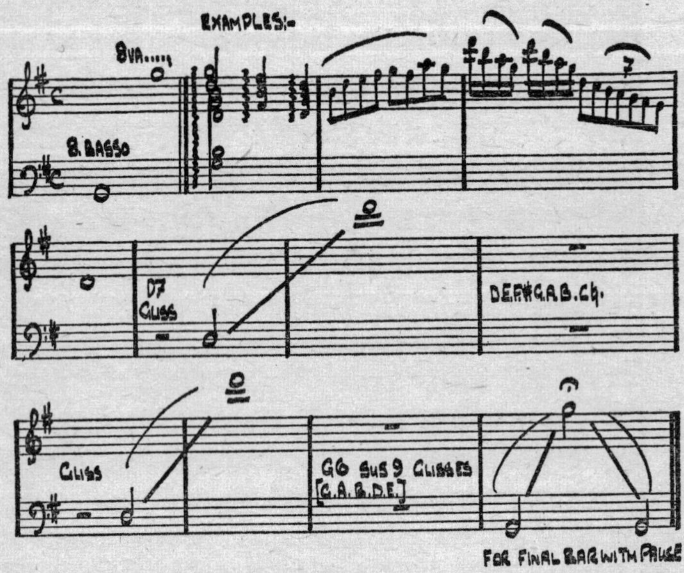

2. THE BRASS

The B♭ Trumpet: Many records feature the sounds of two or three trumpets either in unison or harmony. It's very popular for playing figures but a little heavy for sustained sounds. Various mutes can be used to alter the tone of the instrument. Included in the selection are bucket mutes (soft and warm sounds), cup mutes (soft but with a slight reedy sound), straight mute (thins the sound), tin mute (a very thin sound). Trumpets sound best for pop records from B♭ below middle C to B♭ two octaves above that. The B♭ trumpet is a transposing instrument and everything must be written a tone higher than the concert key. Simple figures always sound best on trumpets.

When using mutes restrict upper range to about F or G.

The B♭ Flugel Horn: A slightly larger instrument than the trumpet with a bigger bore and a more mellow sound. Flugel horn can be written a little lower than the trumpet, say, down to G below middle C but shouldn't be written higher than E♭ or F. Very popular for short staccato unison figures. Can be heard a lot on Burt Bacharach arrangements. Harmony should be restricted to two parts as three gets a little heavy. No mutes are used with the flugel horn. Written like the trumpet, up a tone.

The Tenor Trombone: A beautifully mellow sound in unison or harmony. When used in harmony can support lower strings to provide useful sustained sounds for vocals or higher strings. (Listen to Stylistics records.)

Trombones can be used on their own or with trumpets to provide a fuller brass selection.

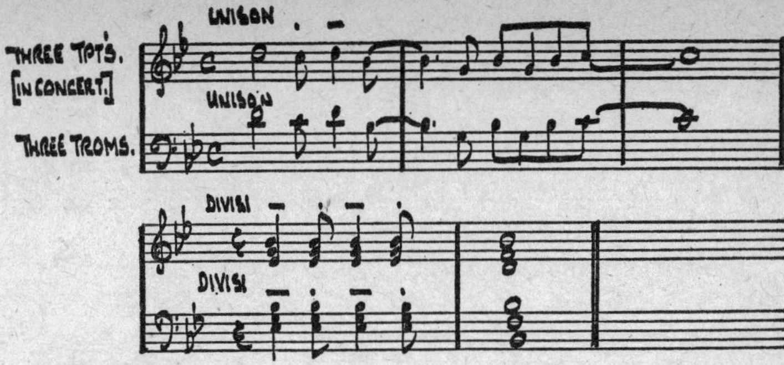

Best effective range is C below middle C to A♭ above middle C.

The Bass Trombone: A larger version of the tenor trombone. Sounds very similar to its smaller brother but has a deep fat sound in the lower register.

Can be used sparingly with bass on the roots of the chords for adding a lot of weight to heavy arrangements.

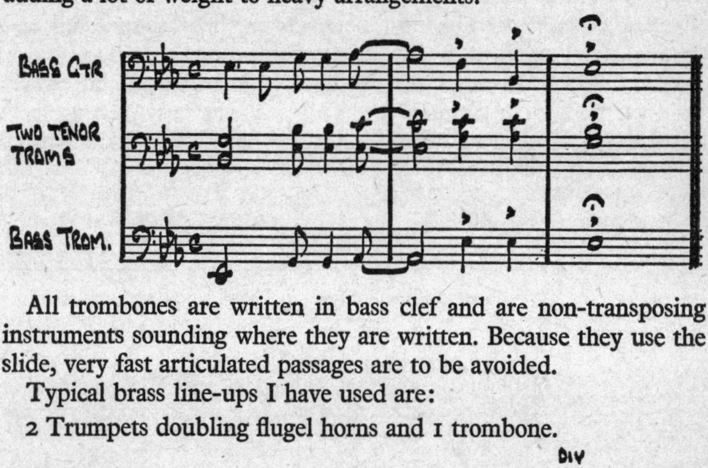

All trombones are written in bass clef and are non-transposing instruments sounding where they are written. Because they use the slide, very fast articulated passages are to be avoided.

Typical brass line-ups I have used are:

2 Trumpets doubling flugel horns and 1 trombone.

3 trumpets, 1 trombone and 1 bass trombone.

3 trumpets. 2 trombones and 1 bass trombone.

French Horn in F: The most mellow of the brass sounds and used frequently in pop records. Sometimes only 1 horn is used for soulful counter lines or two or three can be used in harmony and unison. At their best for pop music when playing long sustained notes. A transposing instrument which sounds a perfect fifth below what is written.

The best practical range is G below middle C to an octave above middle C. The french horn can also be used with trombones. I sometimes use 1 french horn and 2 trombones on a three part sound or if we're really going to town then 3 french horns, 2 trombones and bass trombone is a beautiful sound.

A whole brass section may consist of trumpets, french horns and trombones; or flugel horns, French horns and trombones.

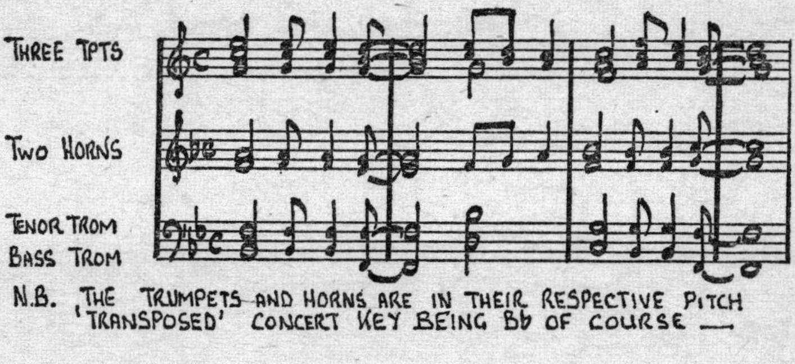

3. THE WOODWIND

This is a slightly erroneous title as some of the woodwind family are made of metal.

The Flute: (Metal or wood. Correct term is 'Concert Flute'.) One of the most popular sounds on pop records. Can be used solo or in sections of two or three or with violins. Fast passages come easily as the instrument has great agility. Warm and soft in its lower register and bright and shrill in the upper.

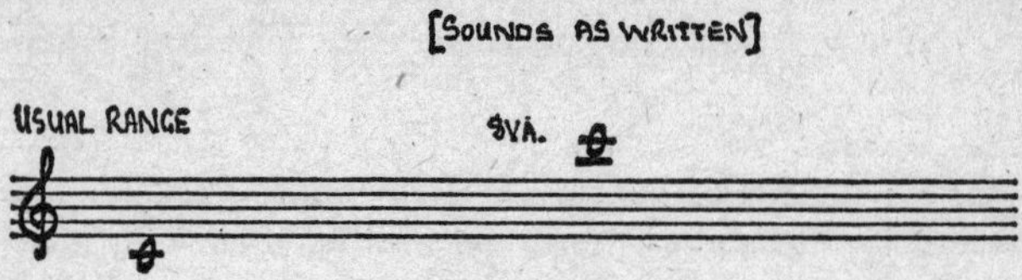

Ex. 1.

Ex. 2.

Ex. 3.

Ex. 4.

Very effective from 1 octave above middle C to 2½ octaves above middle C. A good sound to remember is flute or flutes in unison with flugel horn or flugel horns, one octave above them.

[N.B. FLÜGELS ARE WRITTEN IN CONCERT PITCH FOR SIMPLICITY.]

The flute is warm and soft in the eight notes above middle C.

The Piccolo: (metal or wood) A mini-flute, smaller but even more shrill and agile than its big brother. Sounds good an octave above the flute. Best range is from C above middle for two octaves.

The flute and piccolo are written in the treble clef in the concert key. The piccolo sounds an octave above that which is written.

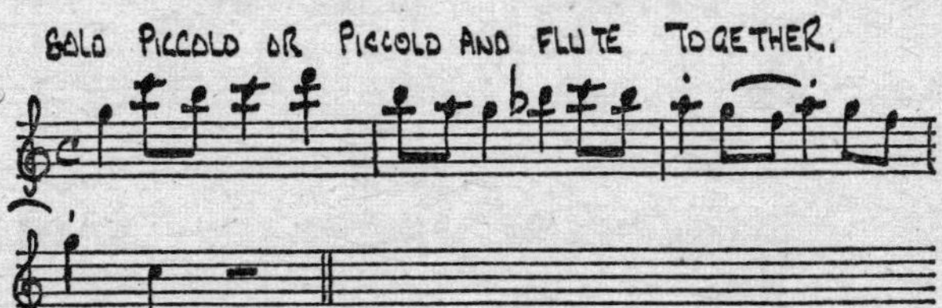

[N.B. THE PICCOLO WILL SOUND AN OCTAVE HIGHER]

The Alto Flute in G: Big brother of the flute. A very soft, warm and mellow sound. Two alto flutes sound good in unison or two part harmony. Little staccato figures or short simple figures are most effective. Even long sustained passages are very attractive. Generally used as a fill-in instrument in soft verses of slow beaty ballads.

The alto flute is written a fourth above concert key. Best range is G below middle C to C above middle C. The instrument can also be used in unison or harmony with the concert flute, although it is more usually heard on its own because of its unique tone.

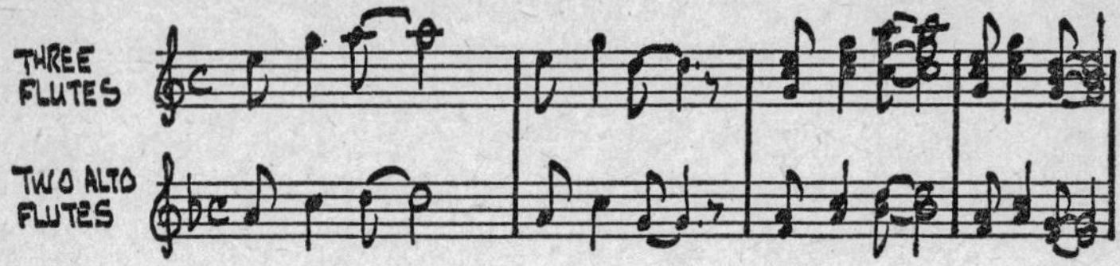

[N.B. ALTO FLUTES ARE IN THEIR TRANSPOSED PITCH]

The B♭ Clarinet: (A single reed woodwind instrument) The clarinet is a transposing instrument written a tone above concert pitch.

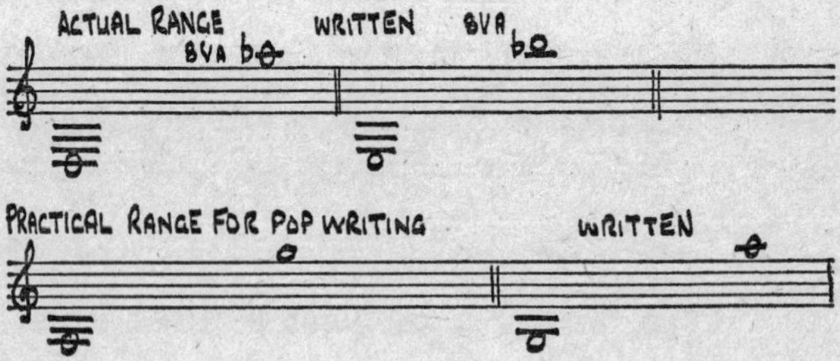

Not used too much on pop records but nevertheless a sound you should know about. G below middle C to an octave above middle C for two or three clarinets in harmony makes a reasonable sustained sound but I wouldn't write them in unison except for special effect.

Clarinets are mostly used as part of a larger woodwind section which might include flutes, oboe, etc.

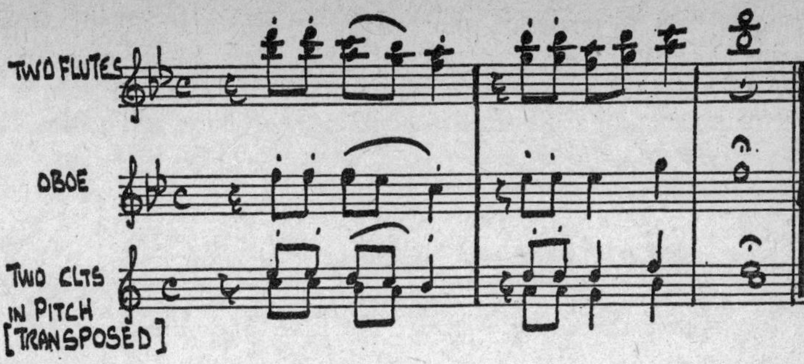

As a solo instrument the clarinet sounds best in its low register (the chalameau register). That's where Acker Bilk played most of 'Stranger On The Shore'.

The B♭ Bass Clarinet: A knockout sound but seldom used in pop records. Very rich and tuneful. Written as the B♭ clarinet but sounds an octave lower. In dance bands one uses three clarinets and a bass clarinet for sustaining behind the vocals or one flute, two clarinets and a bass clarinet. In dance bands the flutes and clarinets are normally played by the saxophone players, this is called 'doubling'. Best range is F 12 notes below middle C to G above middle C.

The Oboe: (A double reed woodwind instrument) A really wonderful solo instrument. Sounds at its best when playing soulful counter lines to vocals or solo passages in rhythmic ballads with strings backing. (My T.V. theme 'Emmerdale Farm' uses solo oboe.) In pop records seldom used as a section of oboes because of its particular sound but its often to be found with flutes and clarinets. A pretty sound is flute and oboe in unison octaves. Best range is from Middle C upwards for $1\frac{1}{2}$ octaves.

The oboe is written in the treble clef in the concert key.

The Cor Anglais: (double reeded) A larger version of the oboe with a lower range and also a more mellow sound. Visually the instrument can be distinguished from the oboe by the bulbous section at the bottom. Used very much as the oboe and most oboe players double cor anglais. The cor anglais is written a fifth above the concert key.

Best range is G below middle C to G two octaves up.

The Bassoon: (double reeded) Seldom used in pop records but very popular in full orchestral writing. It's the big brother of the oboe and is often used in unison an octave below it. The last time I can remember the bassoon being featured on a pop record was Sandy Shaw's 'Puppet On A String'.

It's written in the bass clef and sounds as written. Best effective range is G above middle C to two octaves below.

4. THE SAXOPHONES

This is really a family of brass instruments with reeds, ranging from the soprano down to the baritone saxophone. There is a bass sax and a contra bass sax but they are seldom used.

Soprano Sax in B♭: Not normally used in the section but sometimes heard as a solo instrument. Very shrill, piercing sound, used to the best advantage on very rhythmic pop records with strong Latin orientated rhythm patterns. Best range is two octaves upward from middle C. Written a tone above the concert key.

Alto Sax in E♭: A widely used instrument in solo and section work. Can be heard solo in ballads with a beat or with tenor and baritone saxes and brass in soul or rock records. Best range is 1½ octaves upward from middle C. The alto sax is written a sixth above the concert key.

Tenor Sax in B♭: The most used sound on many types of pop record. Solo on beat ballads or used in pairs (unison or harmony), capable of a hard rocking sound for rock or soul records. Two tenors and a baritone is a very popular section with or without brass. Best range is an octave either side of middle C. The tenor sax is written in the treble clef a tone above the concert key but sounds a ninth lower.

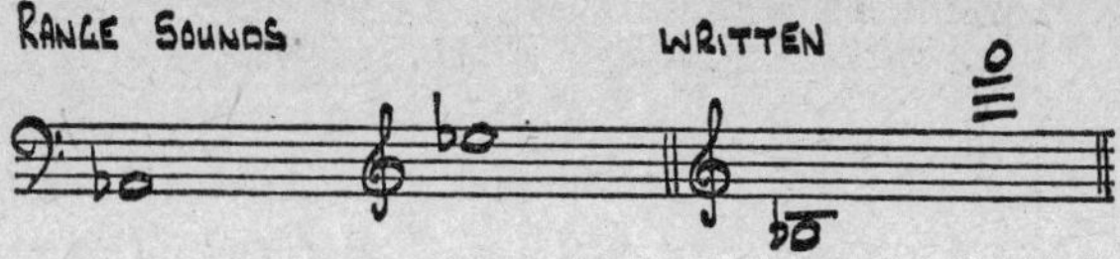

The E♭ Baritone Sax: With a lower range than the alto and tenor saxes the baritone can be used for adding weight to the tenor saxes (or tenors and altos together), providing the bottom of the chord on three, four or five part sax sections or simply for accentuating the bass notes on a heavy rock or solid beaty ballad. It's not often used in a solo capacity. Its best range is from E♭ an octave and six notes below middle C to G above middle C. The baritone sax is written in the treble clef but sounds an octave and six notes lower than the written note.

THE SAXOPHONES.

THINK OF THEM AS A CHOIR. TAKE A PHRASE AND SOME CHORDS THAT YOU WANT TO SCORE AND THIS IS HOW YOU MIGHT APPROACH THE JOB. IN CONCERT PITCH YOU MIGHT HAVE THE FOLLOWING SEQUENCE

EXAMPLE 1: THIS IS HOW YOU COULD WRITE THAT SEQUENCE

EXAMPLE 2'

EXAMPLE 3'

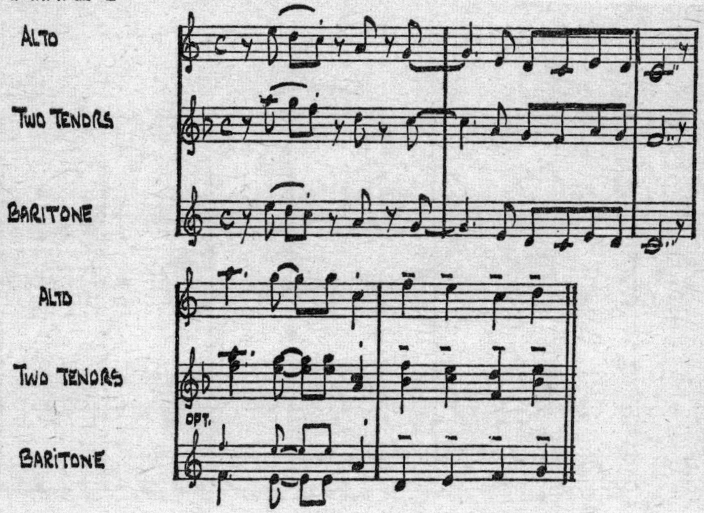

Virtually any combination of brass and saxes can be used to great effect on all types of pop record. Here are a few typical line-ups.

1 trumpet; 1 trombone; 1 alto sax; 1 tenor sax.

2 trumpets; 1 trombone; 1 tenor sax; 1 baritone sax.

3 trumpets; 2 trombones; 1 alto sax; 1 tenor sax; 1 baritone sax.

3 trumpets; 1 trombone; 1 bass trombone; 1 tenor sax; 1 baritone sax.

Here are some ways* of voicing these combinations. I've used the same sequence for illustration.

TPT. 1
TPT. 2.
TPT. 3
TROMS. 1. 2.
ALTO
TNR.
BAR
COL. TPT 1
DIV
TPT. 1.
TPT. 2
TPT. 3.
TROM + BASS TROM
TNR
BAR.
COL TPT. 1

As you will have heard on many records, strings, brass, saxes and woodwind can be used together in various combinations or individually to produce exciting and colourful sounds in conjunction with many different rhythms.

Look at the score of 'Purely By Coincidence' to see how a small brass and sax line-up was used with rhythm and strings.

5. THE PERCUSSION

The Vibraphone (Vibes) A soft, bell-like sound produced by striking strips of metal of varying lengths suspended over tubes. The instrument is struck with beaters (hard or soft depending on choice) and an electric motor drives a revolving vane in each tube which gives the note a vibrato effect, hence the name, vibraphone. Popular for sustained sounds.

The Xylophone (Xylo) A very short percussive sound produced by striking strips of wood of varying lengths corresponding to pitch. The instrument is struck with metal or wood mallets. Not used much in pop records as a featured instrument but can be heard as part of the rhythm section in some Tamla-Motown type sounds.

EXAMPLE

XYLO WITH GTR AND FLG.

The Glockenspiel (Glock) High, brilliant yet pretty bell-like sounds produced by striking strips of metal of various lengths corresponding to pitch with metal or wood mallets. Used a lot on middle-of-the-road 'joggalong' records and with the strings on slower ballads with a beat. An example of the former use in Donny Osmond's 'Why' and the latter, the Stylistics, 'Let's Put It All Together'.

The Marimba: A cross between the xylophone and the vibes where strips of *wood* are suspended over tubes without the revolving vane. Struck with beaters or mallets and used on soft Latin type numbers. The beater or mallet is normally bounced on the instrument (like a roll on the drums) to produce a continuous sound.

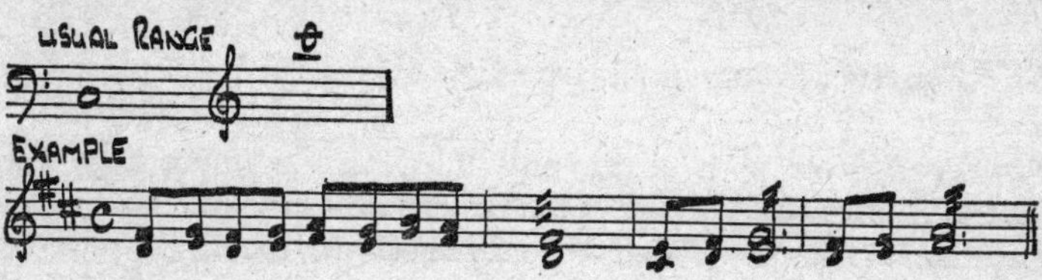

The Tubaphone: A cross between the glock and the vibes but with no vibraphone effect.

Tubular Bells: Tubes of varying lengths corresponding to pitch suspended on a metal frame and struck with leather bound hammers. Sometimes used on pop records for special effects.

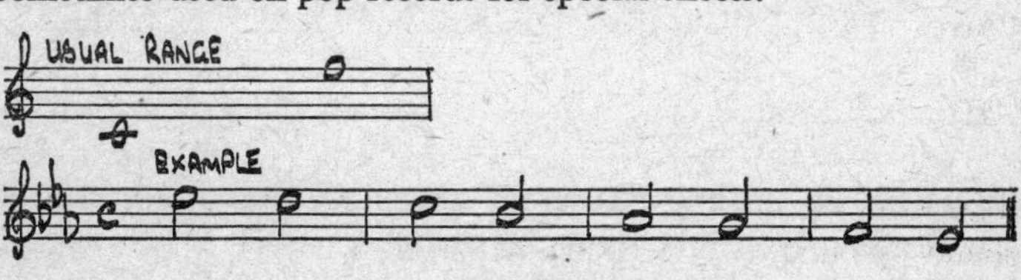

Timpani (sometimes erroneously called Kettle Drums) Timpani come in various sizes but the most commonly used are small, medium and large. They are tuned by tightening the skin of the drum with the 'tap' like handles on top or by the more modern method of a pedal which stretches or slackens the skin as desired. With the pedal the player can even make glissando type effects by depressing the pedal *after* the drum has been struck by the beater.

6. LATIN PERCUSSION

The most widely used. Small Latin percussion instruments include the following:

Tambourine: Comes in all shapes and sizes.

Shaker: Various sizes, a container filled with anything from lead shot to grains of sand. One of the percussion sounds on 'Sad Sweet Dreamer' was a plastic Harpic bottle filled with rice.

Cow Bell: Comes in various sizes. Used frequently in modern rhythm sections. Played with a drum stick, normally by the drummer.

Cabassa: Rows of beads laced over a hollow gourd, played by moving the beads over the surface of the gourd in rhythm.

Res-o Res-o: A hollow piece of wood that is grooved from top to bottom, played by drawing a piece of stiff metal over the surface in rhythm.

Marracas: Used in pairs, hollow, filled with lead shot, rice, etc.

Claves: Two pieces of hard wood knocked together in rhythm.

Castanets: Spanish variety that everyone is familiar with.

Bongos: Two small drums played with the fingers and palms, the drums normally held between the knees.

Conga Drums: Two long drums on stands played with the fingersand palms, used a tremendous amount in modern rhythm sections.

Timbales: Two metal drums on stands used mainly in authentic Latin-American music. Played by hitting the sticks on the metal sides of the drums.

There are several other Latin instruments, but these are the most widely used in modern pop records. They are all written on the bass clef stave like the drums.

7. SCORE LAYOUT

Always lay out your score in an easy-to-read system. Keep the strings together and the brass, etc. on their own and keep the rhythm in one block. It all helps when the score is copied on to individual parts and when you're checking the score during rehearsal.

It's entirely up to you whether you write your score in concert pitch or in transposed pitch.

Concert pitch means that all instruments are written in the concert key or, simply, the key as it is on the piano or guitar, for instance.

This is fairly easy for most of the instruments as they are either already non-transposing instruments such as violins, cellos, flutes, trombones, etc. or the transposition is simple as in the case of trumpets, french horn and cor anglais.

Incidentally, the viola should always be written in the alto clef (unless the passage to be played goes way off the stave). The instrument is not transposing but the alto (or C) clef keeps the notation within the stave.

The difficult instruments for scoring in concert are B♭ tenor sax, and B♭ bass clarinet. You must decide which is easiest for you. They can either be written in the treble clef which would be an octave above the actual sound and when copied taken up a tone or written in the bass clef where they actually sound. The transposition for the copyist in the latter case is difficult as he must go from bass clef to treble clef then up a tone or ignoring the clefs write out the notes a fifth down. If you're going to score in concert I would recommend writing in the treble clef which makes the copyist's job easier.

The E♭ baritone sax should be written in concert in the bass clef then the only change for the transposition is the clef, key signature and any accidentals. The notes will appear in the same place on the stave.

The advantage of scoring in transposed pitch is in the checking of notes. The notes on your score are the same as the notes you want the musicians to play. Also by writing in transposed pitch the notation of many instruments will appear mainly in the stave obviating the necessity for ledger lines.

The advantage of scoring in concert pitch is to make the work simpler at the actual time of scoring. It's one thing to work out figures and harmonies but to have to write them out in various different keys can make the job doubly difficult and twice as time consuming.

Whatever you do, the score must be in one form or the other. Don't mix them up.

CHAPTER ELEVEN

ADVANCED STUDIO RECORDING

Although I've covered the basic technique of modern studio recording in a previous chapter I've no doubt you'll be interested in the use of some of the more advanced gimmicks that are now included on many pop records.

Some records are made absolutely straight, just good natural recording of great sounds. Some add the occasional gimmick to bring extra interest to the overall sound. Others feature the gimmicks in their own right. Here are some of those gimmicks.

1. SYNTHESISERS

These are electronic devices which, using oscillators and sound wave shapes in various combinations, produce musical tones and effects. They are very expensive, starting at about £350 for a simple, fairly unsophisticated unit. They have to be virtually programmed each time they are used. Many groups use them and you can see them frequently in use on BBC's Top of the Pops. Recent records which featured synthesisers are: 'Pop Corn' by Hot Butter and 'Son of my Father' by Chicory Tip.

They can produce an almost endless variety of sounds and I'm sure it's only the beginning of an era as far as the synthesiser is concerned.

2. DELAY

The constant necessity for recording artistes, producers and studios to be one jump ahead of their competitors has produced many startling developments in the recording studio. Some of these developments are only modern versions of older ideas such as tape delay. The very short echo effect on early Presley, Gene Vincent and Carl Perkins records can now be produced electronically. It's still known as delay, but whereas it could only be effected by using a separate tape machine (still widely used) one can now use a device termed generally as 'digital delay'. When using tape delay a separate feed is taken from the vocal line, put on tape (via the recording head) and a feed taken a fraction of a second later off the playback head of the same machine and linked up again with the true voice sound. The length of the delay is governed by the speed of the tape past the two heads. A studio tape-recorder runs at $7\frac{1}{2}$ i.p.s., 15 i.p.s. or

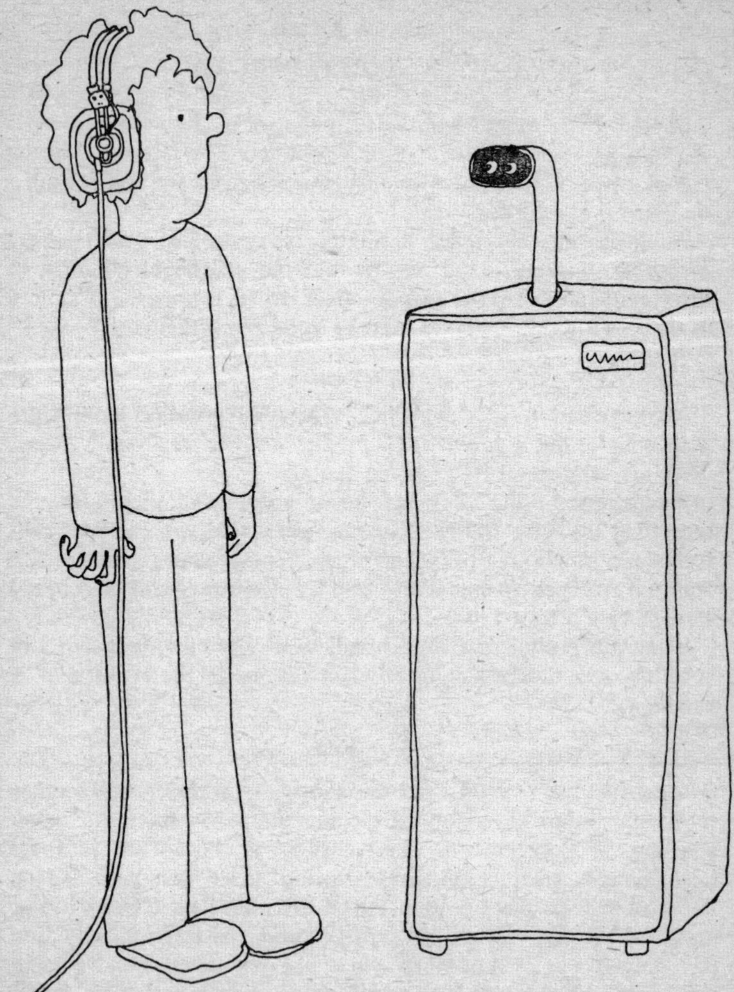

. . . the need to be one jump ahead has produced many startling developments in the studio . . .

30 i.p.s., and this is the disadvantage, you've only got a choice of three lengths of delay. With an electronic digital delay you can determine exactly the length of the delay.

The delay sound is still heard extensively on modern records, not just on the voices but on instruments as well, such as drums. Gary Glitter, The Glitter Band and Alvin Stardust use the delay sound to great effect.

Ordinary echo can be added to the delayed signal or, alternatively, echo can be added to the true signal and the delay then mixed in.

3. DELAY–ECHO

To extend the length of the echo a feed is taken off the echo line and a separate tape machine is used to delay the echo signal by a fraction of a second or more if required. The very long echo on the recorded vocal sound of Andy Williams and Tony Bennett is achieved in this way.

Delay-echo can be used on any of the instruments to be recorded with the exception of bass guitar and bass drum, of course.

4. PHASING

Phasing is probably the most difficult gimmick to describe but the easiest to recognise on a record. The peculiar sound heard on the voices of Queen's 'Killer Queen' is phasing.

The effect can be used on individual sounds (voices, strings, guitars, piano, drums (hi-hat especially)) or the overall sound of the record.

This is not a technical manual and I am no expert on the subject, so a technical description will not be forthcoming.

In its simplest terms it's the same signal reaching the same point at different intervals and as the amount of phase shift is altered so certain frequencies are cancelled out. A phase shifter or delay line is used to control the effect. It doesn't matter if at this point you are none the wiser. Ask a recording engineer to demonstrate the effect for you whilst you're mixing. You'll soon know whether or not to use it.

5. BACKWARD SOUNDS

You've probably heard on a record a sound which you thought was reminiscent of an instrument played backwards. It probably was. This sound is normally confined to solo guitars and parts of the drum kit, perhaps a cymbal roll or hi-hat splash.

It takes a lot of experiment to make it effective. Firstly, the sound is recorded on a separate piece of $\frac{1}{4}''$ tape. The tape is then turned over so that when it is played, any sound upon it will be played backwards. The attraction of the sound is that the die-away comes first and gets louder which is followed by the impact when the instrument was first played. The backward sound can either be dubbed on to the multi-track or included at the time the mix is done. Echo, equalisation and phasing can improve the effect.

6. DIRECT INJECTION

Many recording engineers, producers and musicians prefer to record amplified instruments by direct injection. This involves cutting out the amplifier of the instrument (bass guitar, electric guitar, electric piano, etc.) and taking the signal direct from the instrument to the mixing desk. Many good effects can be discovered by using both amplified and direct sound.

7. LESLIE SPEAKER UNITS

By combining the direct output of, say, an electric piano with a guitar phaser unit and a Leslie speaker unit, some very interesting sounds can be achieved. We're always experimenting with various pieces of equipment and the successful combination of electronic effects can be heard on many hit records. The various amplified keyboard instruments are especially suitable for experimentation.

8. VARIABLE SPEED CONTROL

Many multi-track recorders are equipped with variable speed control. When overdubbing, this can prove to be very useful. For instance, you might want to get a very fast hi-hat rhythm going that's just impossible at the correct speed. You slow the multi-track tape and the musician plays it at the new slower speed. When it's recorded you play back at the original speed and the effect is achieved.

9. KEPEX AND DOLBY

You may see either or both of these units in studios. They are basically noise reduction systems working on different principles. They are not used for special effects. Their job is to put as much signal as possible on the tape and cut down unwanted background or tape noise.

10. QUADROPHONIC SOUND SYSTEMS

This is the ultimate development of stereo, *four* separate channels of sound. As this book is being written, quadrophonic sound is still struggling to really establish itself, partly because world standardisation of systems is still not established.

11. COMPUTER-ASSISTED MIXING

Many studios are now equipped with this facility. It is being developed to assist the difficult work of mixing down as many as 24 tracks of sound from the multitrack recorder. Even with three pairs of hands all helping to manipulate the faders, the co-ordination and organisation required can only achieve a compromised balance, human error being what it is.

Through a computer, all or many of the fader moves can be logged to happen automatically whilst the mix is in progress. Two tracks of the multi-track recorder are used to carry the computer information. Imagine, therefore, on a 16-track mix-down, being able to set twelve of the fourteen remaining faders and only having to think about the remaining two which perhaps would have the lead voice and a solo instrument on them. Time is saved but more important, the final mix can only be better.

CHAPTER TWELVE

THE BACKROOM BOYS

The music business, of course, is not just the personalities out in front of the audience or the hit recording artiste. Behind the scenes many others contribute to the success of the industry. We've already mentioned agents, managers, record producers and music publishers but there are other careers open to the talented individual with imagination and a natural disposition towards hard work.

The most important consideration, need I say, is the willingness to start at the bottom of the ladder, work hard and grab the chances as they come along. It's such a relatively small business compared with the mass employment industries that opportunities to progress will always be there. One needn't necessarily end up in the same branch of the music business as one started out because many areas overlap sufficiently to provide fresh contacts and open new doors.

Let's look at some of the backroom jobs.

1. RECORD PRODUCERS

There are two types of record producers: those that have the ability to produce good records; and those that have the magic touch to produce good *hit* records. After fifteen years of record production I can always guarantee to make a *good* record because I know my craft but I need that extra piece of luck to produce a hit. You can always earn good money being an album producer but it takes a great deal of time building such a reputation that a company will entrust you with several thousand pounds to make an orchestral album for their catalogue.

For myself, I never intended to be a record producer when I left school. I wanted to be in the music business somewhere. I wanted to write songs and orchestrate and conduct but record production never occurred to me. After two and a half years as tea boy, filing clerk and errand boy, with Robert Mellin Music I was offered a job by record producer Dick Rowe to be his assistant. That's where I learnt my trade as a producer, writing songs in my spare time.

So where do the new producers come from? Well they still emerge from music publishers' offices, but so many others try their hands at record production that there's certainly no lack of opportunities. You've got to have experience, you see, and you can get this in so many ways.

. . . bluff your way through for a while . . .

Songwriters, given an opportunity and the funds, can produce their own work, often only starting out with simple demos and developing from there.

Members of groups gather experience while recording for others then turn this experience to their own advantage by producing themselves or others.

Solo singers sometimes produce their own records.

Agents and managers pick up tips while sitting in on their artistes' sessions then decide to have a go themselves.

Musicians, arrangers and conductors benefit from working in the studios and make good record producers.

Balance engineers with their vast technical knowledge become record producers.

In short, you've got to be around, in the right place at the right time to get in. Virtually anywhere in a business close to records. Of course, if you have capital, great ideas and contacts you can set up your own session, bluff your way through for a while, make a few hits then everybody wants to know you.

2. RECORD COMPANY EXECUTIVES

There are three basic areas of executive work: 'creative', 'administrative' and 'Sales'. If it's creative you're after, well, you've got to start at the bottom of the ladder. Creative includes catalogue planning, repertoire management, promotion and art-work.

Administration includes financial control, royalties and contracts, etc. The record business attracts accountants like wasps to a jam-jar (I apologise to all my accountant friends in the record business), because creative personnel are notoriously bad at financial control. Anybody with good management experience and a head for money can do well in the record business, although it won't have much to do with records. With all the 'heavy' deals that have to be done in respect of artistes, managers and licensees, etc. the financial experts are absolutely essential. (Not to mention the administrative expertise which is required to run any major business, of course.)

Sales is another side altogether and the accepted procedure for promotion in any sales force applies equally to the record business. They say that if you can sell soap you can sell records, it's just another commodity to be marketed. I like to think that record company reps have a little more interest than that but it proves the point that to get into the sales side of the record business you don't have to actually begin a career there.

The most challenging area, I guess, is the creative side, but here

. . . creative personnel are notoriously bad at financial control . . .

it's definitely a case of years of experience in the music business before you can hope to achieve a top executive post.

It's a matter of getting in somewhere, the post department, office junior, gofer (go for this, go for that). In time somebody will recognise your burning ambition and give you an opportunity to better yourself.

Some record company executives prove their flair in music publishing before switching to the record business but I would say that the majority of successful executives have spent much of their working lives somewhere in the record business.

3. PROMOTION

Record plugging is an important aspect of the record business, and is really known as record exploitation. You have to use all your powers of persuasion to get producers and deejays to feature your company's product. Many pluggers come from music publishing companies. This is not a job you set out to make as a career. It normally just happens to you by some quirk of fate. You can stay as a plugger all your life or use it as a stepping stone to other activities in the music business. Once again, it's a matter of being in the right place at the right time, but a plugger has to work for someone else for a time to build up his contacts, and no matter how good his contacts and his powers of persuasion, in the end he's only as good as the product he's promoting.

Another important aspect of record promotion is press publicity. The world of journalism itself provides a foothold towards a job in the press office of a record company and many successful press officers are ex-journalists. Alternatively, it's the same old routine of getting any sort of job in a record company and progressing towards your appropriate goal.

4. RECORDING STUDIOS

This is a difficult line of work to break into because there are relatively few opportunities available. The turn-over in balance engineers, for example, is very slow. Once you've made it you can keep a good job as a balance engineer for years, often with the same studio. The only way in is at the bottom but even a tape operator's job is hard to find. Most balance engineers start out as tape operators because from that position you can watch, listen and learn . . . but, as I say, there aren't many vacancies. You can but try, however, if recording work appeals to you.

5. SESSION MUSICIANS

This has got to be the toughest area of all to break into. Rhythm players seem to come from groups who no longer want to keep touring. A producer takes a liking to a particular musician's ability and books him frequently. Another producer gets to know about the musician's work and also gives him a few sessions. The word gets around, a few orchestra bookers recommend the musician and slowly, over several years, another session musician is created.

Brass and sax players come from dance bands, whilst strings, horns, woodwind and harpists come from the symphony and concert orchestras.

Many people constantly knock the BBC for its expenditure but it is a certain fact that the various orchestras which it employs have been the training ground for many of the recording industry's top musicians. It takes years to become a regular session musician and there's no room for incompetence. Only the very best make it and even they are always looking behind them to see who's ready to step into their shoes.

6. DEEJAYS

If you have hopes of joining this select band then you must start at the bottom, gaining experience in local discos and clubs. I concede that many deejays develop from journalists, broadcasters, comedians and singers but we must presume that you are not already a success in one of the associated fields. It's really the gift of the gab that makes a good deejay, especially for radio. The easy-going, friendly, confident style is what it's all about and it takes years for some to develop this.

Of course, there's always the Rosko/Stuart Henry style of 'hit 'em with all you've got for one hour non-stop' technique which seems more appropriate to the disco but, nevertheless, commands a place in our daily listening. I was auditioned to compere Housewives' Choice when it was running and had guest deejays. I failed miserably. Just the sound of my voice was a drag, and I was the first to admit it.

7. AGENTS AND MANAGERS

This is a line of work which depends on experience. You just can't apply for a job offering six 'O' Levels as a qualification. The important thing to remember is that London isn't the only place where agencies and management offices operate. All over the country in connection with places of entertainment (social clubs, working men's

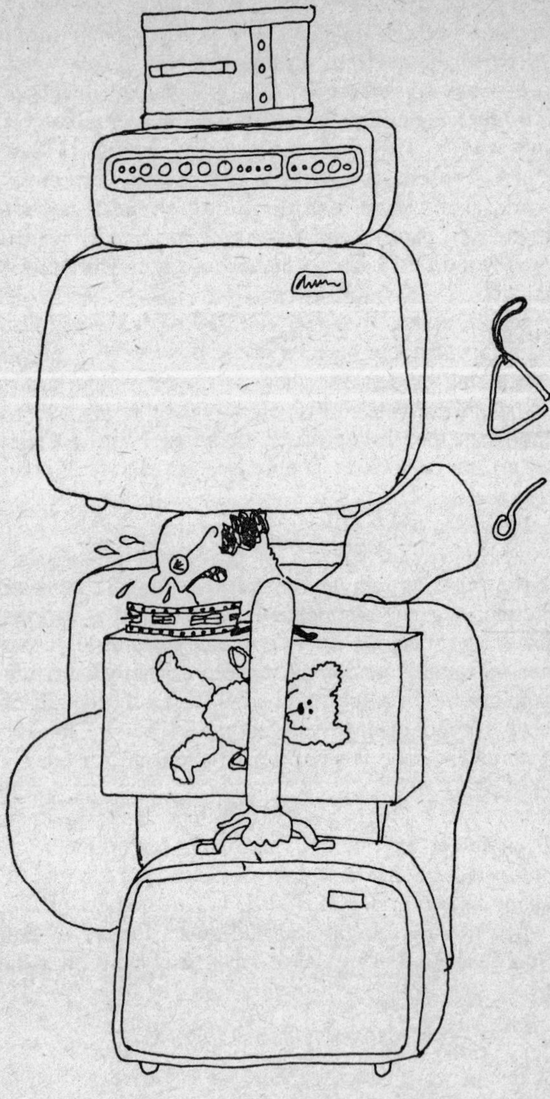

. . . roadies should not be prone to hernias . . .

clubs, cabaret clubs, theatres, pubs and restaurants with live music, etc.), there are agents and managers working to secure engagements for the acts they represent.

Most newcomers get into management and agency work in the provinces via one act which they have faith in and, by making contacts with employers of entertainers (the club owners and concert secretaries, etc.) slowly build up their business to include further acts. It's a laborious process, requiring many evenings hanging around the clubs just in order to meet people.

One can also learn the agency and management business by acquiring a junior position in one of the established firms but the vacancies are few and far between.

8. ROAD MANAGERS

This is really hard work. Most groups that can pay their way have one or two 'roadies' to do the heavy work of humping equipment, organising the set-up in clubs, etc. and looking after the whims of their masters, the star turn. Roadies are normally also the contact between artiste and manager. They drive vans through fog, snow, ice and earthquake to get their artistes to the locations for the gigs.

Road managers normally start out as friends of the group, sometimes frustrated musicians themselves, but trusted. Some agents and managers employ permanent roadies, but these guys have great experience in handling the many problems that beset groups on the road. You can't apply for a job as a roadie just because you've driven ten-tonners and you're built like an ox. The only way to start is to find a new, young, group or act and inquire if they need a chap like you. (Make sure you're not prone to hernias, though!)

POSTSCRIPT

THE PITFALLS OF SUCCESS

When you start making money don't go out and spend it all at once. Sounds simple, doesn't it? But you never know how long your success will last and thriftiness is next to cleanliness. (I like clean and thrifty people!)

Keep a note of all your legitimate expenses incurred in the course of pursuing your career. Put aside something all the time (if you can) just in case of emergency. Self-employed persons in the music business have no automatic pension scheme as one might benefit from whilst working for a company. Building societies, insurance are all safe bets for your money.

Don't think about speculating in property or stocks and shares the day you receive your first royalty cheque or at the end of your first year as a hit recording artiste. Take your time. Seek expert advice. By all means buy a house or a flat. That's always beneficial if you can afford it but don't let other wise guys take you for a ride with flash schemes to make money quickly. You will probably lose more than you'll ever make.

So many people fall into the trap of wasting money on two or three cars when one will suffice. Anything that depreciates rather than appreciates is to be treated with caution.

If you're resident in the U.K. and earning your money there, then you'll be required to pay tax . . . and it ain't getting any easier, matey!

Even though successive Chancellors are plugging the legal loopholes for tax avoidance there are still some perfectly legal ways of paying less tax but that probably means living and working abroad.

Whatever you do, however, consult a good tax adviser on all aspects regarding this subject.

When you have accumulated capital there's no harm in carefully considering business ventures. It's always worth having another string to your bow in the event of the music business deciding it no longer needs your outstanding talent (as often happens).

All I say is, get plenty of good advice.

Try not to let your tax situation get to a point where you have to work twice as hard to pay off any arrears because you still have to pay tax on the current earnings and without a cash windfall the situation can only get worse.

Don't gamble unless you can absolutely afford to lose it. For some that's like an incurable disease, ruining careers, marriages and fouling up everybody else's lives.

Try to avoid letting success in the music business change your personality for the worse. It very often does, of course, and many really nice up-and-coming stars become absolutely objectionable when fame comes their way. You've heard the saying: 'Don't tread on people as you go up, you may need them when you're coming down.' Well, there are quite a few people who walked all over me as they went up that I'm looking forward to watching going down again. (Some of them have disappeared from view even now.) There's never any need to be 'big-time' of 'flash'. A little humility in the biggest star is a joy to behold and if you remember where you started you'll never go wrong.

And one final piece of advice. Stay away from the drugs and the drink. I know some artistes have so little confidence in themselves and feel so insecure that these two crutches are their only comfort, but if one can seek solace in other people and have the will to resist the easy way out then it's quite possible another great talent won't be wasted.

So, remember, on a lighter note: 'When you're alone and life is making you lonely you can always go . . . Downtown.'

May it be *your* name up in the lights when you get there!

APPENDIX A

RECORD COMPANIES

ABBEY RECORDING CO. LTD., 1 Abbey St., Eynsham, Oxford. Tel: (0865) 880240/880222. Labels Owned: Abbey, Abbey Folk, Abbey Street. Tape Labels: As Above.

AD-RHYTHM RECORDS, 13 Denham Way, Rickmansworth, Herts. Tel: Rickmansworth, 72351. Labels Distributed: Lugton & Co., H. R. Taylor, Clyde Factors.

ALASKA RECORDS LTD., 12 The Quadrangle, Cambridge Sq., London W2. Tel: 01-402 4550.

AMBERLEE RECORDS LTD., 387 Harrow Rd., London W9. Tel: 01-866 7748. Labels Owned: Amberlee. Labels Licensed: Dork (USA). Tape Labels: Thornton.

A&M RECORDS LTD., 136/140 New Kings Rd., London SW6. Tel: 01-736 3311. Labels Owned: A&M. Labels Licensed: Ode Records, Dark Horse Records, Firefly Records, Shelter Records.

AMMO PRODUCTIONS LTD., 10 Green Street, Park Lane, London, W1Y 3RF. Tel. 01-493 4523. Labels Owned: Ammo Records.

ANCHOR RECORDS LTD., 140 Wardour St., London W1. Tel: 01-734 8642. Label Owned: Anchor. Labels Licensed: ABC, Dunhill, Impulse, Konk, Dot, Westminster, Duke, Peacock, Backbeat.

APOLLO SOUND, 32 Ellerdale Rd., London NW3 6BB. Tel: 01-435 5255.

APPLE CORPS., 54 St. James's, London SW1A 1JT. Tel: 01-629 8222. Labels Owned: Apple, Zapple.

ARCADE RECORDS LTD., 36/38 Willesden Lane, London NW6 7ST. Tel: 01-328 1911.

ARROWTABS LTD., Humber Rd., London NW2 6EP. Tel: 01-450 2411. Labels Owned: Stream, International Artists. Tape Labels: Stream, International Artists, Arrow.

ASTRON MUSIC, 20 Commercial St., Shipley, W. Yorks. BD18 3SP Tel: (0274) 56829. Labels Owned: NDS, Astron.

AURORA RECORDS, 15 Berkeley St., London W1X 5AE. Tel: 01-493 2506/7.

BAF RECORDS, 253 Edgware Rd., London W2. Tel: 01-262 7128. Labels Owned: BAF, Pineapple, Remi.

BASF, Knightsbridge House, 197 Knightsbridge, London SW7 1SA. Tel: 01-584 5080. Labels Owned: Harmonia Mundi, MPS. Associated Labels: BUK Records.

BBC RECORDS & TAPES, The Langham, Portland Place, London W1A 1AA. Tel: 01-580 4468. Labels Owned: BBC, BEEB. Tape Labels: BBC.

B&C RECORDS LTD., 37 Soho Sq., London W1V 5DE. Tel:

01-434 1351. Labels Owned: Mooncrest. Labels Licensed: Charisma, Trojan (inc. Dragon, Horse, Attack, HJ, People), Ashanti, Sussex. Labels Distributed: Cloud One. Tape Labels: As Above.

BELL RECORDS, 25/28 Old Burlington St., London W1H 2BL. Tel: 01-439 4541. Labels Owned: Bell, Arista. Tape Labels: As Above.

BIG BEAR RECORDS, 190 Monument Rd., Birmingham 16. Tel: (021) 454 7020.

BRADLEY'S RECORDS, 12 Bruton St., London W1. Tel: 01-499 0673. Also 26/27 Regency Sq., Brighton, Sussex. Tel. (0273) 23351.

BRADLEYS TAPEMASTER, Kempsey, Worcester WR5 3PN. Tel: (0905) 820137/352131. Labels Owned: Impression.

BRONZE RECORDS LTD., 100 Chalk Farm Rd., London NW1 8EH. Tel: 01-267 4499.

BUS STOP RECORDS, 10/11 Lower John St., London W1R 3PE. Tel: 01-439 0312.

CAMPBELL CONNELLY & CO LTD., 10 Denmark St., London WC2H 8LU. Tel: 01-836 1653. Labels Owned: Concord, Grampian.

CANON RECORDS LTD., 12 Hillside, New Barnet, Herts, EN5 1LU. Tel: 01-449 1164. Labels: Canon, Charivari.

CAROLINE RECORDS (Export) Ltd., 9–11 Woodfield Rd., London W9 2BA. Tel: 01-286 6090. Labels Owned: Vici Records.

CBS RECORDS, 17/19 Soho Square, London W1B 5PD. Tel: 01-734 8181. Labels Owned: CBS, Epic, Embassy, Harmony. Labels Licensed: Monument, Philadelphia Int., Mums, Blue Sky, Invictus, Neighbourhood. Labels Distributed: WEA, A&M, Young Blood, Birth, Magnet, Hallmark. Tape Labels: As Above.

CHARISMA RECORDS LTD., 37 Soho Square, London W1V 5DG. Tel: 01-434 1351.

CHELSEA RECORDS, 34 Devonshire Mews West, London W.1. Tel: 01-487 5791/2/3.

CHRYSALIS RECORDS LTD., 388/396 Oxford St., London W1. Tel: 01-493 9461. Labels Owned: Chrysalis. Labels Licensed: Scratchy. Tape Labels: As Above.

CIRCLE INTERNATIONAL RECORDS, 89 Chiswick High Rd., London W4. Tel: 01-995 5222/3/4/5.

CLADDAGH RECORDS LTD., Dame House, Damest, Dublin 2. Tel: Dublin 778034. Labels Owned: Claddagh, (Ceirnini Cladaig). Labels Distributed: Release, EMI, Outlet, CRD. Tape Label: Claddagh.

CLOUD ONE RECORD CO., 37 Soho Sq., London W.1. Tel: 01-437 0081. Labels Owned: Cloud One, Cloudburst. Labels Licensed: Babylon, Berserkley.

CMC RECORDS LTD., 17 Savile Row, London W1X 1AE. Tel: 01-734 3251. Labels Owned: CMS, Solid Gold, Feelgood.

COLORTONE RECORDS CO. LTD., 69 Dukes Ave., New Malden, Surrey. Tel: 01-942 1347. Labels Owned: Colortone, Spectrum. Labels Distributed: Colortone, Spectrum.

CONCORD RECORDS, 10 Denmark Street, London WC2H 8LU. Tel: 01-836 1653.

CONTEMPO INTERNATIONAL LTD., 42 Hanway St., London W1. Tel: 01-636 2283. Labels Owned: Contempo, Contempo-Raries, Surrey Int., Labels Licensed: Nashboro Group, Jewel-Paula, Canyon, Alithia, Sunburst.

CONTINENTAL RECORD DISTRIBUTORS LTD., Lyon Estate, Rockware Ave., Greenford, Middx. Labels Owned: CRD. Labels Distributed: Ades, Anthology, Arion, Barclay Group, Barenreiter, Belter, Billinsgate, Biograph/Melodeon/Historical, Blue Googe, Calliope, Caprice, CBS, Chant Du Monde, Claddath/Tara, Collectors Classics, Connoisseur, Deesse, ECM/Japo, Edici, Erato, Freedom, FV Records, Genesis, GNP/Crescendo, Lyrichord, Musidisc, Ocora, Phonogram, Pierre Cardin, Polydor, Fifi, Saydisc/Village Thing, Shandar, Storyville, Tecla, Vista.

CONTOUR RECORDS, 16 St. George St., Hanover Sq., London W1R 9DE. Tel: 01-493 8945.

CREOLE RECORDS LTD., 4 Bank Buildings, High St., Harlesden, London NW10. Tel: 01-965 9223. Labels Owned: Creole, Cactus, Amba, Afrodisc.

CUBE RECORDS LTD., Essex House, 19/20 Poland St., London W1V 3DD.

MIKI DALLON ENTERPRISE LTD., 138 New Bond St., London W1. Tel: 01-493 9681. Labels Owned: Young Blood, Birth.

DAMONT RECORDS LTD., Blyth Rd., Hayes, Middx. Tel: 01-573 5122. Labels Owned: Stereo Gold Award, Happy House.

DANDELION RECORDS LTD., 17 Ronneby Close, Weybridge, Surrey KT13 9SB. Tel: (98) 42689.

DART RECORDS LTD., 23 Haymarket, London SW1. Tel: 01-839 6357. Tape Labels: Dart, Dart Bullseye.

DECCA RECORD CO. LTD., Decca House, 9 Albert Embankment, London SE1 7SW. Tel: 01-735 8111. Labels Owned: Ace of Clubs, Ace Of Diamonds, Ace Of Hearts, Argo, Beltona, Brunswick, Daffodil, Decca, Decca Phase 4, Deram, Eclipse, L'Oiseau Lyre, London, London Globe, Qualiton (Wales), Rex, Telefunken, Threshold. Labels Licensed: BASF, Commodore, Crossover, Emerald, Emerald Gem, Gull, Hi, Hickory, MAM, M&M, Turnabout, UK, Vox, Cube. Tape Labels: As Above.

DEROY RECORDS, Hawk Street, Carnforth, Lancs. Tel: (0524) 73-2273. Labels Owned: Deroy.

DE WOLFE LTD., 80/88 Wardour St., London W1V 3LF. Tel: 01-437 4933. Labels Owned: Hudson, Sylvester, Rogue.

DISCOURSES LTD., 32 High Street, Tunbridge Wells, Kent. Tel: (0892) 26397. Labels Owned: Discourses, All About Music. Labels Distributed: Jupiter, Era, Family Education Records, Graham Collier Music. Tape: Discourses, All About Music, Science Teacher Ed. Project, Kent Mathematics Project.

DISC IMPORTS LTD., 36 John Dalton St., Manchester M2 6LD. Tel: (061) 834 7293. Labels Owned: Euroson. Labels Distributed: Independent World Releases, Beat.

DOVE RECORDS LTD., 15 Berkeley St., London W1X 5AE. Tel: 01-493 2506/7.

EMBER RECORDS (INT) LTD., Suite 4, Carlton Tower Place, Sloane St., London SW1X 9PZ. Tel. 01-235 8243. Labels Owned: Ember, Speciality. Labels Licensed: Everest, Orion. Labels Distributed: Great Voice of the Century, Ember Classics, Famous Artistes.

EMERALD RECORDS LTD., Roughfort, Templepatrick, Belfast BT39 0HB. Tel: (08494) 32711. Labels Owned: Emerald, M&M, Great Bands. Tape Labels: As Above.

EMI RECORDS, EMI House, 20 Manchester Sq., London W1A 1ES. Tel: 01-486 4488. Labels Owned or Controlled: HMV, EMI, Capitol, Columbia, Parlophone, Regal-Zonophone, Rhino, Starline, Waverly, Talisman, Harvest, One Up, Double Up, Encore, World Records, Stateside, Ammo, Asylum, Dot, Elektra, Famous, Fantasy, Green Bottle, GSF, MCA, MCA Coral, Impulse, Mowest, Neighbourhood, Paramount, Probe, Purple, Rak, Rare Earth, Sovereign, Tamla Mowtown, Tumbleweed, Casablanca. Labels Distributed: Alaska, Apple, B&C (including Charisma, Mooncrest, Peg), Bell, Bus Stop, Cactus, Granada, Immediate (inc. Instant), Island, Trojan, United Artists.

ENGLISH FOLK DANCE AND SONG SOCIETY, Cecil Sharp House, 2 Regent's Park Rd., London NW1 7AY. Tel: 01-485 2206. Labels Owned: EFDSS, DTS, Folk Classics. Tape Labels: Folk Tapes, EFDSS.

ENTERPRISE RECORD LTD., Head Office: Kassner House, 1 Westbourne Gdns., Porchester Rd., London W2 5NR. Tel: 01-229 3411. Labels Owned: Enterprise, New World, Double Gold, Sticky. Labels Distributed: President, Jayboy, Joy, Seville, Bulldog, Seven Sun, Crystal, Gemini, Sioux, Request, Rhapsody, Dart, Pickwick, Rediffusion, Hallmark, RCA Camden, Marble Arch, Trojan, Avenue, Ethnic, Lord Koos, Sussex, Fountain Jazz, Kiddicraft, Quality, Supraphon, SRT, Joker, Peter Styvesant Spec., K-Tel. Tape Labels: Ampex, Rhapsody, Enterprise, New World, Pickwick, Rediffusion, Supraphon, Sydney Thompson, Kiddy Cassettes, Remc, Trojan, Jayboy.

ESQUIRE RECORDS TALENT LTD., 76 Bedford Court Mansions, Bedford Ave., London WC1B 3AE. Tel: 01-636 1810. Labels Owned: Esquire, Delmark, Starlite. Labels Licensed: Delmark.

EUROBEAT LTD., 36 John Dalton St., Manchester M2 6LD. Tel: (061) 834 7292. Labels Owned: Beat, Pentaphon, Pony, Perla, Unifunk.

FEELGOOD RECORDS LTD., 17 Savile Row, London W1X 1AE. Tel: 01-734 3251.

FESTIVAL RECORDS, Harley House, Upper Harley St., London W1. Tel: 01-486 4182.

FLAIR RECORDING CO. LTD., 266 Blythe Rd., Hayes, Middx. Tel: 01-848 0460. Labels: Flair, Crotchet.

FLYRIGHT RECORDS, 21 Wickham Avenue, Bexhill-on-Sea, Sussex TN 39 3EP. Tel: (0424) 214390. Labels Owned: Flyright. Labels Distributed: Advent, Muskadine, Adelphi, Swallow, Jin, Lanor, Crazy Cajon, Trix, County, Mamlish, Oblivion, Testament, Takoma, Bomp, Magnolia, Laval, Spivey, Saydisc, Roots, Rounder, Redmont, Ahura Mazda.

FOLK HERITAGE RECORDINGS LTD., Mid-Wales Sound Studios, Castle Caereinion, Welshpool, Montgomeryshire. Tel: Llanfair Caereinion 585. Labels Owned: Folk Heritage, Midas, Country Music Records.

FREE REED RECORDS, Duffield, Derby. Tel: (0332) 840935. (Mail Order).

FRESH AIR RECORDS LTD., 19/20 Noel Street, London W1. Tel: 01-437 1958.

G. M. RECORDS, 90 Wardour St., London W1. Tel: 01-734 4182. Labels Owned: G. M., Cherub. Distributed: Phonogram.

GRAMPIAN RECORDS LTD., Airport Industrial Estate, Wick, Caithness, Scotland. Tel: (0955) 2787. Labels Owned: Grampian, Morven. Tape Label: Grampian.

GTO RECORDS LTD., 17 Barlow Place, Bruton St., London W1X 7AE. Tel: 01-629 6036/6425.

GULL RECORDS, 56 South Molton St., London W1Y 1HF. Tel: 01-629 9869.

HAWK RECORDS, 62 Lower Leeson St., Dublin 2. Tel: Dublin 762862/760569. Labels: Hawk, CMB, Mushroom, Target, Puck.

HERITAGE RECORDS, 10 Hagen Court, Lad Lane, Lower Baggot St., Dublin, Ireland. Tel: Dublin 760928.

HOLLICK & TAYLOR RECORDING CO. LTD., Grosvenor Recording Studios, 16 Grosvenor Rd., Handsworth Wood, Birmingham B20 3NP. Tel: (021) 356 9366/7. Label Owned: Grosvenor.

HOUSE OF WIZZARD LTD., 155/7 Oxford St., London WR1 1TB. Labels Owned: Coconut Records, Marzipan Records.

INCUS RECORDS, 87 Third Cross Rd., Twickenham, Middx. Tel: 01-898 4095.

INDEPENDENT RECORD CO., 39 Harmer St., Gravesend, Kent. Tel: (0474) 65687. Labels Owned: Independent Records. Labels Licensed: Seacruise Productions (UK), Labels Distributed: Southern Sound.

IRISH FACTORS LTD., PO Box 377, 9/10 Hanover Street East, Dublin 2. Tel: 784755. Labels Owned: Rec. Labels Licensed/Distributed: Argo, Ace of Hearts, Chapter One, Contempo, Deram, Emerald, Great Bands, Greenwich, MAM, Nova, L'Oiseau-Lyre, Qualiton, Threshold, Turnabout, UK, Vocalion, Vox, Cube, Basf,

Gael-Linn, Olympic, Globe, Denver, Topic, RCA, Transatlantic, Tangent, Barclay, Rockfield, Grunt, Rubber, Leader, Trailer, Buk, Dolphin, Spoken Arts. Tape Labels: As Above.

ISLAND RECORDS., 22 St. Peters Sq., London W6. Tel: 01-741 1511. Labels Owned: Island. Labels Licensed: Bronze, Rocket. Labels Distributed: Chrysalis, Virgin, Cube.

I.W.R. (MUSIC) LTD., 11 Heron Place, 3 George St., London W1H 5PA. Tel: 01-486 3650.

DICK JAMES ORGANISATION, James House, 71/75 New Oxford Street, London WC1A 1DP. Tel: 01-836 4864. Labels Owned: DJM, Silverline. Distribution: Records: Pye Tape: Precision.

JET RECORDS LTD., 44 Parkside, Wimbledon, London SW19. Tel: 01-947 5505.

J.G. RECORDINGS LTD., 85 Rogers Lane, Stoke Poges, Bucks. Tel: (Farnham Common) 4373.

KESWICK MUSIC, 28 Elfort Rd., London N5 1AZ. Tel: 01-226 4062.

KIDDY KASSETTES LTD., 14 Liverpool Gardens, Worthing, Sussex, England. Tel: (0903) 205053.

TERRY KING ASSOCIATES, 143 Wardour St., London W1V 3TB. Tel: 01-930 1771.

KONK RECORDS, 84/86 Tottenham Lane, Hornsey, London N8 7EE. Tel: 01-340 7873.

K-TEL INTERNATIONAL (UK) LTD., K-Tel House, 620 Western Ave., London W3. Tel: 01-992 8000.

LEADER SOUND LTD., 209 Rochdale Road, Greetland, Halifax, West Yorkshire, HX4 8JE. Tel: (04227) 6161. Labels Owned: Leader, Trailer.

LIVE WIRE RECORDS LTD., 83 New Haw Rd., Addlestone, Weybridge, Surrey KT15 2BZ. Tel: (0932) 51361.

LUCKY RECORDINGS, 3 Havenwood, Wembley, Middx. HA9 9AR. Tel: 01-904 2556. Labels Owned: Lucky, Lucky-Sport.

LYRITA RECORDED EDITION, 99 Green Lane, Burnham, Slough BL1 8EG. Tel: (062-88) 4208. Label Owned: Lyrita.

MAGNET RECORDS LTD., 22 York St., London W1H 1FD. Tel: 01-935 4049/487 3650/487 3667.

MAM RECORDS, 24/25 New Bond St., London W1Y 9HD. Tel: 01-629 9255.

MAUDELLA PATTERNS CO. LTD., Record Division, 39/41 Chapel St., Bradford, BD1 5BZ. West Yorks. Tel: (0274) 21498. Labels Distributed: RCA (Camden), Hallmark/Marble Arch.

MAWSON AND WAREHAM (MUSIC) LTD., Heath House, 11 Blackett Street, Newcastle upon Tyne, NE1 5B6. Tel: (0632) 26461/2. Labels Owned: MWM Records, Rubber Records. Cassettes: MWM.

MIDLAND SOUND RECORDINGS, Meeting House Lane, Balsall Common, Coventry. Tel: (0670) 32468.

MOTOWN RECORDS LTD., 8 Rathbone Place, London W1P 1DE. Tel: 01-323 1225. Labels Owned: Tamla Motown; Rare Earth, Mowest. Tape Labels: As Above.

MULTICORD STUDIOS, 52 Briardene Close, Sunderland SR3 3RU. Tel: (0783) 282353. Labels Owned: Multicord. Tape Label: As Above.

MULTIPLE SOUND LTD., 120 King Street, London W6 0QU. Tel: 01-741 0381. Labels Owned: Windmill, Warwick, Tempo, Dynamic, Pure Gold, Spire, Solid Gold, Top Twenty. Labels Distributed: Robin, Crest. Tape: Windmill, Warwick.

MUSICAL GOSPEL OUTREACH, 10 Seaforth Ave., New Malden, Surrey KT3 6JP. Tel: 01-942 8847. Labels Owned: Key Records, Dovetail Records.

MUSIC FOR PLEASURE LTD., Astronaut House, Hounslow Rd., Feltham, Middx. TW1H 9AR. Tel: 01-890 1344. Labels Owned: Music For Pleasure, Classics For Pleasure, Sounds Superb, Surprise Surprise. Tape Label: Musicway.

MUSIC SOUND ENTERPRISES, The Studio, 30 Marsworth Ave., Hatch End, Middx. HA5 4UB. Tel: 01-428 1341. Labels Owned: MSE.

NEIGHBORHOOD RECORD CO. LTD., 280 Fulham Rd., London SW10 9EW. Tel: 01-352 8535/6.

ORANGE MUSICAL INDUSTRIES LTD., 3/4 New Compton Street, London WC2. Tel: 01-836 7811. Labels Owned: Orange, Amity.

ORYX RECORDINGS LTD., 167 Burwood Road, Walton-on-Thames, Surrey. Tel: Walton-on-Thames 28473. Labels Owned: Exploring The World Of Music, Three Centuries Of Music, Bach Collectors Series, Oryx Baroque, Oryx Romantic, Cosmopolitan and Sunshine Series.

OVAL RECORDS LTD., 156 Kennington Park Road, London SE11 4DJ. Tel: 01-622 3958/735 4747/8808. Labels Owned: Oval. Labels Licensed: Jin, Swallow. Tape: Oval.

PANDA RECORDS (Prop. Lamvale Ltd.,), 25 Montague Mews South, London W1H 1TE. Tel: 01-402 7433. Labels Owned: Panda.

PHONOGRAM LTD., Stanhope House, Stanhope Place, London W2 2HH. Tel: 01-262 7788. Labels Owned: Philips, Fontana, Philips International, Mercury, Universo, Vertigo. Labels Licensed: Avco, All Platinum, Chess/Janus, Tiffany, WWA. Labels Distributed: GM. Tape Labels: As Above.

PICKWICK INTERNATIONAL INC. (GB)., The Hyde Industrial Estate, The Hyde, Edgware Rd., London NW9. Tel: 01-205 5456.

PILGRIM RECORDINGS, 116 Baker St., London W1M 2BB. Tel: 01-486 3271.

POLYDOR LTD., 17/19 Stratford Place, London W1N 0BL. Tel: 01-499 8686. Labels Owned: Polydor, Deutsche Grammophon, Archiv, Debut, Privilege, Heliodor, MGM, Verve. Labels Licensed:

Chelase, Capricorn, Pablo, RSO. Labels Distributed: Track, BBC, GTO, Jet. Tape Labels: As Above.

POLYDOR (IRELAND) LTD., 49 Middle Abbey St., Dublin 1, Ireland. Tel: Dublin 742570. Labels Owned: Polydor, Phonogram, MGM, Mercury. Labels Licensed: Pye, A&M, Island, Bradley's, Sonet, GTO. Tape Labels: Same as above plus Precision Tapes.

POLYGRAM LEISURE LTD., 11 Connaught Place, London W2. Tel: 01-723 2605.

PRECISION TAPES LTD., Precision House, 11 Denmark St., London WC2H 8NR. Tel: 01-836 3104/8 2534/6. Labels Licensed: Ad-Rhythm, Ashanti, B&C, Charisma, Dragon, Horse, Mooncrest, Peg, People, Sussex, Trojan, Bell, Bradleys, Contempo, Cube, Fly, DJM, Jam, Silverline, Damont, Dart Beuna Vista, Disneyland, Ember, Magnet, Precision, Smalltalk, Soundguides, Private Stock, Buddah, Chartbusters, CTI, Daybreak, Dawn Ensayo, Pye 4D, Golden Hour, Pye International, Kama Sutra, Kudu, Marble Arch, Mainstream, Nashville, Ocean, Penny Farthing, Pye Popular, Santa Ponsa, Stax, 20th Century, Vanguard, Shellsound Guides, Kicking Mule, Sonet, Speciality, Spark, Sportdisc, Big Ben, Everest, Nonesuch, Transatlantic, Village Thing, Xtra, Unicorn, Visaphone, Vogue, Conquest, W.R.C.

PRESIDENT RECORDS LTD., Kassner House, 1 Westbourne Gdns., Porchester Rd., London W2 5NR. Tel: 01-229 3411. Labels Owned: President, Jayboy, Joy, Seville, Gemini, Crystal, Rhapsody, Torpedo, Dart, Avenue International. Labels Licensed: Glades, T. K., Cat, Drive, Vee-Jay, Seven Sun, Bulldog. Tape Labels: President, Jayboy, Joy.

PRIVATE STOCK RECORDS, 32 Old Burlington St., London W1X 1LD. Tel: 01-836 3941. Labels Owned: Private Stock. Distributed: EMI. Tape Label Distributed: Precision.

PURE CREAM MUSIC LTD., 43 Welbeck St., London W1. Tel: 01-486 6363. Labels: Pure Cream, Silver Cream.

PYE RECORDS LTD., ATV House, 17 Great Cumberland Place, London W1A 1AG. Tel: 01-262 5502. Labels Owned: Pye Popular, Pye International, Pye Chartbusters, Pye Quadraphonic, Pye Collector, Golden Hour, Golden Guinea, Dawn, Disco Demand, Pye Virtuoso. Labels Licensed: Buddah, Penny Farthing, Stax, Creed Taylor, Vogue, Daybreak, Santa Ponsa, Disney, 20th Century, Ember, Ensayo, Kama Sutra, Kudu, Mainstream, Nashville, Ocean. Labels Distributed: DJM, Bradleys, Sprak, Sonet, Orange, Contempo.

RAK RECORDS LTD., 2 Charles Street, London, W1X 7HA. Tel: 01-492 0654.

READERS DIGEST ASSOCIATION LTD., 25 Berkeley Sq., London W1X 6AB. Tel: 01-629 8144. Labels Owned: Readers Digest, Pegasus.

REDIFFUSION INTERNATIONAL MUSIC LTD., 2–16 Goodge

Street, London W1 P1FF. Tel: 01-580 9506. Labels Owned: Rediffusion, Gold Star. Labels Licensed: Supraphon. Labels Distributed: Supraphon, Panton, CRI, OPUS. Tape: Rediffusion. Cassettes/Cartridges: Rediffusion, Gold Star, Supraphon.

RED LIGHTNIN' RECORDS, 517 Eastern Ave., Ilford, Essex IG2 6LT. Tel: 01-554 5957/590 0391.

REFLECTION RECORDS, 26 Eastbourne Ave., Acton, London W3. Tel: 01-992 6250. Label Owned: Reflection. Distribution: Marshall, Morgan & Scott, Word (UK).

RENFREWSHIRE SOUND SERVICES LTD., Woodlands Road, Thornliebank, Glasgow, Scotland. G46 7SY. Tel: (041) 638 6197. Labels Owned: Renfrewshire Sounds.

REVIVAL RECORDS LTD., 61 Grafton Rd., London NW5. Tel: 01-485 7161/5544. Labels Owned: Revival, Splended (UK), Blue Acre. Labels Licensed: Splended, Southern Sound. Labels Distributed: Lismor, Revival, Splended, Southern Sound, Evasion.

RCA RECORDS, 20 Curzon St., London W1Y 8EU. Tel: 01-499 3901. Labels Owned: RCA. Labels Licensed: Barclay, Prestige, Rockfield, Grunt.

RONCO TELEPRODUCTS (UK) LTD., 6th Floor, 299 Oxford Street, London W1A 4YQ. Tel: 01-499 1925.

RSO RECORDS, 67 Brook Street, London W1Y 1YD. Tel: 01-629 9121. Labels Owned: R.S.O. Records & Tapes Ltd.

RUTLAND RECORDS (Division of Hedley Enterprises), 71 Rutland Rd., Chesterfield S40 1ND. Tel: (0246) 79976.

SAGA RECORDS LTD., 326 Kensal Road, London, W.10. Tel: 01-969 6651. Labels Owned: Saga 5000,6000,7000 Series, Boulevard Opus, Lyrigue, etc.

SATRIL RECORDS, Satril House, 11 Little Newport St., London WC2. Tel: 01-734 7333.

SAYDISC SPECIALIZED RECORDINGS LTD., The Barton, Inglestone Common, Badminton, Glos. GL9 1BX. Tel: Badminton 266. Labels Owned: Saydisc, Amon Ra, Matchbox, Village Thing. Labels Licensed: Ahura Mazda, Roots, Rounders, Kanawha. Labels Distributed: Bornand.

SELECTADISC, 162 Canal St., Nottingham. Tel: (0602) 50693. Labels Owned: Black Magic, Majestic.

SEVEN SUN RECORDS LTD., 133 Broadley St., London NW8. Tel: 01-723 6201/2.

SNAZZ RECORDS, 57A Wimpole St., London W1. Tel: 01-487 3591/3592.

SOLOMON & PERES LTD., 120 Coach Rd., Templepatrick, Belfast, N. Ireland. Tel: (08494) 32711. Labels Owned: Emerald, M&M, Great Bands. Labels Distributed: Decca Group, CBS Group, RCA Group, WEA Group, Emerald & Others.

SONET PRODUCTIONS LTD., 12 Needham Rd., London W11. Tel: 01-229 7267. Labels Owned: Sonet, Kicking Mule. Labels

Licensed: Alligator, Takoma, Gazell (Sweden), Sonet/Sweden. Labels Distributed: Specialty. Tape Labels: Sonet, Specialty, Kicking Mule.

SOVEREIGN RECORDS, The Music Centre, Engineers Way, Wembley, Middx. Tel: 01-903 4611.

SPARK RECORD LTD., 8 Denmark St., London WC2H 8LT. Tel: 01-836 4524. Labels Owned: Spark, Blue Jean.

STAINER & BELL LTD., 82 High Road, East Finchley, London N2 9PW. Tel: 01-444 9135. Labels Owned: Gailliard.

STALLION RECORDS LTD., 87 Brewer St., London W1. Tel: 01-437 8439.

SRT (RECORD) PRODUCTIONS LTD., Bankside, 42 High St., Barnet, Herts. Tel: 01-449 1676. Labels Owned: SRT Records, SRT Custom Pressing. Label Distributed: SRT Records.

SWAN SONG, 484 Kings Road, Chelsea, London, SW10 0LF. Tel: 01-352 0082. Labels Owned: Swan Song.

TANGENT RECORDS LTD., 176a Holland Rd., London W14 8AH. Tel: 01-603 0893. Labels Owned: Tangent, Big Ben.

TEMBO RECORDS LTD., 15 Harley House, Regents Park, London NW1 5HE. Tel: 01-486 5160.

THISTLE RECORDS., 65 Berkeley Street, Glasgow G3 7DX. Tel: (041)-248 2791. Labels Owned: Thistle.

THRESHOLD RECORDS LTD., 53/55 High St., Cobham, Surrey. Tel: Cobham 4142.

TIFFANY PRODUCTIONS LTD., 22 Shaftesbury Avenue, London W1V 8AP. Tel: 01-434 1551. Labels Owned: Tiffany. Tape: Phonogram.

TOPIC RECORDS LTD., 27 Nassington Road, London NW3 2TX. Tel: 01-435 9983. Labels Owned: Topic/Free Reed, Impact.

TRACK RECORDS LTD., 5/7 Carnaby St., London W1. Tel: 01-734 3346. Telex: 946893.

TRANSATLANTIC RECORDS LTD., 86 Marylebone High St., London W1M 4AY. Tel: 01-486 4353/4/5/6. Labels Owned: Transatlantic, Xtra, Transatlantic Singles, Transatlantic Samplers. Labels Licensed: Leader/Trailer, Big Bear, Nonesuch, Everest, Milestone, Village Thing, Black Lion. Labels Distributed: Unicorn, Blue Note, Conversaphone, Big Ben/Tangent, MWM/Rubber. Tape Labels: Transatlantic, Xtra, Nonesuch, Unicorn.

UK RECORDS LTD., 48 Grafton Way, London W1. Tel: 01-387 5851. Labels Owned: UK, UK American.

UNITED ARTISTS RECORDS LTD., Mortimer House, 37/41 Mortimer St., London W1A 2JL. Tel: 01-636 1655. Labels Owned: United Artists, Sunset, Blue Note, Liberty. Tape Labels: As Above.

VIRGIN RECORDS (HOLDING) LTD., 2/4 Vernon Yard, 119 Portobello Rd., London W11. Tel: 01-727 8070.

WALT DISNEY PRODUCTIONS LTD., 68 Pall Mall, London SW1Y 5EX. Tel: 01-839 8010. Labels Owned: Buena Vista, Disneyland.

WINDMILL RECORDS, 120 King Street, London W6 0QU. Tel: 01-741 0381.

WORD (UK) LTD., Park Lane, Hemel Hempstead, Herts. HP2 4TD. Tel: 0442-50132/3. Labels Owned: Canaan, Herald, Light, Myrrh, Sacred, Word.

WORLD RECORDS LTD., Parkbridge House, Little Green, Richmond, Surrey. Tel: 01-940 8331.

ZELLA RECORDS (BIRMINGHAM) LTD., Walker Hall, Ampton Rd., Edgbaston, Birmingham B15 2UJ. Tel: (021) 455 0645. Labels Owned: Zella Records, Ash Records.

APPENDIX B

MUSIC PUBLISHERS

ABBEY RECORDING CO. LTD., 1 Abbey St., Eynsham, Oxford. Tel: (0865) 880240/880222. Affiliate: Oxford Music.

ACUFF-ROSE MUSIC LTD., 16 St George St., London W1. Tel: 01-629 0392. Affiliates: Acuff-Rose World Group.

ACTIVE MANAGEMENT LTD., 3 Townsend House, 22–25 Dean St., London W1V 5AL. Tel: 01-437 7220/8512. Affiliates: Jill Music.

ALASKA MUSIC LTD., 12 The Quadrangle, Cambridge Sq., London W2. Tel: 01-402 4550.

ALAVA MUSIC LTD., 33/37 Wardour St., London W1. Tel: 01-439 2482/3/4.

ALICE MUSIC LTD., 9 Cavendish Sq., London W1M 0DU. Tel: 01-995 1191.

AMBASSADOR MUSIC LTD., 23–24 Greek St., London W1V 5LG. Tel: 01-437 7053. Affiliates: Ambassador/Seven Arts, Bourneville Music, Hallelujah Music, Percy Music, RHM.

AMMO-JAMES MUSIC LTD., 10 Green St., Park Lane, London W1Y 3RF. Tel: 01-493 4523.

ANCHOR MUSIC LTD., 140 Wardour St., London W1. Tel: 01-734 8642. Representation: ABC Dunhill Music, American Broadcasting Music.

APRIL MUSIC LTD., 17/19 Soho Square, London W1. Tel: 01-439 1845. Affiliates: Amazon Music Ltd., Altogether Music, Andover Music Ltd., Bake Music, B. L. Music, Charlie Tunes, Dahlia Music, Finito Music, Geobell Music Co. Ltd., Hotpot Music, Kangaroo Music, Magdalen Music Ltd., Moose Music Ltd., Molloy Music, Omnibus Music, Polygon Music, Prom. Music Verlag, Revelation Music, Paul Robinson Music Ltd., Skin Songs Pub. Ltd., Steville Music Ltd., Tomorrow Music, Victoria Music, Woolfsongs, Wurzon Music, Jeff Wayne Music Ltd., Carrotts Music Ltd., Rock On Music Ltd., Music Maximus, Stonebridge & Profit Ltd.

ARNAKATA MUSIC LTD., 35 Homer St., London W1H 1HL. Tel: 01-723 8424. Affiliates: Ashkorma Music Ltd., Hawkana Music Ltd., Marquee-Dolan Music Ltd., Summerland Songs Ltd.

ARPEGGIO MUSIC, 85 Rogers Lane, Stoke Poges, Bucks. Tel: (Farnham Common) 4373.

THE ASSOCIATED BOARD OF THE ROYAL SCHOOLS OF MUSIC, 14 Bedford Square, London WC1B 3JG. Tel: 01-636 6919.

ATV MUSIC LTD., 12 Bruton St., Mayfair, London W1X 7AH. Tel: 01-499 0673. Affiliates: Axle, Big Secret, Bluey Tunes, Brigitte, Burton, Bryanston, Comet, Cuckoo, Des O'Connor, Future Legends, Hansa Prod., Tony Hiller Music, Lawrence Wright Music, Marble Arch, Metro, Northern Songs, Pamscene, Yisgav.

BARDIS MUSIC LTD., 10 Hagen Court, Lad Lane, Dublin 2. Tel: Dublin 862074/860397.

B&C/MOONCREST MUSIC LTD., 37 Soho Sq., London W1V 5DG. Tel: 01-434 1351. Affiliates: B&C, Mooncrest Music, Ashanti Music, Static Music, Hyasakyte Music.

BEAUTIFUL MUSIC LTD., 23 Haymarket, London SW1. Tel: 01-839 6537.

BEE BEE MUSIC LTD., PO Box 472, London, SW7 2QB. Tel: 01-584 2434/5959.

BELWIN-MILLS MUSIC LTD., 230 Purley Way, Croydon CR9 4QD. Tel: 01-681 0855. Affiliates: Belwin-Mills Publishing Corp, Deshon Music Inc., J. Fischer & Bro., Franco Colombo Publications, H. W. Gray Co., Mel Bay Publications Inc., Musikverlage Hans Sikorski, Southern Music Company, Texas. Sole Selling Agent for Dover Publications Inc., Leeds Music/MCA, E. B. Marks Music Corp.

B. FELDMAN & CO. LTD., 138/140 Charing Cross Rd., London WC2H 0LD. Tel: 01-836 6699. Affiliates: Beano Music, Biscuit Music, Derek Lawrence Music, Dix, Edwards Coletta Music, Gallagher & Lyle Music, Gerrard Music, Hec Music, Herman Darewski Music Publishing Co., Kennedy Street Music, Miles Music, Renaissance Music, Roar Music, Shoot Music, Trident Music, Yardbirds Music, Yellow Springs Music.

BIG BEN MUSIC LTD., The Music Centre, Engineers Way, Wembley, Middx. Tel: 01-903 4611.

BIG EAR PROMOTIONS LTD., Satril House, 11 Little Newport St., London WC2. Tel: 01-734 7333. Affiliates: Big Ear Music.

BIG SECRET MUSIC., 12 Bruton St., London W1X 7AH. Tel: 01-491 7246. Affiliate: Keyhole Music.

BISCUIT MUSIC LTD., 17 Ronneby Close, Weybridge, Surrey KT13 9SB. Tel: (98) 42689.

BLUE MOUNTAIN MUSIC, 47 British Grove, London W4.

BOTTOM DOLLAR MUSIC, 12 Praed Mews, London W2. Tel: 01-262 2067/8.

BOURNE MUSIC LTD., 34–36 Maddox Street, London W1R 9PD. Tel: 01-493 6412/6583. Affiliates: Aeolian Music Ltd.

MARGRET BRACE COPYRIGHT BUREAU LTD., 3rd Floor, 9 Dean St., London W1A 4QD. Tel: 01-437 3711/2. Affiliates: Admiral One Music, Ashtree Holdings Ltd., Brunswick Music, B.W.D. Music, Pearl Connor (Management), Duart Music, Hensley Music, J. B. Music, Kenmar Music, Major Oak Music, M&W Music, P. C. Music, George Porter Music, Proclaim Music, Revelation Tunes Ltd., Revival Music, Sharcha Music, Tepee Musical Industries.

BRAMPTON MUSIC LIMITED, 19–20 Noel Street, London W1. Tel: 01-437 1958.

BRON ASSOCIATED PUBLISHERS LTD., 100 Chalk Farm Rd., London NW1 8HE. Tel: 01-267 4499. Affiliates: BVF Anglo-Continental Ltd., Sydney Bron Music Co. Ltd., Carrie Music Ltd., Debmar Music Pub. Co. Ltd., Earthly Music Ltd., Hazzard Music Ltd., Hit Songs Ltd., Mann Music Publishers Ltd., Marklon Music Ltd., Osibisa Music Ltd., Osibisounds Ltd., Pitney Music Ltd., Tempest Music Ltd., Yale Music Corp. Ltd.

BURLINGTON MUSIC CO LTD., 18 Great Marlborough St., London W1V 2BL. Tel: 01-734 9286. Affiliate: Palace Music.

BURNT ASH MUSIC CO., 152/156 Shaftesbury Ave., London WC2H 83H. Tel: 01-240 1628.

B. V. F. ANGLO-CONTINENTAL MUSIC CO. LTD., 10, Sherlock Mews, Baker Street, London W1. Tel: 01-935 6974.

CAMEL MUSIC LTD., 67 Brook St., London W1. Tel: 01-629 9121.

CAMPBELL CONNELLY & CO LTD., 10 Denmark St., London WC2H 8LU. Tel: 01-836 1653. Affiliates: Berry Ltd., Cinephonic Ltd., Cross Ltd., Dash Ltd., Max Diamond Ltd., Double Top Ltd., Evergreen Ltd., Harrison Ltd., High Fye Ltd., Hournew Ltd., Ivy Ltd., Montclare Ltd., Overseas Ltd., Shere Ltd., Show Ltd., Sikorski Ltd., Glendale Ltd., Vinco Ltd.

CARLIN MUSIC CORPORATION, 17 Savile Row, London W1X 1AE. Tel: 01-734 3251. Affiliates: Abacus Music Ltd., Alan Price Music Ltd., Amen Music Ltd., A.M.P. Music Ltd., Andwella Music Ltd., Anita Music Ltd., Arf Arf Music Ltd., Bandlin Music Ltd., Benday Music Ltd., Bev Bev Music Ltd., Blue Gem Music Ltd., B. S. Music Ltd., Camad Publishers Ltd., Cardinal Music Ltd., Chad & Jeremy Music Ltd., Contempo Music Ltd., Coronet Music Ltd., Curb Music Ltd., Dabe Music Ltd., Dawnbreaker Music (London) Ltd., Daytime Music Ltd., Deoc Music Ltd., Design Music Ltd., Destiny Music Ltd., Early Bird Music Publishing Company Ltd., Eddie Trevett Music Ltd., Engel Songs Ltd., Enquiry Music Ltd., Eric Burden Music Ltd., Far Out Music Ltd., Fiesta Music Ltd., Fluke Music Ltd., Friends Music Ltd., Fugal Songs Ltd., Gamble Huff Music Ltd., Genesis Music Ltd., Getaway Music Ltd., Gloria Music, Gold Disc Musica Ltd., G.T.O. Publishing Ltd., Hercules Music Ltd., Jack Good Music Publishing Company Ltd., Jeff Lynne Music Ltd., Jetstar Publishers Ltd., Joanline Music Ltd., J. C. Music Ltd., Johnny Devlin Music Ltd., Josley Music Ltd., Kalmann Music Ltd., Kenmoss Music Ltd., Kenny Lynch Music Ltd., Kevin Eggers Music Ltd., Kieron Music Ltd., Knox Music Ltd., Lark Music Ltd., Larkworth Ltd., Lee Hazlewood Music Ltd., Leiber-Stoller Songs Ltd., Leon Henry Music., Linvoy Music Ltd., Ludix Music Ltd., Macaulay Music Ltd., The Manor Music Company Ltd., Marilyn Music Company Ltd., Maycroft Music Ltd., Miracle Songs Ltd., Mountain Music Ltd., Mustard Music Ltd., Oaktree Music Ltd., October Music Ltd., Pantryan Songs Ltd., Park Lane Music Co. Ltd., Peterman & Co. Ltd., Pulsar Music Ltd., Quartet Music Ltd., Redwood Music Ltd., Roy Wood Music Ltd., Sam Songs Ltd., Semprini Music Ltd., Shadamm Music Ltd., Shadows Music Ltd., Sidney A. Seidenberg Music Ltd., Slamina Music Ltd., Sledge Music Ltd., Smooth Music Ltd., S.P.R. Music Ltd., Stratsongs Ltd., Stylus Music Ltd., Supreme Music Ltd., Swansong Music Ltd., Sweet City Songs Ltd., Sympathy Music Ltd., Tarot Music Ltd., Tim Holler Productions Ltd., T. M. Music Ltd., Tollak Music Ltd., Tollie Music Ltd., Tone Music Ltd., Toneshire Ltd., Train Publishing Plan Ltd., Trio Music Co. Ltd., Vicki Music Ltd., Visual & Musical Entertainment Company Ltd., Warland Music Ltd., Waterloo Music Ltd., Zan Music Ltd.

CARMEL MUSIC LTD., 4 Cliff Avenue, Westcliff-on-Sea, Essex. Tel: 0702 43682.

HAL CARTER ENTERPRISES, 81a Osbaldeston Rd., London N16. Tel: 01-806 7979/2000. Affiliates: Moggy Music, Kaiser Bill Music.

FRANK CHACKSFIELD MUSIC LTD., Allegro, Elm Walk, Farnborough Park, Orpington, Kent. Tel: (Farnborough) 55500. Affiliates: Eros Music, Medway Music, Senlac Music.

CAESAR MUSIC LTD., 93 Sirdar Rd., London W11. Tel: 01-727 7477.

CHAPPELL & CO. LTD., 50 New Bond St., London W1A 2BR. Tel: 01-629 7600. Affiliates: Acuff Rose, Alliance Music, Anglo-Pic Music, Ascherberg, Hopwood & Crewe, Belafonte Music, Ben Selvin Music, Bradbury Wood, Bregman, Vocco & Conn, Britannia Music, Carnaby Music, L. J. Cary, Chanter Music, Chappell/R&R, Clarence Music, Commair-Chappell Music, Delfont Music, Edwin H. Morris, EFDS Publications, Empire Consul Music, Erle Music, Famous Chappell, Frank Music, Friday Music, Grahple Music, Grob-Chappell, Ipanema Music, Irving Berlin, Jewel Music, Joseph E. Levine Music, Larry Adler Music, Le Vien Music, Midas Music, Our Songs, Patricia Music, P. K. Music, Space Music, Spindrift Music, Sprinfield Music, Stratford Music, Subiddu, Tom-Tom Music, UK Music, Victoria Music, Walton Music, Williamson Music.

CHARISMA RECORDS LTD., 37 Soho Square, London W1V

5DG. Tel: 01-434 1351. Affiliates: Mooncrest Music Ltd., B&C Music Ltd.

CHRYSALIS MUSIC LTD., 388–396 Oxford St., London W1N 9HE. Tel: 01-493 9461.

CLASSIC EDITIONS: 36 John Dalton Street, Manchester M2 6LD. Tel: 061 834 7292/3.

BARRY COLLINGS MUSIC LTD., 15 Claremont Rd., Westcliff-on-Sea, Essex SS0 7OX. Tel: (0702) 43464/47343.

COMPASS MUSIC LTD., 12th Floor, 93 Albert Embankment, London SE1 7TY. Tel: 01-735 9291. Affiliates: Blanedell Ltd., Gull Entertainments Ltd. (Gull Songs), Harmalane Music Ltd., Learoy Music Ltd., Limbridge Music Ltd., Track Music Ltd.

COMPATIBLE RECORDING & PUBLISHING LTD., 87 Third Cross Rd., Twickenham, Middx. Tel: 01-898 4095.

CORUS MUSIC MANAGEMENT LTD., 1 Montague Street, Russell Square, London WC1B 5BS. Tel: 01-323 2787.

CRAIGHALL MUSIC, 68 Craighall Rd., Edinburgh 6. Tel: 031 552 3685.

CREOLE MUSIC LTD., 4 Bank Buildings, High St., Harlesden, London NW10. Tel: 01-965 9223. Cable: Cremus, London, NW10. Affiliate: Cactus Music.

DABE MUSIC LTD., 84–86 Tottenham Lane, Hornsey, London N8 7EE. Tel: 01-340 7873. Affiliates: Davray Music Ltd., Konkwest Music Ltd.

DART RECORDS LTD., 23 Haymarket, London SW1. Tel: 01-839 6537. Affiliate: Beautiful Music.

CHRIS DENNING MUSIC LTD., 83 New Haw Rd., Addlestone, Weybridge, Surrey. KT15 2BZ. Tel: (0932) 51361.

DE WOLFE LTD., 80/88 Wardour St., London W1V 3LF. Tel: 01-437 4933. Affiliates: Hudson Music, Rouge Music, Sylvester Music.

DIAMOND MUSIC LTD., 33 Park Crescent, Enfield, Middx. Tel: 01-366 2018. Affiliates: Diamond Music, Lee Music.

DISC MUSIC LTD., West End House, 11 Hills Place, Oxford Circus, London W1R 2DD. Tel: 01-439 3941.

WALT DISNEY PRODUCTIONS LTD., 68 Pall Mall, London SW1Y 5EX. Tel: 01-839 8010. Affiliates: Walt Disney Music, Wonderland Music.

EDEN STUDIOS MUSIC/VALENTINE, 152/156 Shaftesbury Ave., London WC2. Tel: 01-240 1628.

ELMAN MUSIC PUBLISHING, T.P.A., 22 Denmark St., London WC2. Tel: 01-836 1783.

EMI MUSIC PUBLISHING LTD., 138/140 Charing Cross Rd., London WC2H 0LD. Tel: 01-836 6699. Affiliates: B. Feldman & Co. Ltd., Francis Day and Hunter Ltd., Keith Prowse Music Group, Robbins Music Corporation Ltd.

ENGLISH FOLK DANCE AND SONG SOCIETY, Cecil Sharp

House, 2 Regent's Park Rd., London NW1 7AY. Tel: 01-485 2206. Affiliates: EFDSS, EFDS Pub. Ltd., Galliard/EFDSS.

ESQUIRE MUSIC CO., 76 Bedford Court Mansions, Bedford Ave., London WC1B 3AE. Tel: 01-636 1810.

THE ESSEX MUSIC GROUP, Essex House, 19/20 Poland St., London, W1V 3DD. Tel: 01-734 8121. Affiliates: Bucks Music Ltd, Butterfield Music Ltd., Cauliflower Music Ltd., Coda Music Ltd., Concord Music Ltd., Cromwell Music Ltd., Cube Enterprises Ltd., Cynara Music Ltd., Dorsey Brothers Ltd., Durham Music Ltd., Eden Music Ltd., Essex Music International Ltd., Fabulous Music Ltd., Greenwich Music Ltd., Harmony Music Ltd., Horizon Music Ltd., Hummingbird Productions Ltd., Ivan Mogull Music Ltd., Jubilation Music Ltd., Kensington Music Ltd., Key Music Ltd., Kingston Music Ltd., Lakeview Music Publishing Co. Ltd., Majestic Music Ltd., Mews Music Ltd., Mighty Oak Music Ltd., Musical Comedy Productions Ltd., New Ikon Music Ltd., Noeland Productions Ltd., One Way Productions Ltd., Romney Music Ltd., Rutland Music Ltd., Standard Music Ltd., Straight Ahead Productions Ltd., Tapestry Music Ltd., Tarantula Productions Ltd., Tro Essex Music Ltd., Tuesday Productions Ltd., Tyler Music Ltd., Weekend Music Ltd., Whistle Rhymes Ltd., Wildwood Music Ltd., Writers Workshop Ltd.

EUROBEAT (MUSIC), 36 John Dalton Street, Manchester M2 6LD. Tel: 061-834 7292/3.

EUROPEAN-NORTH AMERICAN MUSIC LTD., 168 New Victoria St., London SW1 E5LB. Tel: 01-828/2861-2-3.

EXPRESS MUSIC (LONDON) LTD., The Studio, 69 Dukes Ave., New Malden, Surrey. Tel: 01-942 1347.

FABER MUSIC LTD., 38 Russell Square, London WC1B 5DA. Tel: 01-278 6881. Agents for J. Curwen & Sons Ltd.

FAMOUS CHAPPELL LTD., 52 Maddox St., London W1. Tel: 01-629 7600.

FLAIR MUSIC CO. LTD., 266 Blythe Rd., Hayes, Middx. Tel: 01-848 0460. Affiliate: Crotchet Music.

FLYRIGHT MUSIC, 21 Wickham Avenue, Bexhill-on-Sea, Sussex TN39 3EP. Tel: 0424 214390.

FRANCIS DAY & HUNTER LTD., 138/140 Charing Cross Rd., London WC2H 0LD. Tel: 01-836 6699. Affiliates: Donna Music, Four Score Music, Kevin Music, Line Music, Magna Music, Sun Music.

FREE REED RECORDS, Duffield, Derby. Tel: (0332) 840935. Affiliates: Free Reed Press, Free Reed Magazine.

FRESH AIR MUSIC LTD., 19–20 Noel Street, London W1. Tel: 01-437 1958.

GEOBELL MUSIC COMPANY LIMITED, Bankside, 42 High Street, Barnet, Herts. Tel: 01-449 1676.

GLOBESOUND LTD., 39a London Rd., Kingston-on-Thames, Surrey KT2 6ND.

GTO PUBLISHING LTD., Regent Arcade House, 252/260 Regent St., London W1R 5DA. Tel: 424 1881. Affiliates: Carlew Music, Indian Brandee Music, Larkworth Macaulay Music, Mustard Music, Sledge Music, Tincabell Music.

GTO RECORDS LTD., 17 Barlow Place, Bruton St., London W1X 7AE. Tel: 01-629 6036/6425. Affiliate: Tincabell Music.

GULL SONGS, 56 South Molten St., London W1Y 1HF. Tel: 01-629 9869.

HAPPY OYSTER LTD., 484 Kings Rd., London SW10 0LF. Tel: 01-352 9881. Affiliates: Mediocre Music, Monocle Music.

HAZY MUSIC LTD., 9 Ravenscroft Ave., London NW11 0SA. Tel: 01-455 4556. Affiliates: Scorpio Music.

HEDLEY MUSIC (Division of Hedley Ent.), 71 Rutland Rd., Chesterfield S40 1ND., Derbys. Affiliates: Fresh Ground Music, Hardwick Music, Hedley Music, Hedleysongs Music, Michael James Music, March Music, Wigwam Music.

HENRY HADAWAY ORGANISATION LTD., Satril House, 11 Little Newport St., London WC2. Tel: 01-734 7333. Affiliates: Satril Music, Torill Music.

HINRICHSEN EDITION LTD., & PETERS EDITION., 10–12 Baches Street, London N1 6DN. Tel. 01-253. Affiliates: Carisch (Italy), De Santis (Italy), Forberge (Germany), Heinrichshofen (Germany), Hug & Co. (Switzerland), Israeli Music Publications, Kneusslin (Switzerland), Lienau (Germany), McGinnis & Marx (U.S.A.), Merseburger (Germany), C. F. Schmidt (Germany), Zanibon (Italy).

HUSH PRODUCTIONS LTD., 8 Albert Gate Court, 124 Knightsbridge, London SW1. Tel: 01-589 6293/4. Affiliates: Hush Music Ltd., Firesign Music Ltd.

INSTANT MUSIC, 21 Beaumont Court, Clapton, London E5 8BG. Tel: 01-806 3126/7. Affiliates: John Edward Music Ltd.

INTERSONG MUSIC LTD., 50 New Bond St., London W1Y 9HA. Tel: 01-499 0067. Affiliates: Ten East Music, Five West Music, Fifth Avenue Music, Gene Chandler & Cachand Music, Defrantz Monique, Schefrin-Zager Publishing, Harry Da Luggage, Tridem Music, Buddah Music, Kama Sutra Music, Kama Rippa Music, Kaskat Music, Kaleidoscope Music, Running Bear Music, Harbot Music, Contention Music, Baron Music, Bob-Cor Music, Hinky Dink Music, Char-Liz Music, March Hare Music, Three Brothers Music, Dynatone Pub. Co., Jadar Music, Golo Pub., Crited Music, Tan Soul Music, Mourbar Music, Barmour Music, Talmot Music, Tuff Music, Fescue Music, Fling Music, Borscht Music, VIP Pub., Wednesday Morning Music, Budd Music, Marks Music, Kenya Music, Matragun Music, Nelson Music, Hilliard Music, Roy Ayres, Charlotte Music, Heavy Music, Andromeda Music, Synergistic Music, Ilza Music, Good Morning Music, Midsong, Diagonal Music, Midland Music, Polypub, Phonopub

Music, Laurie Kay Cohen, Sky Forest Music, Stanyan Music, Editions Chanson, Montcalm, Tomeja Music, Elbomo Music, Leo Leandros, Breeze Music, Coral Rock Music, Coral Rock Pub., Damont Corp., Mobetta Music, Porofino Music, Savona Music. Catalogues Controlled: Intersong Music, Stanhope Music, Landester Music, Bird Music, Deaver Ent., Comma Music, Lynx Music, Tito Music, Buffalo Music, Ryan Music, Dreamway Ltd., Wheeljam Music, Solid Gold Music, G&G Music.

INTUNE LTD., 10/11 Lower John St., London W1R 3PE. Tel: 01-439 0312. Affiliates: Award Music Ltd., Casanova Music Ltd., Golden Egg Music Ltd., Tiger Music Ltd.

ISLAND MUSIC LTD., 155–157 Oxford St., London, W1. Tel: 01-734 9717. Affiliates: Bad Music Ltd., East Memphis Music Corp., Fantasy Songs Ltd., Freedom Songs Ltd., Freshwater Music Ltd., G.O. Music Publishing Ltd., House of Dreams Music Ltd., Jarmanie Music Ltd., Keepers Cottage Music Ltd., Libra Music Ltd., Lunar Music Ltd., Malpas Music Ltd., Porpoise Publishing, Savage Ayris Associates Ltd., Silent Music Ltd., Smash Brothers Ltd., Stocks Music Ltd., Warlock Music Ltd.

JACKSON MUSIC LTD., The Studios, Rickmansworth, Herts. Tel: (Rickmansworth) 72351. Affiliates: Double B. Music Ltd., Freeway Music.

JAILBAIT MUSIC, Orchard House, Mutton Lane, Potters Bar, Herts. Tel: (77) 42433.

DICK JAMES ORGANISATION, James House, 71–75 New Oxford St., London WC1A 1DP. Tel: 01-836 4846. Affiliates: Air (Overworld), Air Mass Music, Alto Music, Ammo-James Music, Cookaway Music, Crest Music, Crystal Music, Spencer Davis Music, Debonair Music, Dominic Music, Filmusic, Gralto Music, Gwyneth Music, Jabirf Music, Jaeb Music, Jamil Music, Jamsham Music, Josid Music, Lords Music, Maribus Music, Medallion Music, Nuova Music, Pacer-Music, Pageant Music, Pall Mall Music, Santa Ponsa Music, Shair Music, This Record Co. Ltd., Together Music, Tudor Music, Utopia Music, WonderMusic, Young Artists, Zoom Music.

JAMSHAM MUSIC LTD., James House, 71/75 New Oxford Street, London WC1A 1DP. Tel: 01-836 4864.

TIFFANY PRODUCTIONS LTD., 22 Shaftesbury Avenue, London W1V 8AP. Tel: 01-434 1551. Affiliates: Tiffany Music.

J. B. CRAMER & CO LTD., 99 St Martin's Lane, London, WC2N 4AZ. Tel: 01-240 1612. Affiliates: Leonard, Gould & Boulttler, F. Pitman Hart & Co. Ltd.

JIG SAW MUSIC LTD., 115 Old Lodge Lane, Purley, Surrey. Tel: 01-668 3457.

JOBETE LONDON MUSIC LTD., 8 Rathbone Place, London W1P 1DE. Tel: 01-323 1225.

STUART JOHNSON PRODUCTIONS LTD., Gledwood Drive,

Hayes, Middx. Tel: 01-573 8744. Affiliates: Guys Music, Tower Bridge Music Ltd.

KASSNER ASSOCIATED PUBLISHERS LTD., Kassner House, 1 Westbourne Gdns., Porchester Rd., London W2 5NR. Tel: 01-229 3411. Affiliates: Bens Music Ltd., Cecil Lennox Ltd., City Music Ltd., Coslow-Kassner Ltd., Cumberland Music Ltd., First Music Ltd., Gale & Gayles Ltd., GLH Music Ltd., Grosvenor Music Co. Ltd., Grant Music Ltd., Ed Kassner Music, Norris Music Ltd., Myers Music Ltd., Rush Music Ltd., Success Music Ltd., Yukon Music Ltd., Schaeffers Kassner Music, Bonney Music, A. J. Music, Mediant Music, Pan Musik.

JOHN KEATING MUSIC LTD., 64 Campden Hill Towers, London W11. Tel: 01-229 7719.

KENBILL MUSIC CO., 16 Hampstead Gardens, Golders Green, London NW11. Tel: 01-340 3598.

KESWICK MUSIC, 28 Elfort Rd., London N5 1AZ. Tel: 01-226 4062.

TERRY KING ASSOCIATES, 143 Wardour St., London W1V 3TB. Tel: 01-930 1771. Affiliates: Aristocrat Music, Crusader Music, Giant Music.

KPM MUSIC GROUP, 21 Denmark St., London WC2H 8NE. Tel: 01-836 6699. Affiliates: Ardmore & Beechwood, Coronado Music, Elstree Music, EMI Film & Theatre Music Ltd., Gallico Music, Peter Maurice Music, Reynolds Music, Sam Fox, World Wide Music World Copyrights.

LANTERN MUSIC, 60 Radford House, Georges Rd., London N7 8HB. Tel: 01-455 3908.

LEEDS MUSIC LTD., 138 Piccadilly, London W1V 9FH. Tel: 01-629 7211. Affiliates: Cat Music Ltd., Eugene Music Ltd., Groovy Music Ltd., London Tree Music Ltd., M.A.M. (Music Publishing) Ltd., Melanie Music Ltd., Rawlou Music Ltd., Shaftesbury Music Co., Spoone Music Ltd., Threshold Music Ltd., Valley Music Ltd.

L.E. MUSIC, Nelson House, Castle Hill Rd., Hindley, Wigan, Lancs. WN2 4BH. Tel: 0942 55500/56121.

ALFRED LENGNICK & CO LTD., Purley Oaks Studio, 421a Brighton Road, South Croydon, Surrey, CR2 6YR. Tel: 01-660 7646. Affiliates: CeBeDeM, Rue de l'Hopital, 31, Brussels 1, Belgium. Stichting Donemus, Jacob Obrechstraat 51, Amsterdam Z, Holland. The Frederick Harris Music Co. Ltd., P.O. Box 670, Oakville, Ontario, Canada. Iceland Music Information Centre, Laufasveg 40, Reykjavik, Iceland.

LIGHT MUSIC LIMITED, Suite 18, 33 Bryanston Square, London W1H 7LR. Tel: 01-402 4810.

LORNA MUSIC CO. LTD., 5 Denmark St., London WC2H 8LP. Tel: 01-836 4741/2. Affiliates: Cinderella Music Ltd., Criterion Music Group, USA, David Rabin (Music) Ltd., DeShufflin Ltd.,

Laurel Music Co. Ltd., Loner Music Ltd., Mayhew Music Co. Ltd., Norrie Paramor Music Ltd., Pattern Music Ltd., Speedee Music Ltd., Woodside Music Ltd.

MAGNET MUSIC LTD., 22 York St., London W1H 1FD. Tel: 01-935 4049/487 3650/487 3667. Adminsters for the world: Bop Music, Bumper Songs.

MARBLE ARCH MUSIC, ATV House, 17 Gt. Cumberland Place, London W1A 1AG. Tel: 01-262 5502.

MARBLE ARCH MUSIC LTD., A.T.V. House, Gt. Cumberland Place, London W1A 1AG. Tel: 01-723 7631/2.

MARROW MUSIC – Gravesend, c/o Margaret Brace Copyright Bureau, Dean St., London W1.

MARSHALL MORGAN E. SCOTT PUBLICATIONS LTD., 116 Baker St., London W1M 2BB. Tel: 01-486 3271.

MARTIN-COULTER MUSIC LTD., 33 Knox St., London W1H 1FS. Tel: 01-723 4242. Affiliates: Mews Music Ltd., Sleepy Dumpling Music Ltd.

MAUTOGLADE MUSIC LTD., 22 Denmark St., London WC2. Tel: 01-240 5349.

MERRY MAKERS MUSIC, 44 Chasefield Rd., Tooting, London SW17. Tel: 01-622 0714/01-672 5436.

MILLION DOLLAR MUSIC, 12 Praed Mews, London W2. Tel: 01-262 2067/8.

M&M MUSIC (Mr & Mrs Music Ltd), 23 Southacre, Hyde Park Crescent, London W2 2QB. Tel: 01-262 5432.

McCARTNEY PRODUCTIONS LTD., 12/13 Greek St., London W1Y 5LE. Tel: 01-439 0386.

MOTIVE MUSIC INTERNATIONAL LTD., 168 New Victoria St., London SW1E 5LB. Tel: 01-828 2861/2/3.

MOUNTAIN MUSIC LTD., Broadbent House, 64/65 Grosvenor St., London W1. Tel: 01-493 4256. Affiliates: Mountain Music, Elger Music, Lead Music.

MULTICORD MUSIC, 52 Briardene Close, Sunderland SR3 3RU. Tel: (0783) 282353.

MULTIPLE MUSIC, 120 King Street, London W6O QU. Tel: 01-741 0381.

MULTIPLE SOUND DISTRIBUTORS LTD., 120 King St., London W6 0QU. Tel: 01-741 0361. Affiliates: Multiple Music, Multiple Sound Music.

MUSICAL GOSPEL OUTREACH, 10 Seaforth Avenue, New Malden, Surrey. KT3 6JP. Tel: 01-942 8847. Associates: Thankyou Music.

MUSIC MANAGEMENT, 33/37 Wardour St., London W1V 3HB. Tel: 01-439 2482. Affiliates: Honest Injun Music, Jenevieve Music, Quarry Music, Shawbury Music.

MUSIC SALES LTD., 78 Newman St., London W1. Tel: 01-636 9033. Affiliates: Amsco Publications, Consolidated Music, Clifford

Essex Publications, Music Sales/Hal Leonard, Music Sales/Alrred Music, Oak Publications.

NEIGHBORHOOD MUSIC, 280 Fulham Rd., London SW10 9EW. Tel: 01-352 8535/6. Affiliates: Reputation Music.

NEW ACME MUSIC CO (UK) LTD., 8 Albert Gate Court, 124 Knightsbridge, London SW1. Tel: 01-589 6293/4.

NOEL GAY MUSIC CO. LTD., 24 Denmark St., London WC2H 8NJ. Tel: 01-836 3941. Affiliates: Audley Music Ltd., Clover Conway Music Co., Gavel Music Co Ltd., Elcien Glebe Music Co. Ltd., Hazlemere Music Ltd., Larissa Music Co. Ltd., Nordic Music Co. Ltd., NWR Music Publishing Co. Ltd., Plantaganet Music Co. Ltd., Two Four Music Publishers Ltd., Wednesday Music Ltd.

NOON MUSIC LTD., 29 Maddox St., London W1R 9LD. Tel: 01-409 2924/2619. Affiliates: John Carter Music Ltd., White Dove Music.

ORANGE PUBLISHING LTD., 3/4 New Compton St., London WC2. Tel: 01-836 7811.

PANDA MUSIC (Prop. Lamvale Ltd.), 25 Montague Mews South, London W1H 1TE. Tel: 01-402 7433.

PEERS MUSIC LTD., 6 Denmark Place, London WC2. Tel: 01-836 6699.

PENDULUM MUSIC LTD., 9 Upper Grosvenor St., London W1. Tel: 01-499 4851.

PENDULUM MUSIC/W.B. Music Ltd., 69 New Oxford St., London W1.

PINK FLOYD MUSIC PUBLISHERS LTD., 69 New Bond St., London W1. Tel: 01-499 4871.

GEORGE PORTER MUSIC, 3rd Floor, 9 Dean Street, London W1A 4QD. Tel: 01-580 9506/01-437 3711.

PURE CREAM MUSIC LTD., 43 Welbeck St., London W1. Tel: 01-486 6363. Affiliates: Pure Cream Music, Silver Cream Music.

QUATERMASS MUSIC, 53 Devonport, Southwick St., London W2 2QF. Tel: 01-402 9642. Affiliate: R.U.G. Music.

RAK PUBLISHING LTD, 2 Charles St., London W1X 7HA. Tel: 01-492 0654. Affiliates: Chinnichap, Chocolate, CCS, Julie Felix Music, Mighty Music, Orange Music, Trigram Music.

RCA RECORDS LTD., 50 Curzon Street, London W1Y 8EU. Tel: 01-499 3901. Affiliates: Sunbury Music.

REDIFFUSION INTERNATIONAL MUSIC LTD., 2–16 Goodge St., London W1 P1FF. Tel: 01-580 9506. Affiliates: Lemmel Music, Mason Music, Rimusic.

REVIVAL MUSIC LIMITED, 61 Grafton Rd., London NW5. Tel: 01-485 7161/5544.

ROBBINS MUSIC CORPORATION LTD., 138/140 Charing Cross Rd., London WC2H 0LD. Tel: 01-836 6699.

PHILIP P. ROBERGE ASSOCIATES INC., 16 Dunraven St., London W1Y 3FE. Tel: 01-499 0671. Affiliates: Alexis Korner

Music, C.C.S. Music, Philip Patrick Music, P.P.R. Music, Thorup Music, Thurd Music.

ROCK MUSIC CO. LTD., 69 New Bond St., London W1. Tel: 01-499 4871. Affiliates: Erinbeam Ltd., Honey Music Co. Ltd., Inkwell Music Ltd.

RONDOR MUSIC (LONDON) LTD., 147 Oxford St., London W1R 1TB. Tel: 01-434 1575. Affiliates: BKM Pub. Ltd., Caledonian Steam, Fair Music, Geronimo Music, Tin Lid Music, Delicate Music.

SALLY MUSIC CO. LTD., 152/156 Shaftesbury Avenue, London WC2H 8JH. Tel: 01-240 1628/1629.

SAYDISC, Specialized Recordings Ltd., The Barton, Inglestone Common, Badminton, Glos. GL9 1BX. Tel: Badminton 266. Affiliates: Matchbox Music, Village Thing Music.

A. SCHROEDER MUSIC PUBLISHING CO. LTD., 15 Berkeley St., London W1X 5AE. Tel: 01-493 2506/7. Affiliates: Aloud, Anim, Arbutus, Arch, Avaris, Bella Godiva, Burlac, Catmother, Dandy Dittys, Emm-Jay, Homecoming, January, Joans Bones, Joint, Levine & Brown, My Babys Music, Newspirit, Savette, Sea-Lark, Stewart-Nims, Summertree, Va-Detta, Vancouver, Yameta.

SEVEN SUN RECORDS LTD., 133 Broadley St., London NW8. Tel: 01-723 6201/2.

SHAFMERE LTD., 4/8 Haunch of Venison Yard, London W1Y 1AF. Tel: 01-493 3238/3346/8733.

CYRIL SHANE MUSIC LTD., 69 Harley House, Marylebone Road, London NW1 5HN. Tel: 01-486 4651/4886. Affiliates: Avemb Songs Ltd., Good Music Ltd., Pedro Music Ltd., Saffron Music Ltd., Shanfidd Music Ltd., Shanklin Music Ltd., Supersongs Ltd., Tip Top Songs Ltd.

SOFT MACHINE PUBLISHING CO. LTD./MCPS., The Studios, 42/46 Victoria Drive, Wimbledon SW19. Tel: 01-789 1464.

SONET PRODUCTIONS LTD., 12 Needham Rd., London W11. Tel: 01-229 7267.

SOUTHERN MUSIC PUBLISHING CO. LTD., 8 Denmark St., London WC2H 8LT. Tel: 01-836 4524. Affiliates: Carter-Lewis Music Publishing Co. Ltd., Cedarwood Music Ltd., Donovan (Music) Ltd., Dunmo Music Pub. Co. Ltd., Latin-American Pub. Co. Ltd., Liber-Southern Ltd., Meteor Music Pub. Ltd., Mirror Music Pub. Co. Ltd., Monique Music Ltd., Most Music Pub. Co. Ltd., Peer International Library Ltd., See Saw Music Ltd., South Eastern Music Pub. Co. Ltd., Southern Library of Recorded Music Ltd., Southern Monarch Film Music Pub. Co. Ltd.

SNAZZ RECORDS, 57A Wimpole St., London W1. Tel: 01-487 3591/3592.

SPARTA FLORDIA MUSIC GROUP LTD., Suite 4, Carlton Tower Place, Sloane St., London SW1. Tel: 01-245 9339. Affiliates: Annie Music, Angel Music, Barton Music, Ding Dong Music,

Double R. Music, Ember Mood Music Recorded Library, Florida Music, Gloucester Music, Loraine Music, Maraville Music, Makamillion Music, Makamint Music, Mildwood Music, Mark Music, Metropole Music, Manshana Music, Mood Music, Newkeys Music, Peppermint Music, Pawnee Rose Music, Ramblin Rose Music, Sands Music, Sharon Music, Trans Music, Woodshed Music.

SQUIRREL MUSIC, 65 Lower Leeson St., Dublin 2. Tel: 763862/3/764925.

SRT (RECORD) PRODUCTIONS LTD., Bankside, 42 High St., Barnet, Herts. Tel: 01-449 1676. Affiliated to Geobell Music Co. Ltd.

STAINER & BELL LTD., 82 High Rd., East Finchley, London N2 9PW. Tel: 01-444 9135. Affiliates: Augener, Galliard Ltd., A. Weekes, Joseph Williams.

THE ROBERT STIGWOOD ORGANISATION LTD., 67 Brook Street, London W1Y 1YD. Tel: 01-629 9121. Affiliates: Abigail Music Ltd., P. E. Baker Music Ltd., Blue Songs Music Ltd., Bruce Music Ltd., Camel Music Ltd., Carnbro Music Ltd., Catrine Music Ltd., Dratleaf Music Ltd., J. G. K. Music Ltd., Luddington House Music Ltd., Marmalade Music Ltd., Montgrove Investments, Mooth Music Ltd., Mushroom Music Ltd., Slamm Music Ltd., Superstar Music Ltd., Throat Music Ltd., Walrus Music Ltd., Windmill Music Ltd.

SUNBURY MUSIC LTD., 5th Floor, 155-157 Oxford St., London W1. Tel: 01-437 2468. Affiliates: Beautiful Music, Blythe Music, Jayman Music, Onkinsmog Music, Very Good Music.

SUN-PACIFIC MUSIC (LONDON) LTD., P.O. Box 78, London SE19. Tel: 01-653 8457. Affiliates: Cameopat Music (Australia), Main Stave (Hollywood U.S.A.), Sun Pacific Music (South Africa).

TANGENT RECORDS LTD., 176a Holland Rd., London W14 8AH. Tel: 01-603 0893.

T.B.H. MUSIC COMPANY LTD., 60–62 Old Compton St., London W.1. Tel: 01-437 3954.

TEMBO MUSIC, 15 Harley House, Regents Park, London NW1 5HE. Tel: 01-486 5160.

TENNESSEE SWAMPFOX MUSIC INC., 56 Suffolk Rd., Barnes, London, SW13. Tel: 01-748 2587. Affiliates: Hilary Music Ltd.

THISTLE RECORDS, 65 Berkeley Street, Glasgow, G3 7DX. Tel: 041-248 2791. Affiliates: Bayley & Ferguson Ltd., James S. Kerr, Scotia Music Ltd.

THRESHOLD RECORDS LTD., 53/55 High St., Cobham, Surrey. Tel: (Cobham) 4142.

TRANSATLANTIC RECORDS LTD., 86 Marylebone High St., London W1M 4AY. Tel: 01-486 4353/4/5/6. Affiliates: Heathside Music, Maypole Music.

UNITED ARTISTS RECORDS LTD., Mortimer House, 37–41

Mortimer St., London W1A 2JL. Tel: 01-636 1655. Affiliates: Arsenal Music, Clowns Music, Dominion Music, Grand Canyon Music, Kama Sutra Music, Metric Music, Mortimer Music, Parnes Music, P.S. Music, Rogers Music, Starfire Music, Sticks Music, Soho Music, Big Three Music, United Artists Music.

UNITED 2 MUSIC LTD., 1 Montague St., Russell Sq., London WC1B 5BS. Tel: 01-580 1100. Affiliates: Corus Music (Publishing), Spool Publishing Co. Ltd.

VALENTINE MUSIC GROUP LTD., 152/156 Shaftesbury Avenue, London WC2H 8JH. Tel: 02-240 1628/1629. Affiliates: Argot Music Co., Arthur's Mother Music Ltd., Buckhorn Music Pubs., Bulldog Music Co., Burnt Ash Music Co., Chapel Farm Music Ltd., Chesdel Music Co. CME Pubg., Cordova Music Co., Corner Stone Music Ltd., Daval Music Co., Derry Music Co., A. Di Martino Music Ltd., Dolphin Music Co., Eden Studios Music Pubg. Co., Equator Music Co., Golora Music Co., Ladysmith Music Co. Ltd., Maiden Music Co., Marathon Music Ltd., Meredith Music Co., Middle Eight Music Co., Monkton Music Ltd., Muggleton Music Co., Nutmeg Music Co., Pickle Music Co., Riding Light Music Co., Sally Music Co. Ltd., Saphire Music Ltd., Silverhill Music Co., St. Francis Music Co., Surrey Music Co. Ltd., Theta Twins Pubg., Valentine Music Co.

VANESSA MUSIC, 62a Locking Rd., Weston-Super-Mare, Avon BS23 3DN. (Publishers of material for children.)

VIRGIN MUSIC (PUBLISHERS) LTD., 2/4 Vernon Yard, 119 Portobello Rd., London W11. Tel: 01-727 8070.

WANTANABE PRODUCTION – Europe, 33A Emperors Gate, London SW7. Tel: 01-373 5626.

WILSON EDITIONS, 36 John Dalton Street, Manchester M2 6LD. Tel: 061-834 7292/3. Affiliates: Agil Music (Germany), Beat, Cromo, Curci, Edizioni '71 Gemelli, Giraffa, I.N.C., Nazionalmusic, Picci, Pinciana Prima, Unifunk (All Italy), Grecophon Editions (Greece).

WIZARD PUBLISHING LTD., 69 New Bond St., London W1. Tel: 01-499 4871.

WOODTOWN MUSIC PUBLICATIONS LTD., 29 Westland Row, Dublin 2.

WORD (UK) LTD., Park Lane, Hemel Hempstead, Hertfordshire, HP2 4TD. Tel: 0442 50132/3. Affiliates: Ward Music (UK).

YOUNG BLOOD MUSIC LTD., 138 New Bond Street, London W1. Tel: 01-493 9681. Affiliates: Birth Music, D.I.G.I.T. Music, Jano Music, Miki Dallon Music.

ZELLA MUSIC CO., Walker Hall, Ampton Rd., Edgbaston, Birmingham B15 2UJ. Tel: (021) 455 0645.

RECORDING STUDIOS

ADVISION LTD., 23 Gosfield St., London W1P 7H3. Tel: 01-580 5707.

AIR RECORDING STUDIOS, 214 Oxford St., London W1. Tel: 01-637 2758.

APPLE STUDIOS, 3 Savile Row, London W1X 1AF. Tel: 01-734 3008.

ANVIL FILM & RECORDING GROUP LTD., Denham Studios, North Orbital Rd., Denham, Middx. Tel: 01-332 3522.

AUDIO INTERNATIONAL RECORDS STUDIOS LTD., 18 Rodmarton St., London W1H 3FW. Tel: 01-486 6466.

BASING STREET STUDIOS, 8/10 Basing St., London W11. Tel: 01-229 1229.

BLENHEIM STUDIOS, 18 Blenheim Rd., London W4 1ES. Tel: 01-995 1661.

CBS RECORDING STUDIOS, 31–37 Whitfield St., London W1P 5RE. Tel: 01-636 3434.

CENTRAL SOUND RECORDING STUDIO LTD., 9 Denmark St., London WC2H 8LP. Tel: 01-836 6061.

CHAPPELL RECORDING STUDIOS, 52 Maddox St., London W1. Tel: 01-629 3117

CHIPPING NORTON RECORDING STUDIOS LTD., 28/30 New Street, Chipping Norton, Oxfordshire. Tel: (0608) 3636.

COLORTONE RECORDING STUDIOS, The Studio, 69 Dukes Ave., New Malden, Surrey. Tel: 01-492 1347.

CORBY STUDIO, Corby Castle, Gt. Corby, Nr. Carlisle. Tel: (0228) 60877/29813.

CRAIGHALL RECORDING STUDIOS, 68 Craighall Rd., Edinburgh 6. Tel: (031) 552 3685.

CTS STUDIOS LTD., see The Music Centre.

DECCA RECORDING STUDIOS, 165 Broadhurst Gdns, West Hampstead, London NW6 3AX. Tel: 01-624 7711.

DE LANE LEA MUSIC LTD, see The Music Centre.

DEROY SOUND, Hawk St., Carnforth, Lancs. PO Box, 3. Tel: (0524-73) 2273.

DE WOLFE LTD., 84 Wardour St., London W1V 3LF. Tel: 01-437 3702.

DJM STUDIOS, James House, 71/75 New Oxford St., London WC1A 1DP. Tel: 01-836 4864.

DISCOTAPE RECORDING STUDIOS, 4 Rushley Close, Dore, Sheffield S17 3EG. Tel: (0742) 367102.

EAR FOR MUSIC (E.F.M.) STUDIOS LTD., 1/3 Berry St., London EC1M 5PJ. Tel: 01-253 6294.

EDEN STUDIOS LTD., 20/24 Beaumont Rd., Chiswick, London W4. Tel: 01-995 5432.

EMI RECORDING STUDIOS, 3 Abbey Rd., St. Johns Wood, London NW8. Tel: 01-286 1161.

EMISON, 23 Redan Place, Queensway, London W2 4SA. Tel: 01-229 0104.

ESSEX STUDIOS, Essex House, 19/20 Poland St., London W1. Te : 01-734 3121.

FRASER-PEACOCK ASSOCIATES LTD., 94 High St., Wimbledon Village, London SW19. Tel: 01-947 2233/1740.

GROSVENOR RECORDING STUDIOS, 16 Grosvenor Rd., Handsworth Wood, Birmingham B20 3NP. Tel: (021) 356 9636/7.

IMPULSE SOUND RECORDING STUDIO, 71 High Street East, Wallsend NE28 7RJ. Tyne & Wear. Tel: (0632) 624 999.

INDEPENDENT RECORDING STUDIOS, 39 Harmer St., Gravesend, Kent. Tel: (0470) 65687.

JACKSON RECORDING CO. LTD., The Studios, Rickmansworth, Herts. Tel: (Rickmansworth) 72351.

KPM STUDIOS LTD., 21 Denmark St., London WC2H 8NE. Tel: 01-836 6699.

KONK, Kinks Recording Enterprises Ltd., 84/86 Tottenham Lane, Hornsey, London N8 7EE. Tel: 01-340 7873.

LEADER SOUND, 209 Rochdale Rd., Greetland, Halifax, West Yorkshire, HX4 8JE. Tel: (0422) 6161.

MAGNUM RECORDING STUDIOS, 117 Colmar Way, Hyde, Cheshire. Tel: (061) 368 0311/2.

MAJESTIC RECORDING STUDIOS LTD., 146 Clapham High St., London SW4. Tel: 01-622 1228.

THE MANOR, Shipton on Cherwell. Tel: 2128/5576.

MARQUEE STUDIOS, 10 Richmond Mews, 1 Dean St., London W1. Tel: 01-437 6731/2.

MAYFAIR SOUND STUDIOS, 64 South Molton St., London W1. Tel: 01-499 7173/4/5.

MIDLAND SOUND RECORDINGS, Meeting House Lane, Balsall Common, Coventry. Tel: (0676) 32468.

MILNER SOUND, 117c Fulham Rd., London SW3 6RL. Tel: 01-589 6477.

MULTICORD STUDIOS, 52 Briardene Close, Sunderland SR3 3RU. Tel: (0783) 282353.

THE MUSIC CENTRE, Engineers Way, Wembley, Middlesex. Tel: 01-903 4611.

NOVA SOUND RECORDING STUDIOS LTD., 27–31 Bryanston St., Marble Arch, London W1H 7AB. Tel: 01-493 7403/4/5.

ORANGE RECORDING STUDIOS, 3/4 New Compton St., London WC2. Tel: 01-836 7811.

PHONOGRAM LTD., Stanhope House, Stanhope Place, London W2 2HH. Tel: 01-262 7788.

POLYDOR STUDIOS LONDON, 17 Stratford Place, London W1 N0BL. Tel: 01-499 8686.

PYE RECORDING STUDIOS, ATV House, 17 Great Cumberland Place, London W1. Tel: 01-262 5502/5495.

RAK RECORD MOBILE, 2 Charles St., Mayfair, London W1X 7HA. Tel: 01-492 0654.

RAMPORT ENTERPRISES LTD., 115 Thessaly Rd., London SW8. Tel: 01-720 5066.

REGENT SOUND STUDIOS, 4 Denmark St., London WC2. Tel: 01-836 6769/6560.

RENFREWSHIRE SOUND SERVICES, Woodlands Rd., Thornliebank, Glasgow, Scotland G46 7SY. Tel: (041) 638 6197.

R. G. JONES RECORDING STUDIOS, Beulah Rd, London SW19 3SB. Tel: 01-540 4441/542 4368.

THE ROUNDHOUSE RECORDING STUDIOS, 100 Chalk Farm Road, London NW1 8HE. Tel: 01-267 4499.

SAGA STUDIOS, 15 Maresfield Gardens, London NW3. Tel: 01-435 1177.

THRESHOLD STUDIOS, Broadhurst Gardens, West Hampstead. Tel: 01-624 7711.

TREND STUDIOS LTD., 10 Hagen Court, Lad Lane, Lower Baggot St., Dublin 2. Ireland. Tel: Dublin 760928.

TRIDENT STUDIOS, Trident House, 17 St. Annes Court, Wardour St., London W1. Tel: 01-734 9901/9.

T.P.A. STUDIOS LTD., 22 Denmark St., London WC2. Tel: 01-836 1783.

SARM (London) LTD., Osborn House, 9–13 Osborn St., London E1 6TD. Tel: 01-247 1311.

SATURN STUDIOS, 12 South Farm Rd., Worthing, Sussex. Tel: (0905) 201767.

SCORPIO SOUND, 19/20 Euston Centre, London NW1 3JH. Tel: 01-388 0263.

SIRIUS MUSIC, Nelson House, Castle Hill Rd., Hindley, Wigan WN2 4BH. Tel: (0942) 58777.

SOUND DEVELOPMENTS STUDIOS, Unit 11, Spencer Court, 7 Chalcot Rd., London NW1 8LH. Tel: 01-586 4488.

SOUND TECHNIQUES LTD., 46A Old Church St., Chelsea, London SW3. Tel: 01-352 2354.

STRAWBERRY RECORDING STUDIOS (UK) LTD., 3 Waterloo Rd., Stockport, Cheshire. Tel: (061) 480 9711/2.

STUART JOHNSON PRODUCTIONS, 1 Gledwood Drive, Hayes, Middx. Tel: 01-573 8744.

SUTTON SOUND LTD., 23 Reden Place, London E2. Tel: 01-727 6681.

WESSEX SOUND STUDIOS, 106 Highway New Park, London N5 2DR. Tel: 01-359 0051/2/3.

WORTHING RECORDING STUDIO LTD. (Saturn), 1A Teville Place, Worthing, Sussex. Tel: (0903) 64859/201767.